D0890831

Illusion vs. Reality

Dialogues with Shri Ranjit Maharaj

A Sadguru Publication

SADGURU

Shri Ranjit Maharaj

Illusion vs. Reality
Volume I

Talks Given From 1996 – 1999
By Shri Ranjit Maharaj

A Sadguru Publication

SADGURU

© 2009 Sadguru Publishing

2009, First Edition

ISBN Number
978-0-578-01623-8

No part of this book may be reproduced or utilized in any form or by any means, electronic or mechanical for commercial use without written permission from Sadguru Publishing

Contact Information:
www.sadguru.us

Email: admin @ sadguru.us or
        bwolffb @ hotmail.com

Cover Design: Andrew Vernon

This book has been previously published in a different form that was originally transcribed and edited by Robert Wolff in the years 1999 and 2000

Preface to *Illusion vs. Reality – Dialogues with Shri Ranjit Maharaj*

This book is a joining and new edition of the two volumes of talks given by Shri Ranjit Maharaj originally printed under the titles of "Illusion vs. Reality" and "Illusion vs. Reality Part II" that were compiled by Robert Wolff during the years 1999 and 2000.

The original printings of two thousand copies of the two "Illusion vs. Reality" books are no longer available outside of India, so it was decided to join the two volumes into a single book in order to make the straightforward and direct teachings of Ranjit Maharaj available to seekers worldwide.

Some minor editing has been done in addition to the editing that was done in the original books. Most of the editing that was done consists mainly of punctuation and grammar. Any additional editing that beyond that was done with the sole intent of making Maharaj's teaching as easy as possible to read and understand for all. The content of the talks has not been changed, and every attempt has been made to keep intact the special way of expression that Maharaj had when he talked with those who sought out his counsel.

It has been a great joy to revisit these talks again and spend time editing and churning the words of the Master while preparing this text for publication. Reading Maharaj's timeless words in this book and reflecting on them in their immediacy in the moment is truly the same as sitting at the feet of the Master. Maharaj always spoke in simple terms and gave very clear and penetrating instruction. By reflecting on his words, or "continuously churning the teaching of the Master," as Maharaj used to say, this text can be an aid to the reader to gain the understanding of one's own Self Nature and come to the realization of Final Reality. This assurance is consistently given by Maharaj throughout these talks.

A special mention of gratitude to Robert Wolff is warranted here for his painstaking work transcribing the talks contained herein. It is a very difficult task to choose selections from the various satsangs and put them together in a such a nice cohesive way such as he has done. Bob has done a great service to Maharaj and to spiritual seekers with his work in getting these talks published originally back in 1999 and 2000, and additionally with his work in cleaning up the scanned-in text of the both volumes in November and December of 2008, and finally with his help proofreading in order to make this current publication possible.

Jai Sadguru Parabrahman

The Editor

Table of Contents

Introduction to *Illusion vs. Reality - Volume 1*

Shri Ranjit Maharaj was born on January 4, 1913. At the age of twelve he met his Master, Shri Siddharameshwar Maharaj, a great Master who was mostly unknown in his own time. Shri Siddharameshwar Maharaj died at the age of 48 in the year 1936. Shri Ranjit Maharaj did not begin to teach until 1983 at the age of 70 when increasing numbers of seekers continued to show up at his door. Shri Ranjit Maharaj was 87 years of age at the time of the first printing of this text.

He gave these dialogues between the summer of 1996 and the winter of 1999. The content of these talks presents the teaching on Final Understanding taught by his Master, which was expressed by Ranjit Maharaj in his own words. What distinguishes this teaching is its simplicity and its directness. In this tradition, it is felt that the teaching should be available to all, with everyday examples and without unnecessarily complicated concepts. The lives of these two great teachers had similar characteristics. There was an openness to all, and their personal lives were simple, without regard for physical comfort or adoration.

Ranjit Maharaj lived in the same one room apartment for over 55 years and only left India for the first time in 1996 when he was invited to teach in the West by his western devotees. For Westerners, a significant distinction about Ranjit Maharaj was that he spoke English, while neither his Master nor Shri Nisargadatta Maharaj spoke English.

The three main aspects of Maharaj's teachings are: 1) understanding through the dialogues and studying the teaching, 2) mantra meditation, and 3) worship. This book is a presentation of his dialogues with his devotees. Mantra meditation is given by the master on an individual basis. Worship of the master is the pinnacle of Maharaj's teaching and is a common theme that is found throughout his dialogues.

Editor's note: I was present at all of the talks that are presented in this book (except one). All of the dialogues in this book come from tape recordings of Maharaj's talks. To put the tapes into book form has required some editing, but the words and ideas are Maharaj's alone. This book would not have been published unless he had approved the entire text. The talks were recorded in Bombay, Paris, Brittany, Germany, Sedona (Arizona), and Berkeley (California). The talks are listed in chronological order. Tapes were selected at random, and the one's having the best audio were translated into English. Some repetition of the material was edited, but most of Maharaj's students find the repetition useful, so it was not eliminated entirely. I have tried, but it is very difficult to bring all of the spontaneous humor and ambience of the talks of the Master into the text. I think it is generally accepted that a direct transmission is the ideal way to hear a master. At the time of the printing of this book Maharaj was still teaching in Bombay, India (or Mumbai as it is now called).

He welcomed all to his small room for his talks, and at times, especially in the winter months it would often get very crowded. Maharaj was fond of saying "Make yourself small." He spoke in English once a day for about one hour, five days a week. On the weekends, he would go to the suburbs of Mumbai and speak in Marathi to his Indian disciples. The samadhi (a memorial shrine) of his Master is in Mumbai and he would go there to worship every Sunday in the early evening. He would also worship his Master every day in his room doing puja, bhajans, and arati, morning, noon and evenings.

Finally, the publication of this book was made possible with the help of many people, and I wish to thank all of them. Listening to his words every day for me was a practice in itself, and I am grateful for the opportunity it has given me to churn the teaching on a daily basis. Words can never express the gratitude that one feels towards the Master. He has said many times that Master and disciple are one, but still...

Robert Wolff

June 1996

Questioner: When I contemplate my real nature, the "I Am," a feeling of love without cause pervades me. Is this feeling correct or is it still an Illusion?

Maharaj: It is the bliss of the Self. You feel the presence of "I Am." You forget everything, the concepts and Illusion. It is a non-conditioned state. This bliss appears when you forget the object, but in the bliss there is still a little touch of the Self. After all, it is still a concept. When you are tired of the outside world you want to be alone, to be in your Self. It is the experience of a higher state, but still of the mind. The Self has no pleasure or displeasure. It is without the "I" sense. The complete forgetfulness of Illusion means that nothing is, nothing exists. It is still there, but for you it has no Reality. That is what is called realization, or Self-Knowledge. It is the realization of the Self without self.

If someone calls you, you say, "I am here." But before saying "I am here," you are. Illusion cannot give something more to Reality. It cannot give something extraordinary to Reality, because Reality is at the base of everything that is. All that exists, all that you see, the objects of your perception, all that is, is due to Reality. There, Ignorance and Knowledge do not exist. They are not. So what expression can you give to them? When you give an expression, that means there is something experienced. As soon as you feel the least existence, it is still Ignorance, and you are away from your Self. You may feel love, and that is okay, but after all, it is still a state, and a state is always conditioned. The non-conditioned is stateless. It is the experience of the non-existence of Illusion. This is very subtle, and then both Ignorance and Knowledge don't remain. It is difficult to understand, but if you really enquire you will get that stateless state. It is and has always been, but you don't know it, that is the difficulty. There is not a single point where Reality is not. You experience its existence through objects, but all this is nothing. It is omnipresent, but you cannot see it. Why? Because you are the Reality itself, so how can you see your Self? To see your face you need a mirror.

Real happiness is inside you, and not outside. In deep sleep you are happy. You forget the world. Therefore, happiness lies in the forgetting of the world. Leave the world as it is, don't destroy it, but know that it is not. Do everything you have to do, but be detached by understanding, because whatever you feel, perceive, and achieve is Illusion. It doesn't exist, and your mind must accept that.

The Saints say, "Since all is nothing, how can this nothing affect you, or touch you?" But what your mind says affects you and touches you. So what to do? The mind is nothing else but Knowledge. People differentiate the mind from Knowledge but this is not correct. There is nothing in the world. It is

Illusion. Only Reality is, and when you understand that the Illusion is really Illusion, how can it affect you?

How can you even feel that it affects you? The lotus leaf lives in water, drinks water, but doesn't take the touch of water. If you pour water on it, the water rolls off, and the leaf is not touched by it. When you understand that nothing remains, there is no more question of love. The bliss of the Self that you feel is still the pleasure of Knowledge. First you must be aware of it, and then you become Reality itself because you are He. Therefore, there is no harm in living in the Illusion, in the world, but as it doesn't exist, you are not touched. The lotus stays in water but doesn't care for it.

In this way you must experience your true nature. I say experience, but there the words do not exist because it is beyond space, beyond Zero. As the words cannot penetrate there, they stop there. In the *Bhagavad Gita*, Lord Krishna said, "From where the words come back, that is my state." He was a king and was ruling, but still he knew that nothing is. You don't understand that everything is nothing, and that this nothing can't touch you. Even when you feel that nothing can touch you, you are still in Illusion. That is the highest point of philosophy, and you can reach there. There, there is no Master, nor disciple, for both are only one. The duality doesn't exist there, only Oneness is, and nothing is outside of it. Therefore, stay in the Illusion but with understanding.

Two friends wanted to play a trick on another friend. One of them started to insult the other one, but he was laughing at the insult. A third friend was troubled, and said, "How can you laugh when he is insulting you?" He was laughing because he had the key to the game, but the third boy didn't understand. In the same way, realized persons, though they are living in the world, understand that all this is nothing, and whatever happens, nothing is happening. Therefore, they are not touched. People are always in fear of what happens, or what will happen. They are afraid of what people will say. They think, "What am I going to do? What will happen to me?" They fight or enjoy. All of this type of bondage is due to the mind.

The one who is out of the circle understands that all is nothing. It doesn't exist, it is only Ignorance. It is said that only the one who dives deep into the ocean can find the pearl. The one who remains on the surface is carried away in the stream of pleasure and suffering. You must dive deep into the depths of the unlimited because that is where you are. Never stop at the limited. The gold doesn't care for the shapes it takes in the ornaments. It may be in the shape of a dog or of a god, it is unconcerned with the form. In the same way, be indifferent to things because they do not exist. Nothing can touch you. You are unattached. The mind must come to the point of the complete understanding of the Illusion. There lies your state. Nothing remains for he who has understood. There is no more gain or loss. Don't ask if you can achieve Reality because you are the Reality, so why say "Can I?" First of all, get out of the circle. Leave everything one after the other, and go deep in your Self. Come back then, and be in the All. What you have described is a good state, no doubt, but go a little farther. When the mind accepts that all is Illusion, and only Illusion, then you are in your Self. The body and the mind are Illusion. You should be happy to know that. Get rid of your identifications. The only thing that the Master does is to show you the real value of the Power which is in you, to which you pay no attention. He does nothing more. It was a only a stone you thought, but the Master reveals its true nature which is a diamond. He makes you the most precious stone.

"I am omnipresent and almighty. I am the Creator of all that is." When you are at the base of all, you are in the All. Therefore, even a murderer cannot be considered as bad. Know that whatever is happening, it is by "my" order. Be the Master, not the slave! You are the Master.

Questioner: I would like to know why some realized persons reincarnate in order to help others to realize themselves?

Maharaj: Nobody comes, nobody goes. Who told you that? You have read books and you repeat. It is said that the greatest man is the one who dies unknown. Rama and Krishna were secondary heroes. The accomplished man lives in silence and dies in silence. Then their thoughts work in someone else. But the idea that they come back is nonsense.

Nobody comes, nobody goes. All is a dream. In a dream you can become a great Master, but when you wake up, you come back to your ordinary state. Who has gone there and who has come back? Nothing has happened. The concept of a great Master has come upon you and you become this "great Master," but when you wake up you feel, "Ah, all this is nonsense. How can I be a great Master? I know nothing!" Still, in the dream you were giving lectures and were talking easily of all these things, but when awakening comes, all of this knowledge vanishes. It was a dream. From where has it come, and to where has it disappeared? When nothing is, all is only beliefs and concepts of the mind. The so-called sage who says, "I am the reincarnation of God" doesn't know Him, doesn't know Reality. On the contrary, he is the slave of his ego, of Illusion. When Knowledge itself has no entity, there is no question of all these things.

He who understands gets rid of everything. This person looks like an ordinary one, but his heart is quite different. If you stay outside, how can you understand? To become the owner of the house you must enter it. In the same way, you must penetrate your own Self to become the owner. But there the "I" doesn't remain as "I." There is no more question of Master and disciple. The thought of a Master can inspire whoever takes a body, because he and the one who is in silence are one. Penetrate the heart of the "realized one" and you don't remain as "you," because only He is. So, it is said that those who teach are incarnations of God. The Master gives out Knowledge to all, but doesn't value it because he knows that Knowledge is the greatest Ignorance. Therefore don't be touched by anything.

Questioner: If all is Illusion, are you yourself an Illusion?

Maharaj: Oh, yes! I am the "Greatest Illusion"! All that I say with full heart and so frankly is all false! But the false that the Master tells you can make you reach "that point." The address of the person is not real, only the person is real. When you reach the house thanks to the address that you have been given, the address is true only until the moment you enter the house. As soon as you come in, the address vanishes. Words are nothing else but indicators, they have no Reality in themselves. If "I" remains, then Illusion remains. Don't remain as "I." That is the highest understanding of philosophy. Saint Tukaram said, "I have seen my own death, and what I have seen there, the joy that was revealed, That I know." First of all, you must die. You means Illusion. Therefore, what I say is false, but at the same time true, because I speak for That. The address is false, but when you reach the destination, it is the Reality. In the same way, all the scriptures and the mythological books are meant only to indicate that point, and when you reach it, they become non-existent, empty. Words are false, only the meaning that they convey is true. They are Illusion but they give meaning. Therefore all is Illusion but to understand the Illusion, Illusion is needed. For example, to remove a thorn in your finger you use another thorn. Then you throw both of them away. But if you keep the second thorn which was used to remove the first one, you'll surely be pricked again. To remove Ignorance, Knowledge is necessary, but finally both must dissolve into Reality. Your Self is without Ignorance and without Knowledge.

Therefore, the Master and the seeker are Illusion because they are "One." The false can be removed only by the false. If you keep the second thorn, which means Knowledge, even if it is a golden thorn, you'll be pricked (by the second thorn). The ego is only Illusion, and ego is Knowledge. It is said that to catch a thief, you must become a thief. Then you can tell him: "Be aware, I am here and I know you are a thief so you won't be able to rob me." But you cannot catch the thief because he has four eyes and you have only two eyes. At a glance the thief notices the valuables, and if you are not aware, he robs you. Illusion is like the thief, so you must be stronger than the thief. Your mind must accept that all is Illusion, and only Illusion. Then you'll be the greatest of the greatest.

Knowledge is a great thing but it must be only a remedy. When the fever goes off thanks to the medicine you take, you must stop taking it. Don't prolong the treatment or you will create more problems. Knowledge is necessary only to remove the disease of Ignorance. The doctor will always prescribe a limited dosage. First of all, understand that the "I" is Illusion and that what the "I" says is also Illusion. The Master and what he says are also Illusion, because in Reality there is only Oneness and no duality. "I" and "the other" do not exist anymore. Go deep within yourself; so deep that you disappear. Otherwise, what will happen is like if a goat comes into your house and to make it go out, you open the door. The goat goes out but a camel comes in. The camel is just like Knowledge. So to get rid of the camel, you must break down the walls of the house. Then you are out of Illusion.

Whatever happens in Illusion, is only Illusion, and in fact nothing ever happens. So many things happen in this world, birth and death, but it is only a dream. You must accept that. Your mind should not be touched. When someone dies, people cry. The realized being won't laugh, he just keeps mum and remains quiet. He knows that nothing has happened. Nothing is lost. Matter is never lost. The five elements that compose the body return to the five elements, and the "Power" returns to the Power. Only the name and form, which are Illusion disappear. Be formless. Be nameless. If someone asks you your name, answer, no harm, but be conscious that you are not that. You must go beyond Illusion because it is not, and it doesn't remain. Understand that it is fire, but don't touch it. Don't try to extinguish the fire, or you will be burned. Just understand that "Nothing can touch me, nothing can limit me, nothing can fathom me, and nothing can evaluate me. Because it is all Illusion." Due to the "I" thought, you feel a sense of importance. There you say, "This is my house, it's my chair, these are my things," etc. The things themselves never say that they belong to you. They are mute and inanimate. Be mute. Stay in your Self and don't speak. I teach, but I never have the feeling that this one or that one should understand, because it is only by chance that one or the other will rise to this level. By his own luck he will find the key, and he will be the happiest of all beings. Everything depends on his capability, or capacity to accept. You must always go straight to the essence of things. The essence of what is said has true meaning. Take the essence of the flower and be happy, but know that even the essence is not true.

Questioner: If a beggar asks for money from a realized being what will he do?

Maharaj: It is his choice whether to give or not. Because after all, everything is Illusion. He can seem merciless to the point of not giving water to a dying man. If a man is moaning "water, water," he won't give it because the man is going to die anyway, and giving water will only prolong his suffering. You think you are good by giving water, but you only add to his suffering. Due to the dying man's ignorance he wants to live longer. But what can you get by breathing a little more? I don't advise you to be merciless, but understand that by giving into his wish you give him more suffering. The one who thinks that by doing this he has done a good deed, is misled.

If you give a hundred francs to a beggar, he won't be a rich man the next day. He will continue to beg because this habit of begging has become so deeply ingrained in him that his begging has become second nature. All beings beg to get happiness from the time of birth on, and then finally they die without attaining it. Even when you go to the church or temple to pray, you become a beggar in front of God. First you beg for yourself, then for your wife, and then for your children. First for you, and then for others. Everyone is primarily concerned with his own happiness, but you cannot get it because your methods to obtain it are wrong. Be always on the path that your Master shows you, and you will be one with him. These habits are nothing but the results of a narrow mind. The mind is Knowledge. When this Knowledge comes into contact with matter (sense objects), it takes the form of passions and habits. These habits and passions make you miserable. So, have the understanding that when you enter the prison you are not the culprit. Stay in the world but say "Nothing is true." Don't cater to your passions. Understand what they are, and you will be free in life as long as the body is there. One day the body will disappear, but actually nobody takes birth, and nobody dies. Blessed is the one who realizes himself. Realization means understanding, and if you understand that all is Illusion, you will always be happy.

* * * * * * * * * *

June 1997

Questioner: Is a person who is realized in a state of great happiness or joy? Is Reality expressed through great joy or love, or is this still Illusion?

Maharaj: Reality is always Reality. It is Oneness, so why speak of its expression through happiness? For example, if you have lost your wallet and someone returns it to you, you are happy. But in fact he has only returned to you what has always belonged to you. This happiness is a temporary state and if you understand correctly, it has nothing to do with Reality. You only imagine that Reality was lost, but it was never lost. This feeling is due to Ignorance. When you know yourself, there is no question of joy. Therefore, this expression of happiness is also Illusion. Who is there to express this joy, and to whom? Reality is non-duality, Oneness.

It is because you have forgotten yourself that this question of happiness comes up for you. But even in Ignorance, you are He. Clouds may be there so you cannot see the sun. Then, the clouds disappear. Why would the sun be happy? The sun doesn't have to worry about anything. When the clouds were there no one saw the sun, but it was still there. Thus, the joy and peace you feel when the clouds disappear are also an Illusion because the sun was never covered by anything. It was only that you couldn't see it. Why should it feel joy? Joy and happiness are still symptoms of Illusion. You get your wallet back but it was already yours. It is true that by the Master's grace you find yourself, but the Master does not feel that it is thanks to him. You respect him for that because he has given you the Knowledge, and that Knowledge, if you accept it with full conviction, takes you to the Reality. But if he takes responsibility for it, saying "I did it," that means he is not realized. You have forgotten yourself and he tells you this. But Reality was never lost.

You feel that you are limited or bound but that is only a thought. Because of Ignorance you feel imprisoned and suffer, but problems are an Illusion, they don't exist. Whenever unhappiness or problems come to you in the Illusion accept what happens. Don't fight with what comes. In this way, the ego will dissolve. The ignorant person never accepts when misfortune happens. One who understands says, "Let all misfortune come to me!" because he knows that whatever happens is not true. The ego is always looking for some benefit for itself. For example, "I must be respected, loved, or recognized." Whenever your ego experiences hurt, it is due to a lack of understanding. Ego is the problem for you, so let it die. If it dies, it is for the best. It is the Illusion that dies. If the ego dies, then only He, the Reality, remains.

Questioner: I have heard that the evolution of humanity should change from "I" into "We," and that the individual consciousness must become "Universal Consciousness." Is this true?

Maharaj: In fact it is a misunderstanding that makes you believe you are a separate entity. Everyone functions in Consciousness (Knowledge). You also do. If you understand that you are not the body, your consciousness becomes Universal. All limitation disappears. If you break the vase, the space contained in the vase becomes as big as the space of the room, and if you break down the walls of the house, it becomes vast cosmic space. It is all together as one "Great Space," or "Mahakasha." In the same way, if the consciousness of the ego ("I am this or that," etc.) is broken, you become Universal Consciousness, the "All." But here you must understand that this Consciousness is also Illusion, or Ignorance. In effect, Ignorance is the source of Consciousness or Knowledge. So the source of Consciousness itself is the forgetting, or ignorance of the "Final Reality." You become the total creation, the Consciousness (Knowledge) of the world, but this is still Illusion. This ego that becomes Universal Consciousness is the worst of egos. "I am the creator of the world, I am omnipotent, etc." But this Creator only creates Illusion. So what is the use of it? Knowledge creates more Illusion. This understanding must ripen with the help of the Master, and this Knowledge itself will be absorbed in the Reality.

In the Final Reality there is neither Consciousness (Knowledge) nor Ignorance, and that is what you are, your "True Nature." It is because of Ignorance that you say. "I am this or that." And it is also because of Ignorance that you say, "I am consciousness." This is the obstacle on the path to Reality. So the statement, "Individual consciousness must become Universal," is correct. But you must understand it completely. If you say, "I am not this little creature, I am omnipresent," think about "Where am I not?" You are equally present in the ignorant person and in the person who has Knowledge.

Every creature in the world has this Consciousness. So why should I say "I know, I have realized," etc.? That only feeds the Illusion. It is correct to say that individual consciousness must become Universal Consciousness, but the mind, or ego, is an obstacle for you because it does not want to die. Break the limitations that you yourself have created by your own thought. Feel that you are the creator of the world, and that you can also destroy it. Break the limitations imposed by Illusion and you become Reality. It is Oneness, non-duality, no-mind. Why would the ocean be troubled by bubbles that appear on its surface? It knows that the bubbles are nothing but ocean, and there is no gain or loss to the ocean whether the bubbles are there or not.

In the same way, Final Reality is not affected by anything. Nothing can happen to it. It cannot be greater or lesser. Only the Illusion of ego hides it from you. The sun doesn't need to be worried about clouds for they cannot stop it from shining. In the same way, Reality has nothing to do with the Illusion of ego which has made you so small. The movie screen doesn't care if the film projected upon it is good or bad. There is neither good nor bad for the person who is out of the "Circle of Ignorance." The realized being lives in the world but is never touched by it. Why is he not touched? Because he knows that it is Illusion. How can you be touched by something which is not real?

Because of Ignorance you say that you are touched by the world. But if you awaken, nothing will bother you or affect you. In a dream, a lion appears and you are afraid, but then you wake up. Where did the fear go? In the same way, you cry when your ego is hurt. But when you awaken everything disappears in an instant. In fact, when your ego is hurt you make progress on the path to Reality. The ignorant person cries when his house is destroyed but the realized person says, "Now the whole world is mine, I can sleep anywhere." So all limitation and bondage disappears from your mind.

To be "Universal Consciousness" (and therefore, universal mind) is a good sign. But here, "knowing" means that you are in all beings and things. If you try to use this Power by reading the minds of others for instance, you will fall back into Illusion. Ignorant people will be impressed by your powers of prediction or mind readings, and the ego becomes stronger then, and says, "I have Knowledge and others are ignorant." So, understand that Universal Consciousness will bring you more problems in this case, because the nature of Consciousness is expansion, to know more and more. Understand that you are Universal Consciousness, but do not try to use this Power or the ego will return with greater force, and although you are close to Reality, you will be even worse off than if you were just ignorant.

When the Power is at your disposal, the mind gets stronger and is eager to use it. "I can do this or that. I can see this or that. I can make it rain. Etc." When this opening happens in you, you know that, "I am the Creator, it is my will," but if this understanding stays at the level of "I," it is ego. So whatever Powers come to you, do not use them. The realized being says, "I know that I do not know." If you say, "I am everything, I know the mind of all," it is still ego.

And when the Power is there, one has the desire to use it. At this level be very vigilant. Do not accept the ego of Power. To have Universal Consciousness is a good sign, but know that the "Universal Being" is also Illusion. The danger lies in thinking that you are "All-Powerful." Let all these things be, and understand that nothing is. Universal Consciousness means "the Great Illusion" (Mahamaya). To accept the Great Illusion means that you attract great problems. He who wears the crown carries the weight of problems. Why master Illusion? Illusion is nothing, so you master nothing. Then where is the mastery? So what is the use of Universal Consciousness? Know that it is nothing. All is nothing. Consciousness itself is not true. Submerge your ego, do not be afraid of it. He who says, "I am All-Powerful!" is sounding his trumpet in the desert.

Go out of the ego. Do not be too big, or like the balloon that is over-inflated, you will burst. Whenever the mind affirms, "This is true," go against it and say, "No, it is false." Do not let your enemy enter your home. When you open yourself to Knowledge you have the impression that you can know everything. But pay attention. First understand your own mind or you will forget yourself. You will be as if under the influence of a strong emotion. You will do worse things than you ever thought yourself capable of doing.

I heard about a sage in Bombay who was making miracles. He could walk on water or through fire without being burned, etc. But one day, and this day always comes, his Powers stopped working and people made such a mockery of him that he committed suicide. Ignorant people can drive a sage crazy. He became their prey. Ignorant people spread all sorts of false ideas about sages. For example, they say that a sage should not feel pain. But the sage is alive, he is not a corpse. He must therefore feel the burn upon contact with fire. The sage feels pain but he knows that it is his body that feels it and not himself, because he is not identified with the body. But if the so-called sage says that he does not feel pain, it is still his ego speaking. This body is not a corpse, it is alive, thus pain must be felt. As long as the electricity is connected, the bulb must give light. The same is true for the body. As long as the Power is connected to the body, it must feel pain, or feel something. Certain sages fall into this trap if they truly think that they must not feel anything.

Jani was a poor maid servant, but she was an awakened being. She lived in a village and like everyone else she put cow manure patties to dry on her wall in the sunshine for later use as fuel. Her neighbor who was always against her, stole them from her one day. Jani complained to the village judge who said to her: "How can you recognize the ones that belong to you?" She answered, "Put your ear near them and if you hear the name of Lord Vitthala, that means they are mine." In this way they trapped the thief. Of course people asked how a cow manure patty could talk, but in fact, it was Jani's Power that spoke, for she was in all things. Everything that says "I am Reality" is mine, and that which says "I am the body" is not. She had total faith in God and her Power was in everything.

He who understands, says, "I am not the body." The body is nothing other than a cow manure patty. If the Knowledge "I am Reality" penetrates you, everything is yours. Do not say that only realized beings are great. You yourself are great. Christ said, "I am God." If you understand that you are not the body, you are as great as He. But the ignorant person always feels powerless. "Oh, he is so great, and I am so small." It is the ego that makes you believe that you are a tiny creature. Throw off this false idea from your mind. You are as Powerful as Christ but you do not understand that. "I am Reality" is the understanding you must have. That is what the Master wants to make you understand, and that is what the Master teaches, nothing else. But then what is the meaning of this understanding? Understand, and then forget everything, and you are He.

If the ego blocks your path, crush it. Let others make their comments. When you understand that you are not a beggar, you instantly become rich. You all have the highest Power in you, so welcome it. The mind must completely accept that. If you accept it with all your might, how can Illusion persist? That which is nothing cannot persist. The problem is that you always have the habit of complaining, "Oh, I can't do this or that." That is ego. It is Maya; Illusion. Be very strong in your Self. I tell you that you are the Reality and that you can experience this. Try to accept it until there are no more limitations for you. You are unlimited. No one can limit you. But in spite of it all, you have put yourself in bondage. Forget all limitation and be He, the Reality. Try to understand so profoundly that your mind cannot fight you. Then you will be able to defeat the ego. Otherwise it is impossible. When a doubt comes upon you (for example, "How can I be the Reality?"), you lose your strength. You need strength and Power to overcome it, or it will never disappear, I tell you. Only the Power of Understanding can defeat it. "Let the world go to heaven or hell, I don't care." Be this determined! But you are afraid to leave Illusion. What to do? Why do you fear that which is nothing? Everyone who comes to me says the same thing, "I live in fear. I am powerless. I can't do this or that. What can I do?" Forget all that.

In an Indian text it is said that a man can get drunk for a few rupees with one glass of alcohol. That power makes him dance and hallucinate and say, "I am a king, I am everything." He is under the influence of Ignorance. But if under the influence of the "Power of Knowledge" given by the Master, a man says the same thing, is it possible to control him? The Power that you have is much greater than that of alcohol. This Power, the effect of Knowledge, must penetrate the mind. "I am the Reality." If you understand correctly, nothing and nobody can stop you. Be like Saint Jani who declared forcefully: "There, where you hear the name of God, that belongs to me." Therefore, if I tell you that you are Reality, you must accept it. Have that strength within yourself. The problem is that you only accept it halfway because your ego won't let you go too far. That means you do not drink the glass of wine down to the bottom. An ignorant man will never say "I am king" if he is not drunk. He who drinks the "Wine of Knowledge" says "I am Reality," and no one has power over him. Be strong and have fear of nothing and no one, for everything is nothing. So how can nothing make you afraid? Many people say they have had these experiences and yet become caught again by the world. But what is the world? The Master tells you that the world is only Illusion. So why be bothered by it? Then, if you remember the world, just like remembering a dream, there is no harm. If you have a nightmare, upon awakening and remembering the bad dream, you feel nothing because you know that it has no hold on you. If you kill someone in a dream, you don't take responsibility upon awakening. The world is Illusion. Why bother with it? If this determination penetrates you, no one can stop you. If not, that means you are giving preference to nothing, and you become a small creature.

You must have the courage to accept what the Master says, and to act accordingly. When you play cards there is a king and a queen, but are they real? They are only paper. It is your concept that crowns them king and queen, but they have no real power. In the same way, this world is not real, so what can it do to you? Have this conviction, this determination, within yourself.

The so-called sages who give you methods to follow only reinforce Illusion in you. You go to see a Master in order to get out of Illusion, and they plunge you more deeply into it. These are not true Masters, and in this case, it is better to remain in Ignorance than to have false Knowledge. Understand and be "That."

Questioner: Maharaj, if the body suffers, you say, "The body is suffering, but I am not suffering." Is that correct?

Maharaj: Yes. The body suffers, but I do not suffer. If your neighbor has problems you say "My neighbor has problems," but you don't feel anything. Consider your body as your neighbor. Thus, the problems of your body are the problems of your neighbor. It is when you say "I am the body" that you suffer. If the body is burnt, it is the body that feels the burn, not you. When you are anesthetized for an operation where does the pain go? The pain is there, but the mind sleeps. It forgets. Upon awakening, contact with the mind makes the pain reappear. The body has pain, not "I." So, don't identify yourself with the body. This body, being alive, must feel pain. Otherwise, it is a corpse.

One day Kabir was bitten on the leg by a dog. His disciples went wild. "Oh Maharaj, what has happened to you?" Kabir answered, "The dog knows, the body knows, why should I know?" But since you identify yourself as a body, you accept the pain as being yours. Kabir knew that the bite had happened to the body and not to him. He thought of his body as his neighbor. It is only because you accept the idea "I am the body" that you suffer. It is ego. The sage says, "Let things happen." When your neighbor dies, you are not affected. But your body is the most precious thing to you. You refuse to accept its disappearance, its death. The realized being says, "Oh how wonderful, my problems are disappearing." For the body is a problem, nothing else. If you get a boil on your leg for example, you ask the doctor to cut it out even though this boil is part of your body. But because it is making you suffer you are ready to part with it. In the same way, if you understand that the body is only a boil that has grown on you, you will be very happy to see it disappear. But since you identify yourself with the body, you suffer at its death and refuse to let it disappear.

The realized being also says, "At this very moment my body is a dead body." It only functions because the Power is connected. When a light bulb is burned out, you throw it away. The electricity doesn't object. It doesn't care. So you yourself are this "Inner Power"! Then death will be nothing to you. Understand that the body is dead right now.

In these two ways you can understand. It is the nature of Knowledge to be dualistic. The body is an instrument. You must know how to use it. If you use it to understand Reality you will become Reality. If you say, "I am the body" you will go to hell. Hell means the garbage can, for the body is nothing more than a shit mill. Don't be the owner of a shit mill. Be the owner of Reality.

Questioner: How can we purify ourselves? How to get rid of ego in the quest for Reality?

Maharaj: Ego is Ignorance. By understanding you can overcome Ignorance. When ego disappears, understanding remains. But this Knowledge is also a state. You must dissolve this Knowledge in Reality. All that the mind has accumulated and accepted as truth during so many years, understand that all of it is false. You believe in the truth of what you say, but that is wrong. It is because of Knowledge that you have this feeling, but Knowledge comes from Ignorance. From where does this come? From Zero. Thus, its origin is nothingness, just as when you are in deep sleep and you are in Ignorance, and then suddenly a thought arises, and a dream happens. All that you have acquired through Knowledge is nothing more than Illusion. Do nothing, but understand where Reality is. When you feel nothing, it is there and you are certainly tempted to say, "Reality is thus nothingness." But this is not correct, for it is beyond Zero.

Everything that you see and perceive is false. By this understanding, the mind is purified. How did the mind become impure? It did so by believing the world is real. It takes itself as the Reality, and thus Reality is lost. The world is only the reflection of Reality and a reflection is not true. Suppose you see your face reflected in a mirror. The real one is your face and not your reflection. But if you say that the reflection is Reality, you are lost. If you understand that the reflection is false, you are Reality. That is purification of the mind. "Everything that I see and perceive is false." But, in fact how can the mind be purified? It is itself a concept, and how can a concept be true? What is not real is always impure. Everything is superimposed on your True Nature, but you, Reality, are never altered. You are so clear, so pure.

So, the mind takes everything as true and that is the impurity. But when you understand that everything is false, the mind itself disappears. The mind is nothing other than your thought. It can be a thought of God or any thought, but a thought is only a thought. It comes from Ignorance. So forget the thought, forget the Knowledge and you are He. You take the false for true, and the true as false. That is the mistake. That is the impurity. This is like being in a courtroom and swearing on the bible to tell the truth and nothing but the truth when in fact everything that you say is false. What to do? It is the nature of the mind to see and say only the false. So one can say that purity of mind is nothing other than forgetting the mind, for it doesn't exist. It is only a concept. By forgetting the mind, you are Reality. The mind means thoughts. When they disappear, you are there.

Questioner: You speak of doing nothing, to be the non-doer, but for me this is the most difficult. My mind is always active. What to do?

Maharaj: Forget your mind. Do you think during deep sleep? Do you do anything? No. So why do you say that it is impossible for you to do nothing? It doesn't make any difference if the body and mind are there. The problem is that in the waking state you always want to do something. You feel that you are taking action when in fact you are doing nothing. Just like in the dream state you think you are taking action, but when you wake up you understand that you have done nothing. It is the same thing here. In the waking state, if you awaken, you understand that you have done nothing. You say to yourself, "Although I thought I was doing something, I did nothing." The mind is always in action but let it die. For when the mind disappears, there is no more action. So be "no-mind" and Reality is. The problem is that you want to be "no-mind," and at the same time be the mind. Is this possible? You are in action because of Ignorance. In the waking state you must reach "no-mind" by understanding that all is Illusion. This is the understanding.

Nobody does anything. Ignorance is in thinking that you are the doer. If you kill someone in a dream do you take responsibility for it when you awaken? You are certain that you didn't kill anyone and yet in the dream this experience seemed real. Whatever you do is nothing anyway. So do nothing. For your true nature there is nothing to do, because you are always there and everywhere. Anything can be lost but you yourself. You are never lost. So, my Master, Siddharameshwar Maharaj said, "You report at the police station that you have lost something, your money, your child, your wife, etc. But until now, no one has ever reported losing himself." Even in Ignorance you never say that, for if you say it the police will answer, "But you are here in front of me! How can you be lost?" So you are never lost. Then why do anything to find yourself? It is always for something which is not (which doesn't exist) that you must do something. For that which is always there, there is nothing to do. Philosophy is like that. It is very easy and very difficult at the same time because you can't accept it.

If you do something, you are in bondage. If you do nothing you are free. "Although I am doing, I am not doing." This is the "true samadhi." **Sama** means "As I am" and **dhi** means "before." You are That but you persist in saying "I am the doer." This Ignorance can be overcome by understanding only. Forget everything, because nothing exists. In this way everything disappears. Nothing is left. It is exactly like when you wake up from a dream and say, "I didn't do anything." Understand that everything you see and perceive is only a dream. From deep sleep a thought arises and the dream appears. You feel like you are acting in the dream, but in fact you are not doing anything. If in the waking state you understand that although I do something, I do nothing, then you are Reality at that moment. That is the trick of understanding. If you think you are the doer you are lost, because you believe that Illusion is true.

Questioner: Listening to you, is it doing something or not doing anything?

Maharaj: You are doing nothing because everything is Illusion. To listen is Illusion and what I say is also Illusion. But for *whom* I speak, that is True. To speak is also Illusion. I can tell you that what I say is a lie, but what I speak about, "Reality," is True. Words are false because they cannot reach Reality. But, we need them in order to understand. The address written on paper has no Reality. Only the designated place is true, and when you reach it the address has no more use. The words disappear. Only the meaning remains. The steps of the staircase no longer exist when you enter the room. In that way, words are spoken to understand Reality, but the words are in themselves false. When you see the person you were looking for, the address has no more use. Since all is Illusion, I also am Illusion. I cannot be an exception to that. The person who speaks, and the person who listens are both Illusion, but Reality is. You and I do not exist.

It is a very good question. Understand that words can give you a certain understanding of Reality but then you must experience it yourself. The Master teaches you up to a certain point. Beyond that point, you must understand for yourself. Then there is no more duality. There is only Oneness. So who can understand whom? Can you have an experience of yourself? So the Master and the aspirant are both Illusion, like the heroes in a movie. Only the screen is true. If the heroine wanted to know herself, she would disappear and only the screen would remain. If what I say and what you hear are Illusion then what is left? Only the Final Reality exists. If the understanding penetrates you, this is the Truth. In Reality there is neither Truth nor Ignorance, there is nothing. Reality is always Reality. This is the magic and the miracle of the world. Even though everything seems to be, nothing is. It is exactly like a card trick. What you see doesn't exist, but to get rid of Illusion, the trick of understanding is necessary.

How can something that doesn't exist be real? It is by the trick of understanding that you will get rid of it. Many people speak of their experiences, but whatever can be experienced is Illusion. So what to do?

As soon as there is an experience the trio appears: the experiencer, the object to be experienced, and the experience. But Reality is only Oneness. In Reality there is no world even though the world appears. To experience Oneness is always Illusion. To say, "I have experienced Oneness," is a false statement, because Oneness cannot be experienced. Forget all that, and Reality is. You only have an idea of Reality from words and teachings. The one who is Reality doesn't need an address. So everything is false, and Illusion is seen upon Reality. If you stay on the staircase how can you enter the room? Forget the staircase. The room is there. Because of Ignorance you say, "I do something." Reality lies in not doing anything. Reaching Reality requires nothing because it is always there. You simply must be rid of the Illusion of "doing" that is imprinted on your mind. The mind does not accept this because it does not want to die. The mind by nature likes to think, and believes it is the "doer." Everything you like and don't like, and all of your habits disappear when you understand, because they are nothing.

Questioner: Maharaj, if everything is Illusion, why are we here? Why can't we remain in the silence or deep sleep?

Maharaj: You don't understand what deep sleep is. In deep sleep there is nothing. It is Zero. Why are you here? To understand. Let everything happen, but know that it is nothing. Because of Ignorance you go to Zero in deep sleep. But here in the waking state, you must first go to this Zero point, and then go beyond this nothingness, because Reality is beyond that. Go beyond the Zero point and Reality is. You are here to understand that "Although I am doing, I am not doing."

That is what I am talking about. There is neither "I" nor "am," there is only Reality. Everything that I see and perceive is nothing, even at this very moment. In deep sleep you cannot understand that the waking state is only a dream. People are all in Ignorance. They are born in Ignorance, they live in Ignorance and die in Ignorance. You are here in order to get out of this "Circle of Ignorance." In deep sleep you forget everything. Here, (in the waking state) forgetting is remembering, and remembering is forgetting. That's the trick. To remember is to forget, to forget is to remember. Do not try to find Reality or to recall it, for it is always there. As soon as you remember you are lost, for you are seeing something other than Reality. You make it an object. These two states of waking and sleeping appear different, but they are the same. Reality is not a state, it is stateless.

* * * * * * * * * *

December 18, 1997

Maharaj: So let thoughts come and go; high tide, low tide. If low tide comes to the ocean, the ocean never worries about it. So whatever thoughts come and go, why should you worry? You are beyond thoughts. So first one should know "Who am I?" That is called "Knowledge of the Self" (AtmaJnana). Just as with a dream, you say it's not true when you wake up, it is the same here. You see the world, you experience everything but who experiences? The world is just your thoughts, or ego, and ego sees and experiences everything. This world is nothing but a long dream, take it for granted. Everybody says, "I'm So-and-so." Is your name anywhere written on you? If it were written on you there would be no need for anyone to ask your name. Many thoughts trouble you. But all thoughts, whether good or bad, pleasant or unpleasant, come and go. Whatever comes and goes, and whatever doesn't remain, how can it be true? It's all the mind's work. The mind has the habit to see wrong things and then accept them as true. You say you exist. Prove it.

The five elements and the Power (Chaitanya) have come up, and a name is given to you by your parents. No object of the world says that "I am this or that." A table never says it's a table. It is all only your thoughts. So how can you be a name? There is something in there, that Power that is in you. First know That. Know yourself as That, and the world as That, nothing else. Bad and good, right and wrong, is all the mind's work, so you must examine your mind. Many people come here and leave, but I remain. You are never lost, you always remain. So many thoughts good and bad, pleasant and unpleasant come and go. Why to worry? Whatever appears and disappears and doesn't remain cannot be True. Thoughts are the mind's work, and the mind has the habit to accept wrong things as true. This body you have is just playing a part. Some play a man's part, and some a woman's. But the Knowledge in both is the same. She and he both work with that Knowledge. In this way one should understand. First the Master teaches you, then finally you understand that you are He, capital H, and everybody is He. So why to worry? Nobody is bad, nobody is good. You have five fingers, some are smaller some are bigger. Which one is good or bad? All are made of flesh and blood. If you have a 100 or a 50-watt bulb, both work with electricity. Electricity is one. You all breathe air and eat with your mouths, so everything is common for all. The Power that works in every body is the same, that's the main point. Everything is a thought. Thought means Knowledge, and Knowledge is mind. It all works with the Power. But you are neither the mind nor the Power, you are He.

Everyone is running after wrong things. They live in a ruthless way. Everyone lives because of the breathing. No breathing and then everything goes off. So everyone is desiring the breathing. If you are sick you call the doctor right away. "Give me medicine so I can breathe more and more." So, as long as the Power is there you are happy. But, the breathing takes place in a dream.

Every day you do the same things. You get up and brush your teeth, take breakfast, take tea, go to work, come home, take your dinner and sleep. You do the same things, and then create duties for yourself, and live like that endlessly. "I have to do this, I have to do that" But when you were born you had no sense of duty. You didn't know if you were a girl or a boy. All these actions are the mind's work. You must find out what is not you. The mind is not you. Your thoughts are always changing, how can that be you? You never change. The Power in you as a baby is the same Power that is in you as an adult. That same Power is working in you. The problem is that you do all these things, but don't know yourself. So, people go to the realized person because they want some understanding of who they are. Then the realized person says to know yourself first before you try and understand the world.

All the time you are going around the world with an identity card. A passport is your validity card. But that validity card which is stamped wherever you go is not true. To be the Reality, a passport is not required. You are He, so wherever you go it's okay. You say, "I'm so many years old, I live in America," and so on. But you don't exist, and your identity card is a fraud. Only the Master can say that you are an imposter. Everyone else are mad and foolish. You have to think about these things as you have the discrimination power to know what you are not. The human being is always after money. If you throw money to a dog will he care about it? Only man cares for pieces of paper. All other creatures want something to eat. In Ignorance you have become so small; smaller than a dog, I say. You run after money you can't eat, and then you hoard it and never give it to anybody. You are just like a dog in the manger. He doesn't eat and won't allow anyone else to eat. You'll never give a cent to anybody unless you want something. So you are just like a dog in the manger, hoarding and barking at anyone who comes near. Reality never eats, and He never wants anything. Knowledge wants to eat more and more. Knowledge wants money and everything. When you sleep you don't want anything for eight hours, but when you awake you want juice, biscuits, etc. You don't need anything. I want to say that! Body needs. You don't need.

(At this point a man came late into the room and began asking questions.)

Questioner: I have been here for 20 years and I have not heard of you. I think only the lucky ones know about you. (The questioner is a Mohammedan; a Muslim.)

Maharaj: I don't advertise myself because I don't exist.

Questioner: You remind me of Krishnamurti, and for a moment I was taken aback.

Maharaj: Yes, from the face people say that, but I have never seen him.

Questioner: Maybe he has seen you.

Maharaj: Many people have come to see me, but I don't remember everybody. Some people agree with you about the resemblance.

Questioner: Yes, yes, but the Atman (Self; Soul) is still the same.

Maharaj: Atman is the same, okay, but Atman is also not true. Reality is true. Allah is true, but Knowledge is the Atman.

Questioner: But when one dies, the Ruh (Atman) goes off.

Maharaj: Yes. Atman goes in the Power. Power is Atman, nothing else.

Questioner: In English what is the meaning of the Atman?

Maharaj: Atma means "Soul." Ruh is a wish. It is also a thought.

Questioner: It is not Ruhani Tagnat, "Soul Power"?

Maharaj: Ruh is also not Final Power. Ruhani Tagnat is also the Power of Knowledge. Knowledge itself is also not true. So in your Mohammedism (Islam) they say that you can't be Allah, but they don't understand the meaning of that. When you are there, Allah cannot be there. Let the "I" disappear and Allah is there.

Questioner: Allah is the Creator and we are his creatures.

Maharaj: No, they are not creatures. The Power is the same for you and the Creator. The Power in you is that Power. You create many things, but you don't understand. You create dreams, and the dream comes. Who creates the dream? It is in yourself. You create many things by thoughts also. So the Creator is not true. Creator of the wrong is not true. Who created the dream that you saw? You were sleeping.

Questioner: The sub-conscious.

Maharaj: Sub-conscious is also a thought. So thought created the dream, and thought itself is wrong. Thought cannot be true. The world itself is an Illusion.

Questioner: When the Rishis (ancient seers; sages) said that all is Illusion, the whole of India started going inwards. Hence India is backwards, but the West developed outside.

Maharaj: Because they are in Maya. They are always in Illusion. They don't know that the Power that is in me is the same Power which created the world. Why is it called Atma? Because you are in the body. When you leave the body Atma becomes one with Brahman. So you are also the Creator. You have created many things. Who has created all these contrivances? Inward development is greater than outer. Now these foreigners run to India because they want the inner development. They are tired of the outer development. After the Second World War they realized that happiness lies in knowing yourself and not in the material life. My Master in 1926 published a book called the "Golden Day." It is about the same subject that we are talking about now, but nobody wanted to hear it then. Now, the Westerners come looking for inner development. Outer development appears to be true while you are living, but where is outer development when the body goes off? It has no entity at all. Saints say that "The world is not true," and "Come with me to my side. Then you will understand the Power that is in everybody." So the one who develops this Power can understand. You're a foreigner if you don't have this understanding, no matter which country you're from.

Questioner: Is there a place called hell?

Maharaj: Hell is here. When you say, "I'm the body," you are in hell. When you understand you are not the body, then you are in heaven. Heaven is not in the sky. Heaven is in yourself. Heaven starts from you. If you don't take a birth then where is the world? You may have crores (tens of millions) of rupees in the bank, but what is the use of it to your body after it dies?

Questioner: In the Bible it is said that it is more difficult for a rich man to enter the kingdom of heaven than it is for a camel to pass through the eye of a needle.

Maharaj: Rich people cannot accept this because they don't know that the world is not true. If you understand that the world is Illusion then you can understand what Reality, or what Khuda, or God is. Khud is Khuda. It means the one who signs is the Reality and not the hand that is doing the signing. (The person or the name). Follow me? You are He, but you don't understand, so you say that He is in heaven, and we are in hell.

Questioner: With which part of Islam do you not agree?

Maharaj: I agree with them. God is one only. So Kabir says, "Allah Tu he Tu he re Allah, Tu he Tu he re Allah." You are only this. So one should know Oneness, Reality. So it is told, "United we stand, divided you fall" You are the Reality. You never fall, you never die. Nobody dies. Birth and death are both an Illusion.

Questioner: I lost my mother and father. How can I regard them as an Illusion?

Maharaj: They have gone. Because they were not there. Where have they gone? Tell me. You have put their bodies in the earth.

Questioner: So they merged with the five elements.

Maharaj: Even the five elements don't exist. In a dream you saw everything, does it exist? In the same way, this world doesn't exist. Where are your mother and father? They have no entity now. They came, took birth and a name was given. So you became a son and he became a father. Nothing is there and no connection exists. Nobody can go with anybody. Everybody wants to live. Nobody wants to die.

Questioner: The life in this world is a sport and pastime and real life is to come.

Maharaj: Yes, yes. Real life is to come means you should understand what is Reality. So I say that the world is fun and fair, nothing else.

Questioner: You shouldn't take it seriously?

Maharaj: No, since it is not, what to take seriously and what not to take seriously? True is the Reality, and that is yourself.

Questioner: But Sir, it takes time to come to that stage. How can you look at the bat and say it's not true? You may take the bat and hit my head with it. It's very real!

Maharaj: No, not to worry. You can think that.

Questioner: But I can't say it is an Illusion. They give the example of the Master who said the same thing and finally the pupil beat him. He said to the Master, do you still believe that the world is Illusion! Still, the Master said "Yes."

Maharaj: Let that beating be an Illusion, why should you worry? Master doesn't worry. If someone calls you a fool, say "I'm a double fool." When I was in America they asked if I was also an Illusion. I told them I was a first class Illusion. First class means Maha Illusion (Great Illusion, or Mahamaya). What I speak and what I tell is all wrong, but for *whom* I speak is the Truth.

Questioner: But are you talking to our Atman? Who are you talking to?

Maharaj: Nobody, nothing is there. All is Illusion, what to do? Speaker and listener are both false. If one comes up to that point then they become realized.

Questioner: Then what is the opposite of Illusion?

Maharaj: That is your Self without self.

Questioner: But when the self itself is an Illusion?

Maharaj: Reality has nothing to do with all these questions. It's just like a screen. Reality doesn't take the touch of all these pictures. That's why what comes and goes is called a dream. Nobody can take the world with him when he dies. You can't dream the dream then. Whether you are a rich person in the dream or a Saint, where has it gone? Now come on! Listen, if Illusion is wrong, not true, then the one who understands that, is He. He becomes He. He doesn't remain himself also. Only Final Reality remains. You can give any name for that. Call it Khuda.

Questioner: When we study all of this and think this way, it has put India fifty years behind the West.

Maharaj: Let it be. When it is a dream, fifty years back or forward is only in your mind.

Questioner: In the Olympics we are nowhere, in recognition we are nowhere.

Maharaj: Nehru wanted to put India in the best place. So he did everything. He himself doesn't exist now, what to do?

Questioner: His statue is there.

Maharaj: What is the meaning of a statue? A statue can't do anything.

Questioner: Every year we celebrate his birthday.

Maharaj: You can honor him, no harm. Honoring him is of no use whatsoever. What does he get? Where is he?

Questioner: Okay, the memory I have of him, that is not an Illusion.

Maharaj: Memory is Illusion. Memory itself is an Illusion. Memory means what? Knowledge.

Questioner: If I pinch myself, I feel the pain and it is real to me.

Maharaj: Pain is not real.

Questioner: It is true that I can't show you the pain, but I can feel it.

Maharaj: Pain happens to the body, not to you. Suppose you are operated on and you are in pain. You ask for medication to sleep. In sleep everything goes off, and when you awake again you say, "Ahhh!" So the pain is nothing but the touch of mind (the identification of the mind with the body).

Questioner: But it's real to the person who feels it.

Maharaj: You don't follow what I want to say.

Questioner: That's is why I'm waiting and sitting at your feet

Maharaj: In a dream somebody slaps you. You feel the pain of the slap in the dream. You awake and there is only a pillow next to you. So how did you get the slap, and who felt it? Follow me? So the pain you felt in the dream is not true. Same way here with the world also. It is not there. This is nothing but a long dream. When you awake, the picture is going on like one on a TV screen. When you turn it off, the picture goes off. When you turn it on again, the picture comes. When you die the picture goes off. When you take birth again, the picture turns on. That is all that happens. Understanding this is required. It is not a simple thing, but if you listen, and accept what the Master says, it can happen in a second. On the other hand, people go after the Reality, but they lack the ability to grasp what the Master says. The Master says that you yourself are He. There is nothing to get. Come with me, nothing else is required. Time is an Illusion, so fifty years one way or another is meaningless. No matter where you are, you are always there, everywhere you are. There is nothing that exists that is apart from you. Myself is everywhere and anywhere.

Questioner: Everybody wants a short cut to Reality. So is the idea of Shaktipat (transmission of energy), like what Swami Ramakrishna did to Swami Vivekananda, possible? He became great overnight.

Maharaj: I don't believe in Shaktipat. You must listen to the Master. Ignorance has come by hearing. Therefore you must listen to a realized person and then realization is possible. By hearing, Ignorance has come up, and by hearing it goes off. How can Shaktipat help? If I put my hand on someone's head, can he know anything? For example, suppose one boy is running and another boy doesn't want to run. Can you put your hand on his head and make him run? How can you get energy in his mind and body to run by just doing that?

Questioner: What I mean is the transfer of energy from your Chakras (energy centers) to another person.

Maharaj: No, that cannot be done. When the Master guides you and if you grasp what he says, and put it in practice, then yes, you can get the understanding.

Questioner: Then what do you make of what those swamis have said?

Maharaj: I am not saying that they are not great. What they say is their business. I just don't agree with this concept. What to do!

Questioner: I agree that by hearing one can see the light. But now have we got the time? In this rat race of a world, have we the time to become enlightened? There is only twenty four hours in a day. I believe that Swami Vivekananda wouldn't lie.

Maharaj: I don't say anybody lied. I told you that what I speak is wrong, it doesn't exist, but for *whom* I speak is true. That's the meaning in it. Right or wrong, I don't criticize anyone. I don't care what others say. I know what my Master has told me, and I have experienced that. A young boy doesn't have to learn his mother tongue because he hears it from his parents. It happens automatically. Other languages he must learn. When you were born, you didn't know what Ignorance was, or what Knowledge is. The child gets imprints on his mind from what he hears, and then he understands. So imprints come on the mind, and the mind replies. Then he speaks. Follow me? Same way here also. By hearing, Ignorance has come, and it can only go by hearing. Shaktipat actually means a Master speaks and if the disciple listens and takes it to heart, then he can also be a Master himself. If he is attentive and has a clear-cut understanding then why not ? You are He.

Questioner: I am That!

Maharaj: Yes. When the ego doesn't remain, only Reality is there. But "I" and "That" are both wrong. They are words. You have to go beyond words. Words come back from there. Reality is beyond words.

Questioner: Reality is always emphasized, but nobody explains how to get there and what it is.

Maharaj: Reality is Reality. How can you say what it is? When you say something about Reality you are in a dream. How can a person who is sleeping know who he is? This world is the Creator's dream. The Creator's creation is also a dream. The Creator itself is also wrong.

Questioner: Dreams do have significance.

Maharaj: A dream is always a dream, no matter who dreams it. The realized person understands it is all a dream, and that it is not true. That is the difference. (The phone rings and Maharaj answers it).

Questioner: You just talked to someone on the phone. Is that real or an Illusion?

Maharaj: It's an Illusion.

Questioner: But you talked on the phone.

Maharaj: I should talk. While I am living, I have to talk. A dead body cannot talk. As long as the body is living, he lives in Knowledge and in Final Reality. But the realized person in fact doesn't do anything. He understands that when he talks, he doesn't talk. He sleeps but he doesn't sleep. That he understands. Nothing exists, and yet you say it is there, what to do? That's Knowledge, or the lack of it.

Questioner: In darkness we see a rope and say it is a snake.

Maharaj: Yes, that is Ignorance. Even at the moment you say it's a snake, it is still a rope. Due to Ignorance, or darkness, you say that what is not true is true. You say the world is not an Illusion, that it is true. By the grace of the Master, you get the understanding, and if you accept what the Master says, the world becomes nothing. It's only your thought. Thought has come upon you. You are the thoughtless Reality; Self without self.

Questioner: But is thought material or non-material?

Maharaj: It doesn't exist. It has no real existence. Many thoughts have come, where are they now? They come and they go. Guests come and go, the host always remains.

Questioner: People emphasize what is called "Higher Reality," or Truth.

Maharaj: Reality is Truth. Truth is not a thing. In a dream you did many things. Can you say it's true or "the Truth"? Suppose you kill someone in the dream and go to the police station and say, "I've killed someone." Then they put handcuffs on you. But when you tell them it was in a dream, you're set free.

Questioner: But why does one dream of violence?

Maharaj: Why means? There is no question of why of that which is not. For that which doesn't exist, how can there be a why? The question doesn't arise. First, try to understand the point I am trying to make, and then argue. No harm. I don't mind arguing.

Questioner: I am not arguing with you sir. I am trying to clarify my doubts.

Maharaj: So I am clarifying your doubts. Yes, yes. I understand. So when doubts are there, your ego is there. One who has doubts is not He. One who has no doubts is He always. Everyone in fact is He whether he doubts or not. It is the ego that has these concerns. So, as you don't know, you have to ask questions, anybody can ask questions, why not? One should not worry about it. I always say that I speak like a loudspeaker. If you hear or don't hear, it's your choice.

Questioner: That is why you see Westerners. They have a thirst for spiritual Knowledge.

Maharaj: Why is that?

Questioner: Because in the previous birth they might have been Indian.

Maharaj: No, no. Forget about that previous life. How can it be? When you take the birth you become the smallest creature. The ego takes birth. Your body does not come back again. What good have you done with this body anyway? You all tell lies. You say, "I'm So-and-so." Your signature is a forgery. You are in prison many years for this. Only in this human form can you think of what is real and unreal. Once you forget your real Self, then the world becomes real for you. Your heaven is lost, and you live in hell. Hell means you live in fear and you become the smallest creature. Always say "I am He, and not this." You may be a bad person, or a pious person, but still you are He. Your fear is for what you think exists. That is Ignorance. Nothing can touch or affect you. How can nothing touch nothing? When you feel that that which is nothing is touching me, that is Ignorance. If you understand that nothing cannot touch me, then you are a realized person.

Questioner: Can you tell me about Stitapragna in the Bhagavad Gita?

Maharaj: Stitapragna means that one understands that everybody is myself. He lives in That. He doesn't say anything. He understands that all are myself.

Questioner: So if you are fearless you can reach that stage?

Maharaj: Yes, then you can be Stitapragna.

Questioner: Like Bhagat Singh. (Historical patriot) When he was sentenced to death, he saw it as dying for his country.

Maharaj: That is okay. They don't know anything. They know the country only. You should not speak for anybody. He gave his life, that much he did. You can't do it, so you praise him. Follow me? A realized person doesn't praise him. What is there? What dies? The body dies, he didn't die.

* * * * * * * * * *

December 22, 1997

Questioner: My mind is always noisy, what to do?

Maharaj: The mind is always noisy. It wants to think all the time. Water must move, otherwise it's not water. In the same way, mind is a thought, nothing else. Thoughts come to you and then they go. You are not the mind. When you sleep, mind sleeps, so thoughts don't come. So, when mind is working, thoughts must come. One should know what is the mind. If you understand your thoughts or mind, then you can understand yourself, otherwise not. What kind of thoughts come in your mind?

Questioner: Work, what I have to do, what will happen. I seem to live in the future.

Maharaj: Everyone lives in the future. The mind should be taught not to think more. Why does the mind think? Because you take everything to be true. The world is true, myself is true. What is your name? Mary. Is Mary true? Is it anywhere written on your body. Can you point it out? So what you are not, you always think of more and more. That is mind. The mind always thinks of what doesn't exist. When you were born you didn't know anything. Your father and mother gave you the name. You had no name at that time. You took the birth, not knowing "I am a child" or anything. Existence came in your mind as "I am here." That "I" is ego, nothing else. You should know "Who am I?" So, in the Bible it is said, "Know thyself, and you will know the world." The world is very big. How can you know everybody or everything? See yourself first. Go to the source from where it starts. The world starts from where? When you awake, the world starts, otherwise it is not there at all. When you are sleeping there is no world, and no Mary. You forget everything. When you get up, then you say, "Oh, I'm Mary." In the beginning you are not able to say your name, so your father and mother prod you to say your name over and over again. At that time you are not at all attached to anything.

Suppose a boy sees the ocean but says it is water. He is told that it is not water, it is called ocean. Then he takes that in his mind. It is only water but you give the names to things. Has this table over here ever told you, "I'm a table"? You say it's a table, but it's nothing but the Power. If you put a match to it, it goes off in a second. It starts from Zero and ends in Zero. Go to the source from where it has started. If you go to the source, the thing itself doesn't remain. You take it true when it's not true. The mind always thinks wrong things. When you sleep, your body and mind both sleep. You go into Zero. There's nothing you say. Something told you that nothing is there, and that's the Power. So one should know what I am, and what I'm not. You are not the body, and you're not the name of the body. Suppose instead someone had called you Elizabeth, you would have become Elizabeth. There is nothing in a name. Changing your name doesn't change you. You are what you are. First, find out "Who am I?" The mind is a thought, nothing else. What you say is the mind. If you say, "I'm Mary," then you are Mary, what to do? You are not always merry, sometimes you are unhappy. If you're given the name Krishna, are you Krishna? The name is there. The name cannot be He. By name you cannot be That. Go to the source. If you go to the source of the river, does it still remain a river? When you go to the source of yourself you also disappear. That is called "Power."

For example, electricity is the Power and when connected to the bulb it gives the light. It doesn't know it's the light. In the same way, when Power enters the body it becomes Knowledge. If you touch electricity you die, if you touch the Knowledge, Knowledge goes off. Knowledge doesn't remain because you are beyond Knowledge. Final Reality is beyond Knowledge, and beyond Ignorance. If you understand or touch the Knowledge, it goes off, and you remain. Knowledge has no value at all. It is nothing but your ego. You say, "I know. I do everything." but it is in a dream. Who is the doer now? Nobody is the doer. If you put electricity in a fan, or a computer, or anything, it works. Does electricity say I do it? It is just the Power.

So the Power connects to the body and Knowledge comes. Knowledge means "I know, I understand." Then ego comes. The "I" comes when you say, "I know." Understand "Who am I?" first. That's the main point. Say as Socrates said, "I know I know nothing." What you know is nothing. What Reality is, you cannot know. Why? Because you are He. How can you know yourself? This body is made of five elements. When one dies, what happens? Scientists say that matter never dies. The body goes to the earth, or ashes in my country (India). The Power goes to the Power, and the elements go to the elements.

Questioner: Why then do all the religions talk about destiny and predestination?

Maharaj: Because they don't know. They don't know the inner meaning of their own teachings. They teach the wrong things, I tell you. Be He, and then teach.

Questioner: We're all educated here, and we can understand the philosophy, but the experience of it is different.

Maharaj: Make that experience yourself. Everything is nothing, everything is Illusion. Then you can understand "Who am I," otherwise not. When it is Illusion, how can it be destined? The Creator of the world is also Illusion. You are having a dream. You are not doing anything. Who is the creator of the dream? Tell me! Can you find him? Nobody is there. Only your thought is there. And then, you see many, many things there. But someone might ask, "Who gives the thought?" The thought comes from Ignorance.

Questioner: How can that be? On the contrary, the more learned you are the more thoughts you have.

Maharaj: Ignorant persons have many thoughts. That's the difficulty. What you understand up to now is all wrong. The mind must be changed, and that is what the Master does. You are always free, but you say, "I'm in bondage," what to do? As you have forgotten yourself, I say these things. Who am I to give anybody liberation? If a boy is ignorant he goes to school. If he's not ignorant then?

There is a story in Marathi of a realized man who had a son about 14 years old. His wife wanted the boy to go to school to learn about the world, so they sent the boy to school. One day the boy was taught the Sloka, "Om Nama Siddha" (What is true, I bow down to you). Just on that one verse, the boy wrote 1500 verses. So, the man asked his wife, "What to teach him now?!" If you have the wrong things in your mind, it is difficult to change it. In a way, the mind should be blank, or open, then acceptance comes very fast.

Questioner: When you sit in meditation and you have experiences, is that also Illusion?

Maharaj: Yes, yes! Everything is Illusion. The Knowledge that you have is playing with itself. What you see is just Knowledge. If you remember yourself, you forget Him. Forget Him, and "you" are there. Forget "I," and He is there. You want to see Him, but "you" can't see Him. You want to understand Him, but then the mind comes in. When you are He, what to achieve and what not to achieve? So much has come in the mind, how can you leave it? When the Master says, "You are He," how can you believe it? Mohammedans say one thing, Hindus another. Everyone has their own ideas. Who is right? Nobody is right because it is all nothing. If you see someone being killed, and you are asked, "What has happened?," one who understands says, "I don't know anything." The one who is killed is He, and the killer is He. What to do, and what to tell? Nothing has happened, everything is wrong. You want to say it's all true. How can it be true? Eyes always show the wrong things. What to do? When you see a dream, the eyes are closed. A thought comes and everything happens. Is it true? With which eye did you see the dream?

When you have understanding, the mind becomes satisfied, and no thoughts come. The mind always thinks of others and not of itself. If the mind thought of the Self, it wouldn't exist. So, you asked earlier about your noisy mind. The mind doesn't exist, but it's always noisy. It's always noisy because you think of the wrong things. Someone tells a lie, and to maintain that one lie, you tell a 100 more lies. The one who understands says, "I haven't seen. I don't know." If you ask him 1000 times, he will say, "I've not seen." What you witness is always wrong. So, what you see and perceive is all wrong. The eyes cannot see in darkness. The Power in you can see the darkness and the light. You see with the Power, not the eyes. The eyes don't work in darkness.

Understand the Power that is in you. Understand "Who am I?" first. Then you can get the heaven. But "you" must die first. You doesn't mean the body. The body can't go to heaven. The body starts from Zero and ends in Zero. The Self is heaven. There is no heaven in the sky. Everything starts from you.

The mind always thinks, but if that mind is given the understanding, then the mind becomes quiet. The boy is crying and crying, but if you give him chocolate he is happy. He forgets crying. So, if the mind is given the correct thoughts it automatically stops. The mind searches for the wrong thoughts. If you understand your mind, it can take you up to the Reality. Realized persons understand by mind, "I am not this, or anything else." Bondage and liberation is also the mind's work. Why do you want liberation? No need for it. This Knowledge can be understood by the grace of the Master, and nothing else. Siddharameshwar Maharaj is my Master, and he gave that understanding. But you must want to understand.

All religions say to know yourself. Kabir says, "What is the point of going to sacred places if you don't know yourself." If you understand, then every place becomes sacred. He pervades everywhere. He is in everybody. Every bubble in the ocean is nothing but ocean. So break yourself now from the ego and you are He. Nothing to do, only a change of understanding is required. Be out of the "Circle of Ignorance." You take birth in Ignorance and die in Ignorance. Ignorance means nothing, Zero. Space is also Zero, everything comes into space. If there is no space, then how can anything happen? The Self is spaceless and thoughtless. So, mind can be thoughtless if you understand yourself. You say the world is true, the Saint says that the world is not true. That is the difference. There may be many noises in the world, but the one who understands remains noiseless.

Questioner: Is there any such thing as the spirit world when the body goes?

Maharaj: The Power is there but the Power is wrong. It's not true! In the Power you see gods, and you see demons. Both are there. Both are false. God is Power, the Knowledge. Reality is there, and on that Reality you see everything. Unless the basement (foundation) is there, no floors can come.

Questioner: Religions talk of life after death. Is that just a concept?

Maharaj: Yes, it is simply your wish.
(There was an interruption and some new people came into the room.)

Maharaj: Saints say many things. Some say "do this" or "do that," but that's not correct. One should know oneself first. Everything is wrong, but "You" are right. You without you, is the Reality. How much time does it take to know oneself? Some teachers say the understanding will come later. I don't agree with that. They say that if you do this and that, then understanding will come. You are always there.

His name is Bob. Suppose he has some brandy and gets the kick of the drink. He then does and says silly things. Someone comes along and gives him a slap. Then he comes around or not? What the Master says is just like a slap. You can understand at this very moment! (Maharaj then recounts the story of the tenth man.) Ten men had crossed the river and when they got to the other side they each only counted nine men. They assumed that one man had drowned crossing the river. Each person counted and they all came to the same conclusion that one man was lost. Some wise man came along and saw that the men were crying, so he asked what was the matter. He said after hearing the story that there are ten men here. So he asked one of them to count. He counted nine. He then gave a slap to the man who was counting and he said, "Oh, the tenth is found." The others were still in doubt. When each men got a slap, they understood the tenth man. When you forget yourself, then all troubles come.

So, if you are unconscious and you get the injection from the doctor, you come to your senses or not? Finding yourself can be very easy. The wrong thoughts of the mind should be taken out, that is all. To say that after some time, or after many births you can know yourself, I don't agree. You never forget yourself anywhere in the world. I take it a little further now. If the body goes to the cemetery You remain. You don't die. Everyone is the same. People have different skin color but everyone eats, everyone breathes the same air, everyone wants water. The five elements are required. Existence rides on the breath for all. When there is understanding, Oneness comes in the mind. There is no duality at all. So it is said, "Common sense is not a common thing." Differences and separation are the mind's work. Everyone is He.

* * * * * * * * * *

December 23, 1997

Questioner: Should the practice of meditation be with effort or effortless?

Maharaj: Meditation is there only to make your mind subtle. The mind has become very objective. So, in the beginning, only in the beginning, meditation is necessary to understand what the Master is saying. It is an initial stage. It's not the final stage. Meditation can lead you to the Final Reality, but it is a long and very hard discipline. In the beginning it is useful, but eventually it gets absorbed in the Final Reality. In our tradition, meditation is referred to as the "ant's way," and understanding is called the "bird's way." Birds can fly from tree to tree and ants of course move very slowly. The bird's way is by thinking only. In meditation you have to practice many hours a day and there are also many restrictions. Sleep and food are restricted, and it is a very difficult practice. So Saints who have realized by understanding say to meditate in the beginning to prepare your mind for understanding. So both ways are necessary.

When a realized person speaks he talks beyond sky, beyond Zero. An objective mind will not understand so fast. Most important in the beginning is the notion that he is my Master and what he says is correct. Faith and dedication is essential. In the beginning the Master says that Knowledge is necessary. But in the end that Knowledge must be submerged in the Final Reality. Knowledge belongs to the ego. But gaining that Knowledge is an important step you must go through. You have to practice "I'm not the body, not the mind, not the Knowledge, not the ego." Your habits must be changed, so practice is necessary, otherwise it's impossible. In everyone's mind is the concept, "I am So-and-so." You must practice with the understanding, "by doing, I am not doing," and "by eating, I am not eating."

There are three kinds of karma (see appendix). Karma means action. When you do an action, at that moment it becomes actionless; it doesn't remain (Akarma). You've done it, and it is over at that moment. You then think many things about your actions. Suppose you hurt someone and many thoughts come in your mind. As a result of that, it becomes karma. Action and reaction are opposite and equal. Karma is a function of your mind only. If you say "I've done it," then you're stuck with karma. So how to get out of the circle of Ignorance? By understanding only. When nothing is true, and you don't exist, then what remains? As long as you are there, everything exists. When the body dies, does everything go off or not? If you have many dollars in the bank, what is the use of it there? Can you sign a cheque?

When one dies, one thinks of the good and bad actions that one has done. This is carried with you in the mind, nowhere else. These thoughts have no real existence, but because you say it exists, it follows you. If you come to India and some things are required for your personal habits, you bring these things with you or not? It's the same way when you die and leave the body. You bring your good and bad actions with you only in your mind. They don't exist, but your mind says that they do. "I've done these things."

Nothing is good, and nothing is bad in the world. Why? Because it's not true. There is no barren woman's son. He never existed. The ego is like the barren woman's son. It doesn't exist, but still you say, "I've done it." The ego should be understood and left. "I don't exist, I am not," should be your understanding. In this way, all actions are actionless in the moment .

If in a dream you kill somebody, when you awake where is your action, and who did the action? Who is responsible? You are sleeping. You've done nothing and you can't even remember your name. Your mind is at rest and you forget everything. Only Ignorance remains, and Knowledge also, in a latent form. They always go together. If Ignorance goes off then Knowledge must go too. They are two sides of one coin. They are two sides, still they are one.

(Someone came in late and was standing outside the door, but Maharaj asked the person to come in so he could hear.) One who comes must hear the Master's words. Ignorance has come by hearing. Without hearing it's not possible to get the understanding. When you took the body you didn't know anything. Afterwards, everything has come upon you. Your name, where I am, who I am; all these things have entered your mind. All of your Knowledge has come from your parent, teachers, and everyone else you meet. All of them are in Ignorance, what to do? Only a realized person can say none of this is true. "Come with me," he says. "All are going to the east side, come with me to the west side." Everything you have learned is wrong, nothing is true, and this world you experience is nothing but a long dream. Take it for granted. So you've done something good or bad in the past. Does it exist in this moment? It is only in your mind that "I've done good or bad." Somewhere people are celebrating their marriage, or maybe their birthday. Where is it? There is no time or space in the Final Reality. This should be your understanding. Then actions become actionless at the moment. Once done, its finished. So it is said, "When you spit you can't take it back." When you say something bad to someone, you often say "I'm sorry," but you can't take it back. What is said, is said. All these fathers and forefathers, where have they gone? Do they write to you?

So, in the beginning you must go to the school for the understanding. You can't meditate for the whole day. At first you encounter some resistance to learning, and sometimes one has to bribe the child to go to school. But after a while when you get the taste of what the Master has said, that nothing is true, not even yourself, you'll never care for the world. What is there? It starts in Zero and ends in Zero. Zero is always Zero. It is nothing. In Reality there is only Oneness, no duality at all. Due to Ignorance you say, "I am an American," or "I am a Frenchman." Where is it written anywhere? It's only in your mind. You're always in bondage.

When you go to sleep you close all the doors and windows. So you make yourself a prisoner or not? By your own wish you become a prisoner. You lock the door from the inside and willingly do it. I tell you nothing exists. Just as in a dream, it's all in your mind. Tell me, with which eyes did you see the dream, and who made it? You did nothing. Your thoughts made it, take it for granted. Some thought came and it all happened, who can say? There is no entity there, and where did it happen? Who can say?

Understanding should come, that's all. The sky is very big. When you close your eyes where is the sky? It's the biggest thing, but close your eyes and it's gone. Only the Power remains. To demolish the sky, close your eyes. Only You and the Power remain. Due to the sky or space, our eyes can see everything. In one second everything can go off. Put a match to this table and it becomes ashes. It has no existence. The wind comes and goes. Where has it come from, and where will it end? Understanding should come. Your mind is nothing but your thoughts. Understand your thoughts and thoughts won't remain.

When a guest comes to your house and doesn't go, he is no longer a guest, but the host. Then he claims to be the owner of the house. Now we are partners, he says. The body is the same. The body is only a guest. The guest is not the owner of the house. The body wants everything. It's not even a good guest. When it goes, does it ever say thank you for all the sustenance and care that you've provided? Does it ever say "bye, bye"? You've entertained it all your life, and it goes without a word. But still you say, "I'm this." What to do? A change of mind is required, nothing else. The mind itself is bondage, and mind itself is liberation. So meditation is required in the beginning, but after a while the Master tells you, "No need, forget that meditation also." Understanding makes you He, and you don't remain. When that happens, what to do and what not to do? The Power in you is the Creator of the world. What happens is your choice, and not the Creator's choice. Understand that way and you'll never feel anything. "I am nothing." Due to the body, you have become a very small creature. Forget the bondage, nothing else.

In France, once we went to see the Eiffel tower. In front of the tower there was a man standing there. He looked like a statue, but he was a mime. His face was painted white. Then he began to move so everyone knew that he wasn't a statue. And when he was finished with his act, he asked for money. Everybody wants something, they do something, create some Illusion, and then they expect something in return. It's essential to have a real Master for the understanding. If a Master does like the mime he's no Master I tell you. To make a show, or to create miracles is all nonsense. What miracles can you do? There is no miracle at all. Can you make anything more than the five elements? If there is a miracle the body itself is a miracle. The five senses are extremely close to one another, but their abilities are quite different. So what more miracles can you make? Why try to attract people, where is the necessity? It's only the Power, the sixth element that does anything. Suppose you have a dream that it's raining like hell. When you wake up, is anything wet? So when you are awakened by the Master you will say the same thing: "It's not true." The mind can be awakened, nothing else. Understand your thoughts and they won't remain. Go to the source. In one little seed the whole tree is there, so go to the source. The mind makes noise because you say everything is true. Nothing is true, myself is not true. "I" don't exist. A dead man doesn't think anything. Can he ask for water? Nothing is nothing.

You are beyond space and time. When you say "I am" then everything comes, what to do? You must think again and again. By not thinking, you have become a small creature. By thinking, you can become the greatest of the greatest. Finally, that thinking gets absorbed in the Reality, and you don't remain. Say, "I'm the Creator of the world." Be big. No harm. But also say, "What I have created is not true. I am not." Understand "Who am I" first, and then that "I" will be absorbed by understanding. If you examine the ego it doesn't remain. You say, "ego is myself." Understand finally that even understanding is not true. Everything starts from Zero. Multiply or add or divide, Zero remains Zero. You can never see yourself, you can only see your reflection in the looking glass. Nothing is to be done, only understanding is required. There is no doer, and nothing is done. But the ego does not want to die. There are certain worms that when you cut them, they don't die. The ego is just like that. Thought is ego. Knowledge is ego. If "I" goes off, then He is there. He is always there, nothing to worry.

One who goes to the depths of the ocean gets the pearl. Go to the depth of yourself and He remains. One who gets the understanding doesn't feel anything. Whatever happens let it happen. It's okay. It's my choice now. The understanding should be so strong that if someone wants to kill you, let it happen. So, go to the death of that ego and Knowledge, and the one who wants to kill you will not hurt you because you say, "Go ahead, I'm not going to die." You must be watchful here, because the Knowledge you get from the Master is also wrong. And if you then say, "I'm the Master now," that is also wrong. There is only Oneness in the world, no duality at all. Everybody is He, why to worry? Nothing is bad, nothing is good. These are all thoughts. All are liars, so where is the Truth? Can you find Truth in all these lies? Everyone says the wrong things. You say this is a table. It's not a table. Many names are given. There is a name given to you, but you are not that. So whatever you do, good or bad, is all wrong. Knowledge is wrong. The mind must be changed, that is all. When you are in deep sleep, does Knowledge go off or not? If you die, whether you're a doctor or lawyer, and you take another birth, you still have to relearn your ABC's all over again. Where has the Knowledge gone? One should think in this way.

* * * * * * * * * *

December 26, 1997

Questioner: Yesterday you said that the mind does not want to die. So is it a good way to repeat to ourselves that, "I am not the body, not the mind?" Is this a way to get rid of the mind?

Maharaj: It's okay, that is a way. But "I" myself, is also a thought. That "I" thought must finally be absorbed in the Reality. It's okay to say, "I'm not this, not this." Discriminate everything first. The mind says yes, but understand that you are not doing anything. You are not sleeping, you are not talking, and so on. What you feel is also mind, forget that too. That thought, "I am not doing," is just like a thorn that helps you to discriminate. Then that thought gets absorbed in the Reality. "I don't exist, and I am not doing this or that." What you have said up to now is nothing but an Illusion. You are really not doing anything, but the mind thinks the opposite. That mind must also be absorbed. Discrimination is the main point. Then you will understand that "I am everywhere." Where am I not? The mind must be taken out by nullifying thoughts such as, "I know. I do. I understand." etc. Nothing is true.

In a dream you've seen many things, but you've not seen. Your eyes are closed. Then who saw? So what you see and perceive is nothing but your thoughts. The Master tells you these things so the "I" or ego doesn't remain. Final Reality has nothing to do with all these things. "I" is only a thought. Thoughtless Reality has no emotions and no concepts in it.

Everything comes upon it. The screen doesn't think of anything, good or bad. The screen doesn't say yes or no. It shows everything, but it doesn't take the touch of it. Don't take the touch of anything. All the ornaments are nothing but gold. Agree? You give it different names, that's all. So, the name has no entity at all. Shape and name are given, but it is nothing but an ornament.

So practice by saying, "I do nothing." Just like in sleep, everything happens but you do nothing. When you awake you know that you haven't done anything. You know that. Same way here. "I am not speaking, I am not eating," that should be your understanding. All of these thoughts such as "I am right, he is wrong," come in your mind. So when emotion or thoughts come in your mind, to take out these wrong notions, understand that you do nothing and that the "I" doesn't exist. Everything starts from Zero and returns to Zero, and nothing remains because it's not true. One thorn can take out another, but if you keep the second thorn it will pinch you. Finally that emotion of the "I" thought should be absorbed. If you are not, then who is the doer? The "I" has no entity at all. That is what you must ponder over. If you don't, how can you understand this philosophy?

The thinking is the second thorn, and that also must go. Thinking is not you. Who thinks? Here, the thinker is not found. In the beginning, one must look at what the "I" is doing, but what is done by "I" is not you. You don't do anything. The "I" thought exists in a dream, nothing else. So if you understand that this is not true then why to worry? So say, "I don't do anything," then there is no doer. Finally, the "I" goes off. You must be careful here because if you say, "I've got the Knowledge," or "I'm a Master," that is ego.

People often make a show of their Knowledge. Some renounce and put on special clothes. Showing anything is not correct. Understanding is what is required, nothing else. If a man puts on women's clothes, that does not make him a woman, and vice-versa. Thinking is the first obstacle that has come upon you, but you are thoughtless. Thoughts are of the mind only. Thinking is like a boil that has appeared on you. It must be removed by understanding, and then forgotten. But without understanding you remain in Ignorance and can't do anything. In the beginning Knowledge needs to be acquired. To remove Ignorance, or darkness, light is necessary. Both are wrong, however. When there is light, there is darkness, and when there is Knowledge there is Ignorance. But you are neither Knowledge, nor Ignorance, nor light, nor darkness. The world doesn't exist. Who exists? He exists, or my Self without self. One should leave the room, otherwise He can't enter. As long as space is there, you see everything. No space, then there is nobody and nothing. If you understand that space is nothing, then everything in it is wrong. Ego is Knowledge, ego is mind, and mind is nothing but your thoughts. The mind is the greatest factor. The mind is Knowledge. When real understanding comes, then everything is thrown off.

Doubts are many in the world. The mind always has doubts. The Master says, "You are God." You say, "How can I be that? I am a simple person. What you say is impossible!" The mind won't accept it. You may be a sinner, a thief, or anything, but the realized person doesn't worry because he knows that you are All. He sees ornaments as gold. Suppose you put gold in shit, does it change its nature? Gold is gold. Same way here. Reality is always Reality. Don't be something, be everything! Something is ego. People ask me, "What time is darshan?" What is the meaning in it? By giving darshan you become something. I am not this. The temple is ever open and everyone is He. Anyone can go to the graveyard or temple at anytime. There is no bondage for anyone. Everyone is He, so who will give darshan to whom? So, I tell people that if they want to hear something in English come at 3:30 p.m. When you go to your own place, do you need permission? Be open and everything is your choice. In your own home you can do anything. You are not bound by any laws. You are He, so why to doubt? You are in everybody. Your Self is so open, but you have forgotten yourself and say, "I'm this."

You are everywhere and nobody can stop you. Can you stop the wind? You are the shit, and the God also. When you become subtle, nothing comes in your mind. Be subtle. But as you have forgotten yourself, you have to go to the Master. To take out Ignorance you have to go. You have taken Ignorance on yourself. In Ignorance you say that everything which is not, is true. A drunkard gets the kick and says, "I'm a king." Give him a good slap and he'll remember himself. A slap from the Master is the mind's slap, nothing else. And he gives you such a good slap that your mind doesn't remain. You are always in everybody, and everything is okay. Choose a Master that is free from everything, who doesn't worry for anything. In a dream you accept what comes. Here, do the same. Accept everything. Things come and go, but nothing stays. The guest must go, the host remains. The guest cannot say, "This is my house." If you are everywhere how can you be a devil, a Saint, or God? Or, you are all these things. All are your thoughts. So, he knows that there is nothing good in him and nothing bad in him. For the Saint, everybody can come in. He is open and welcomes everyone. Everyone is Himself. And why even say "my house?" Be out of everything. Throw off all the appearances on you. The mind, knowledge, intellect, possessions; all of these are appearances on you. Only then can you see yourself.

The temple and the graveyard are always open. The graveyard is also a temple. Dead bodies go off, and what remains is true. Some people go to the graveyard to meditate. Nobody disturbs you, it's quiet. However, if you understand your body is a dead body at this very moment, no need for the graveyard. You may live in a cottage or a palace, take it for granted that it's still a graveyard. All of the dead bodies are moving in the world. Everybody cries in the world. All are unhappy. Saints don't cry because they know everything is wrong. Unnecessarily people worry. People worry for the death while they are living. A Saint was told that he was going to die tomorrow. He said, "I'll worry about it tomorrow." Tomorrow never comes, take it for granted. Every day is today. There is no time or space in the Reality. No today, tomorrow, or yesterday. In the beginning you have to give all of this some thought and attention. Welcome everything, and then throw it off. Bondage is when you take it as true. (To the original questioner.) What you said is okay, but still it is a thought. You are not that. Be out of the "Circle of Ignorance" and then re-enter, no harm. Ignorance cannot come to you if you have understood that you don't exist.

Questioner: Before awakening, does what you eat or drink make a difference, helpful or harmful?

Maharaj: Whatever you like to eat or drink, who is there to stop you?

Questioner: Nobody but me.

Maharaj: That "me" is the dirty thing, take out that "me." If the snake is there take out its poisonous tooth, and then you can play with him. Even if he bites you, you know you are not going to die because it's not true.

Questioner: I don't know that now.

Maharaj: So now what?

Questioner: Some people say that certain food and drink block the subtle body, so they suggest a vegetarian diet.

Maharaj: These are all thoughts. In your Christian tradition wasn't wine brought at Christ's birth? Wasn't he God? In the Indian tradition they never put wine before God. So, water is also the basis of wine, and both water and wine help to digest food. Are they one or not? If you take brandy and get a kick you forget yourself, but that is not the real forgetting because you remember after the kick wears off. Real forgetting is when you take the brandy and you don't get the kick in your mind. A man who drinks and says, "Give me the change, I can count it." He is not intoxicated. In the same way, accept anything in the world, but don't get the kick in the mind. If you say it's true then you get the kick. When you say it's not, then what harms you?

Questioner: It was a teaching of my previous Master that being a vegetarian was helpful. It was good for the vibrations in the body. Is that true?

Maharaj: Suppose you drink and eat non-vegetarian food, can you not understand? These are all bodily affairs. By taking only good things have you become good? Are those people realized by all of this? Bodily affairs are not my concern, be out of it.

Questioner: Are there any Masters who eat meat?

Maharaj: Understand yourself, that's the point. The body is not you. You see yourself as a body. You are not the body. What is good and what is bad? These are all nonsense thoughts, I tell you. Get out of your mind. Good and bad is the mind's work.

My own Master asked his disciples, "Bring me anything that is bad in the world." They couldn't find anything bad, but finally someone brought shit. But without shit you can't get food. Fertilizers are required. Nothing is bad in the world, nothing is good. The "I" that judges what is good and what is bad, and that doesn't accept, is what is bad. That's the meaning in it. Good and bad is according to circumstances.

Questioner: So what you are saying is total separation between body and God?

Maharaj: He pervades everywhere. Where is He not? He may even be in the brandy or in the shit, why not? I don't eat meat, or drink. That's my choice. Suppose someone is sitting next to me eating meat and drinking wine. Should I say he's bad? I should not feel anything. Then the idea of Oneness comes in your mind.

One of Siddharameshwar's disciples was playing cards with him, and he was in the habit of smoking. So he excused himself so as not to smoke in front of the Master. So, the Master gave him a bidi (an Indian cigarette) to smoke. The Master didn't mind. That's the meaning in it. One can be so open, but due to the body you become a small creature. Why all this worry? When you say good food and good things bring good ideas, that is bondage. A dog eats meat and so does a tiger. One is a faithful companion, and the other is dangerous. They both eat the same things. Is one bad and one good? So nothing is bad, take it for granted. Good is bondage. Reality is everywhere. Accept it. Krishna always told lies and never told the truth. And Rama was always telling the truth. Krishna is considered a full incarnation, and Rama a half incarnation. Everything is in me, good and bad. If you don't drink, that is your choice, but don't judge others. Everything is simply okay. This is real freedom. If you are in the jail all you think of is being in jail. When you are out of jail what to think of and what not to think of? You're ever free.

* * * * * * * * * * *

January 6, 1998

Maharaj: When Siddharameshwar Maharaj was there, there were no cassettes. The Master must be a complete Master, and he was a complete Master. He gave everything, and that was his greatness. Many teachers don't give the final understanding. One has to go beyond Knowledge, where the Knowledge becomes Ignorance. That stage he explained to us, and made us understand. Krishna had a friend, a bosom friend, and when Krishna was going to leave the body he asked Krishna to take him with him. Krishna said, "Where I'm going I can't take you." Though he was a close friend of Krishna, he didn't know the heart of Krishna. He insisted that Krishna take him with him, so Krishna began to teach him, to give him the Knowledge, the understanding. You cannot remain in the body. When it's time, the body must go. So the friend said to Krishna, "You are a very shrewd fellow, only when I wanted to go with you did you tell me these things. And now that I understand, and you have given this precious Knowledge to me, I must praise you for this. You must show me your heart as well." After liberation one should worship. Once you have understood, what is left for you to do? There is nothing to be done. Only praise the one who has taught you these things. He is in your heart no doubt, and you and he are one. Make duality there, make incompleteness, but only for the thanking. When you have the final understanding, and then you worship, that is the best.

Questioner: Is it true that the guru does everything and the disciple does nothing?

Maharaj: Yes. But the disciple must enter the door. That is his responsibility. But you must meet the right guru. Otherwise you are lost in heaven. Lost in heaven means lost in hell. One must be very shrewd to see how the Master acts and what he does. And then you can accept his heart in you. Then the friend told Krishna, "I'm not going with you because you are not going anywhere." All the bubbles are ocean, nothing but ocean. The Master cannot give you anything. He guides you to the right place. Nothing is to be achieved here. As you have forgotten yourself he gives you the right understanding. I don't criticize anybody, but a Master must give the right understanding. But in Reality, how can the Master give you anything? There is only Oneness in the world, so who is the giver and who will be given to? If you get the right address and you don't knock on the door, who is responsible? You have to knock, then you get the final understanding without doing anything, and then you are He.

So in the beginning faith is required, complete faith in the Master. Meditation is also required in the beginning. It is an initial stage. Then you can feel, "He is my Master." If you don't go to the school you can't learn. My Master always said this is a college or school for ignorant persons. What the Master says accept it. Master sometimes says wrong things also to test your faith. You as the aspirant must always be on the alert, otherwise you won't understand the Master. The Master says so many things, some of them are beyond the sky. Many teachers go up to the sky, but they don't go beyond Zero, or the sky (Space). Don't take your Master as an ordinary person. That's the main point. What he does is okay. He can make you all Gods. He makes you aware of your own Power and then you can act any way you like, because a king has no law. If the Power is used wrongly then the ego comes. If you are after fame and name, or whatever, you are misguided. When there is only Oneness how can you separate yourself from others?

In this way, Siddharameshwar Maharaj gave us the understanding. Everybody is myself, so who to bow down to, and who not to? So Lord Krishna gave his heart and showed how to act after understanding, how to live and what to do, and what not to do. There is no duality at all, only Oneness. If the Master makes the duality, he has not understood. All the ornaments are nothing but gold. No matter where you are you are always He. But as long as the body is there one should always be an aspirant. Even if you make duality, still it's only one. If you put money in your left pocket or in your right pocket it's still yours. Is it one or not? Everything is yours anyway. When you understand that you are He, you are always free, and you are independent of what happens or doesn't happen. The screen has nothing to do with the pictures. Be touchless (untouched). Why? Because it is nothing. If "nothing" touches you, you are in Ignorance. The highest understanding is that there is nobody but me, everyone is myself, so who to care for and who not to care for?

Questioner: Maharaj, did you get the understanding before or after your Master left his body?

Maharaj: Don't ask that question. Why? Nothing is to be done. I saw him and he conquered me. I was an ignorant person. I was just twelve years old. I didn't know anything. I saw him and that's all. All are He, what to understand more? If an ant concentrates on a bee one day the ant will fly without wings, why not!

Questioner: All I can do is meditate on you?

Maharaj: Meditate on Me, not the body. Then He is in the form of the Reality. The Master is in the form of Reality, because he is always in Reality. "I" should be taken off, nothing else. "I" is the black cloud before the sun. Because of the ego you can't see the sun. There was a saint who over many lifetimes was wandering here and there but still could not reach the destination. If a real person meets you, he is the destination, nothing else. Understand that you are He then you can do anything. Once you get the degree, the college has no authority over you. Do what you like. When you understand your own Power, to whom can you show the Power? There is nothing of any importance afterwards. When everything is Illusion, what is there to be impressed by? Illusion cannot be true. I agree. Concentrate on the Master, but the Master is not Master. The Master doesn't remain Master, otherwise he's lost. If I say, "I'm the Master" then I'm not a Master. Nobody is separate! Separation is gone. Be out of the Circle of Ignorance, then re-enter and the ego won't remain. Don't say "I'm something." The disease of Knowledge is the worst. Don't be an entity. Something is nothing, take it for granted. Self without self is the Final Reality. Say, "I'm nothing." Socrates said, "I know I know nothing."

All the people sitting here are all one; only the shape and names differ. When you sleep you don't exist, why say more? The "I" doesn't exist. When a king and a poor chap sleep, they both forget who they are. Awakening comes, and then he says "I'm a king" or "I'm a beggar." So, due to the mind everything is going on. The mind should be made "no-mind." no-mind means "I do nothing." People run to see what has happened, what is going on. When one understands that nothing has happened, then, no-mind. The world is nothing. Understand at the moment this is a dead body. As long as the Power is there, the body works, and when disconnection comes, it's finished. If you understand that which is not, at the moment it frees you from the worry of death also. So, to be a Master is also an Illusion. Don't be the Master. You can play your part as a Master if somebody wants to hear, no harm. Give the right understanding. Some teachers say that after many births you can get the Reality, or do this or that, and then you can get it. That's all nonsense. Foolishness!

So, she asked me when I got to the destination? I was He before I met him, and after I met him he conquered me, that's all. Have complete faith in the Master and afterwards faith is not required. The one who keeps the faith becomes He. If you have ten lahks (one lahk is equal to 100,000) in the bank, and I say keep faith in it, is there any meaning in it? I know I've got it, why tell me? You see the whole dream, and when you get up, you say it never happened. It never existed. It is nothing. Nothing is always nothing. You say nothing is something, and that is Ignorance. First know yourself, otherwise how can you know others? So in the Bible, Christ says, "Know thyself and you'll know the world." All of the fruits of the tree come from one seed. In the same way, all are the fruits of the Oneness. Attributes may be in different combinations, but still there is only Oneness. Everything is mine; all hands, legs and minds, they're all mine. Then opposition doesn't remain. Nothing is bad in the world, and nothing is good also. I have two hands. That which one is bad and which one is good? When there is nothing, everything comes in. It all comes from Zero. Virtue, sin, right and wrong, all come from nothing. Be ignorant to the world and knowledgeable to the Reality. Say, "I'm not this" and the ego goes off. Ego has no entity, what to do? Everybody says "I," can you show your "I"? You can't see your face, so a looking glass is required. All senses work with the Power, yet you can't see the Power.

Understand what is the source, where everything starts. It all starts from Zero. The world is nothing but Zero. The sky is Zero, so everything comes from Zero. And Reality is beyond Zero, that's why researchers will never find Him, because He is beyond Zero. The Power that is so subtle, which makes everything work, can you feel it? Why? Because it is nothing. How can you feel it? The Power starts from Zero, but Reality is beyond Zero. So everything can be forgotten in a fraction of a second, just as you see it in a dream. The year 1997 came, now it is gone. Where has it gone? And where has 1998 come from, and where will it go? You cannot say anything. As long as Consciousness is there you say everything. Everything is in Consciousness, nothing else. Time, place, distance, everything comes there. The Power is in everybody and everybody works with that Power. Understand that and you are out of the Circle of Ignorance. In the Final Reality there is no time or place or distance. You cannot forget yourself. You are always there. You never forget "I," because you are the source of all these things. If you are not there, who will say anything? A dead man cannot say anything. So, you have to die. When I am not, then who is there? He is there. Nobody wants to die, what to do?

Questioner: Is it true that only the guru can remove the fear of death?

Maharaj: Because you don't die. Death is to the body. You are not the body. What comes must go, but you are ever there. Electricity doesn't worry if a bulb goes off. Put in another bulb and you get the light. You are everywhere. You are the source of everything. How can you die? The Master makes you He, and there is no death for you. I still go ahead, and say this is a dead body at the moment. The Power is connected, so it speaks. In a fraction of second the Power can be disconnected. Be He, that's the main point. Everybody fears death. Don't be an ant, be a lion, and say, "No death for me." All these notions of birth and death, come from the mind. They are the pictures in the mind. Be the producer. These pictures are made by me. Everything starts from you, but then you identify with the picture. You forget that you are the producer of these thoughts. If you are not there, who can say anything? Have the Knowledge but say, "I am an ignorant person. I know that I know nothing." The Master plays a part and teaches you, that is all. The kick of Ignorance has come in the mind, what to do? The kick of the drink comes and you can say anything. You can create the whole world. The Power is such. That which is nothing can make many things. Many varieties come in nothing. How can there be variety when there is only One? Only Oneness is there, so there is no variety. People want variety because they're ignorant. What you see is only your thoughts, it starts from nothing and ends in nothing. Gold doesn't say, "I'm an earring, or a chain." Gold is gold. Understand everything is one and then nothing remains.

* * * * * * * * * *

January 9, 1998

Questioner: My son who was sixteen died last year in a motorcycle accident. I now feel lost in the world, and I am looking for the meaning in life because I want to find peace and serenity. I would like to meet my son again by the way of the spirit. Is that possible? Why is there so much suffering in the world? And why is there no equality between people in the world? Why did my son die so young? He had so much to do in life.

Maharaj: He died by a mistake, mistakes happen. Why him? The question doesn't arise. One is not born at all. The question of death doesn't come in. An ignorant person thinks, "I am born." When you are born you must die. Birth means death. Suppose one says, "Why should I have to pass the stools?" Because you eat. If you eat you must pass the shit. Why are people unhappy and why no equality? That which is not true, which is incomplete, how can it give happiness? Why did he die so young? He had so much to do, she says. He doesn't say anything now. Suppose you are in a dream and you want to become a great manager of a company. Where does the wish go? Only thoughts remain. Same way here also, people want to do many things in life and be fulfilled. But they can't complete or finish what they want. Why? It is just not true, that's the main point. There cannot be completion in the Illusion. Illusion means "nothing." All have different wishes, and if all the wishes are fulfilled, how can the world remain? Nobody wants to be poor, but poverty is there. Nobody wants to die, but still they die. What to do? The world is not complete. Many ideas come in the mind. Suppose one wants to be a dog. Can you be a dog? I always give bad examples. The problem is that the wishes are for the wrong things. What is real has nothing to do with all these desires and fears.

You are sleeping, and you get the dream. When you awake you say, "It's only a dream." Nothing is there. The world starts from Zero and ends in Zero and all you get is Zero. She says many things are to be done. For what? When you give birth to a child, he must die sooner or later. And can I see him again? People think such nonsense things. Where is he now? He has become Zero. Name and shape have gone off. If you understand that which is not, then the question of death doesn't arise. People are in Ignorance. They don't understand, so they ask all these questions. Nobody wants to die. Why should I die? The dream comes, and the dream goes. This world is nothing but a long dream. That which is not can never be true. It feels solid to you now due to your gross body and your sensations. In a dream if someone slaps you, when you awake only your pillow is there. Nothing is there, but you experience it due to the dream. There is no meaning in these questions, I tell you. These questions are correct according to the Ignorance of the person. The root of birth is nothing but misery and problems, so how can the fruits of pleasure come? Duality is the cause of all this.

There was a man who in Marathi his name translates as "dust," meaning no value. Then he got some money and became rich. Then, instead of being called by his given name, they referred to him as Mister Dust. Then he became even richer and they called him, "Master Dust." So the man said, "The name is given to money, and not to me. When I had no money I was called dust, and now due to my circumstances they give me a title, an honor." The root is sour, so how can the fruits be sweet? It's impossible. It's a wish for all who take birth that they have something better in the next life. That's the main point. And this desire is what makes you take birth again and again. You want to be great but how can you be great? The desire takes a body, which comes from Zero. The dream is always wrong, it can never be right. And how can you see that boy again? How will you recognize him? He has become dust. It is all simply wrong ideas in the mind. Death is nothing. There is no death for anybody. The five elements go to the five elements, and the Power goes to Power. The boy hasn't gone anywhere. He didn't exist in the first place. Suppose you have a child in a dream. Do you cry for it when you wake up? (Pointing to a flower.) This is a nice flower, I agree. When it dies and turns to dust would you like to see it?

Questioner: Why do we suffer so much when our children die?

Maharaj: It is the love for Illusion, the love for nothing. Why suffer? You say you're the body, I say you're not the body. The body is only a covering on you. For two or three minutes of pleasure you make a child and then it suffers for a whole life. No one dies for you, and when you die you become dust. Christ said, "Thou are dust, you eat dust, and finally you go into dust." The body is nothing but dust. When the body is working, it is working only on the breath. And when the breath goes, nothing remains. Not even a thank you, or a goodbye!

One Saint's son died. He was giving sermons and he said the following day, "So many people die in the world everyday, why should I cry for one only?" When you say, "It's my child," you cry. One who understands that I'm not the body is happy, otherwise not. When you say, "I'm the body," the ego comes. The body is nothing but flesh, blood and bones. If the body is nicely finished you like it. Ignorance is the concept "I am the body." Everything is false, nothing is true. Suppose you have a bundle weighing ten kilos and you give the contents away. Where is the bundle then, where has it gone? This body is nothing but a bundle of blood, flesh, wind, and bones. They have all come together and your parents have given it a name. What's a name? All names are false. His name is Bob, show me Bob. So many different names and they all are of no value.

If you break this flowerpot it becomes earth. Why are names given? Just to understand, and for convenience. Birth and death are only your thoughts. Suppose your dearest dies and someone tells you, "You loved him so much, keep him with you for a few days more." You of course say, "No, put him in the ground so we don't have to see him again." Nobody wants to be around dead bodies. The only solution to death is to forget. There are many bubbles in the ocean. If one breaks does the ocean cry? Why don't Saints cry? Because they have become the ocean, so why to worry?

Questioner: Is any of this true, like our being with you?

Maharaj: No, nothing is true. Everything comes from Ignorance. Due to Ignorance you say that I am a Master and you are an aspirant, but in fact the Reality is you! Due to the identification with the body-mind you think you don't know anything. So, then you are compelled to come to a Master and hear what he has to say. It is nothing but a dream. What I speak is also wrong. But I speak for the Truth. The address is wrong when you meet the person. There are no words in the stateless state. It really is quite different. All words come back from there. If someone sees an arrow pointing to the bathroom, the pointer is not the place. You can get an understanding through words, but words are no longer true when you reach the destination. What I tell you is wrong, but what I speak about is true. Words are only pointers. Your Self is He without self, Absolute Reality. Your separation is due to body-mind identification. You say, "I am this bubble." Due to mind you have become small, so you need to expand your thoughts and become bigger and bigger. Eventually the balloon will burst and you will become He. Break down the walls of your mind and you become the sky.

Bondage is only your thoughts, that's why the Master has to change your thinking. You are not the body, you are the Power. That is what you must think again and again. Then the understanding will come. Everyone wants to see a picture, a photo of himself, no matter how he looks. But the photo is not you. It is a shadow of the Reality. If you focus on the shadow you can't see the Reality. Forget the shadow and you are He. Nothing is happening or ever happens, but still you think so. Take it as a dream. The eyes have the habit to see what is not there. What to do? This is a dead body at the moment. If the Power is there, it speaks, otherwise not. If the bulb is bad you simply change it. The Power doesn't go off. And the woman who lost her child, when she sleeps does she forget or not? Due to the wrong idea in the mind you say it's mine, and then you suffer.

When you are away from the Master you may remember some things and forget others. Take it for granted that everything is nothing. The Master is also not the body. So you must churn what the Master says. If you don't then you will forget. That is the practice wherever you may be. Think again and again. He is everywhere, He is not the body, and you are He. When you sleep you forget everything. Are you not happy? Forget you are an American, or an Indian, or whatever it may be. Understanding is the practice that everything is Zero and an Illusion. How much time does it take to know yourself? You are He at this very moment. Nothing you see and perceive is true. That should be your understanding. All is nothing. It all depends on your mind and how you accept it. The Master does everything you do. He eats and sleeps, but his mind has been converted, nothing else. Then, good or bad thoughts may come, but you won't feel anything, because it is nothing.

If a rich man puts on dirty clothes, it does not make him poor. If you know your own wealth, what does it matter what people say? Know that you are the Creator of the world. Make the mind bigger and bigger and then it will go off. Then, only He remains. Doing and not doing will no longer be your concern. By doing, you're not doing, that is the basic understanding. A king gives orders others carry them out. Accordingly, the king gets the pleasure while others are doing the work. Don't be a small creature. Don't say "It's true." That is the mistake people make. Accept what the teacher says and your mind will always be at rest. Don't be a slave of the Illusion. Don't give it value. Keep it in your pocket but don't take the touch of it. Then nothing can harm you. If he says he's Bob, then he's lost. If he says he's not Bob, he's the Creator of the world. Overnight a beggar can become a king, why not? If you say, "It's all wrong," you're the king, and if you say, "It's true," you're a slave. So be the Master, not the slave.

* * * * * * * * * * *

January 10, 1998

Questioner: A few days ago when someone said, "I see," you said, "the Power sees." Also you said if two people are given the same address, and if one person gets there and one doesn't, the reason is the ego. Could you explain that in terms of the Power that is the same for both?

Maharaj: The Power doesn't do anything. Power is Power. Where you put it, it works. Like electricity, if you put it in a fan, or in a bulb it works. Electricity doesn't do anything, agree? In any contrivance it will work. But without Power you can't do anything. So who is the doer? The doer is not found. So for all the good and bad actions, nobody is the doer. Power doesn't know anything. Suppose electricity kills someone, can you file a lawsuit against it? Hands cannot move without the Power. Who does it then? That is the ego that says, "I do it, I see," and so on. Who is this "I"? Find out for yourself.

He says he's Bob. Where is he? He is a name only. A name is not true. But with that Power he does everything. If the culprit is not found, then the case is dismissed. You have become the culprit yourself. You say, "I do it, I see, I kill," but it is the hand that kills. Then, if you say, "I killed," the sentence of death comes to you. You consider the ego to be yourself but you are not that. The seed is one, and many fruits come out of it. Some are sour, some are sweet, and some turn out bad. Can the seed be blamed? Due to the mind you say good or bad. The mind is the agent of your Power. The mind does everything. The mind makes the discrimination. It's the same way with the Creator and the Creation. The Creator is not found. What to do? The Creator doesn't exist as told in our mythological books. He's called "Mahamaya." Maha means "big," and Maya means "that which is not." That which is not is a big nothing. That's the meaning of it. But this which is not, this nothing, can do many things.

In a dream you are sleeping. Your eyes are closed and in your dream you kill someone. Who did it? When awakening comes, who is the killer? You say, "How can I kill someone?" and then you say, "It was only a dream." The world is nothing but a long dream. You don't exist but still you say, "I did it." The one who doesn't exist does everything. When you say, "I am the doer," then you must get the sentence. Electricity doesn't know, "I run the fan." The sun doesn't know, "I give the light." If the sun says, "I give the light," then it's not the sun. If a mango says, "I'm sweet," then it's not a mango. So where is the "I"? The doer is not found here. The name comes and you say, "I'm this."

When you die it is written in a book that So-and-so died. The name which has come, has gone. Nobody dies, take it for granted. Still, you fear death because you say, "I'm the body," what to do? If you say, "I'm the body," then death must come. The body has taken the birth, you have not taken the birth. Power is there, so light comes. And when the bulb goes off, you put in another bulb. Electricity doesn't know if a bulb is good or bad, or if there is light. Power doesn't know anything. How can it know? Power is Knowledge now, Knowledge is Power. If Power is not there, you can't do anything. With the Power you can do everything.

So who is the doer? Who made the dream, tell me? You are sleeping in complete Ignorance, agree? Some thought comes and then anything happens. A king dreams that he's a beggar, and vice-versa. Who did it? From Ignorance a thought came, and everything happens. So when you awake, you say it was a wrong thing. It was a dream. Here (in the waking state), it is a dream also. Your father and mother gave you a name and you became that because you accepted that. What was your name before birth, tell me? And what will be your name after death? Due to the Power, you do everything. It doesn't take the blame or credit for anything. Power doesn't know, "I'm Power." These are all subtle things one should understand. If you say, "I see," who is it that sees? With that Power, you see. The Power doesn't see. With the Power, all of the senses work. What you do is only in your thoughts. Without your thoughts can you do anything? Thought means mind. Without mind you can't do anything. The mind works with that Power. I agree.

Questioner: Where do your thoughts come from?

Maharaj: From Zero. When you are sleeping you are in complete Ignorance. Then a thought comes. It's automatic. Both Knowledge and Ignorance are there in a very subtle form. As long as you are breathing, Knowledge is there. Breathing is Power, nothing else. It's a sub-Power station. Everything is mixed-up, so how to find the doer? Nobody is there. Why? It doesn't exist. It's an Illusion. If it's an Illusion, how can it be true? You say the Power does it. The Power doesn't do anything. When you dry your clothes in the sun, does the sun know this? The sun doesn't know either light or darkness. There is no discrimination in the Power.

Questioner: Is the mind separate from the ego?

Maharaj: The mind is ego. The mind is the sub-agent of ego. The manager should be there, and the clerk should be there. All are required, otherwise the factory can't run. This body is a factory of shit. Agree? What do you produce? So, then you say that I am the owner of this shit mill. Ego says, "I'm this." He will say, "I'm Bob," at once. You must think about these things, and maybe go a little further where there is no thought, the Final Reality. Without thinking, you are not a man, you're an animal. You have the discrimination power to know what is true and what is not true, or what is Reality. Who does everything? Who speaks? The "I" can't speak. Only if the Power is there can there be speech. No Power, then nothing. "Thinking is not myself, Knowledge is not myself, and Ignorance is not myself." It is all nothing but your thoughts. Knowledge and Ignorance are two sides of one coin. If you want to know something, Knowledge must be there to ask, "What is this?" With Knowledge you ask. He, the Reality, doesn't do anything. But you say, "I've done it." The eyes cannot see. A dead man has eyes, can he see? You must go beyond all these things.

Knowledge is just a thought. Reality has been forgotten and all this Knowledge has come up. From Ignorance and forgetfulness Knowledge has come up. How can it be true? If the source is bitter then what you drink is bitter. Everything is Knowledge, nothing else. But Knowledge is not true. That is what one should understand. I am talking about the last state now. When Knowledge is there, everything is done by that Knowledge. But from where does this Knowledge come? It comes from Zero. You must understand who you are. Christ says, "Know yourself and you will know the world."
You don't know yourself, and you still say, "I'm that." It creates a mess. If the "I" doesn't exist, who sees, who hears? Actually nothing happens, but you say, "I experienced it" at that time. Just like in a dream, you see, hear and experience, but when awakening comes, what is true? This world is a living dream, Mahamaya. The Creator is also Mahamaya. It is nothing, and from nothing many things have come. There is no end to it. From Zero a thousand crores are counted. (One hundred lakhs makes one crore; one crore equals 100 X 100,000 or ten million.) If no Zero, then the "I" cannot come. The Reality has nothing to do with all these things.

You sing, you dance, you cry, you laugh; what has the screen to do with all these events? The screen always remains the screen. Understand that it is nothing. It all starts from Zero. You say it's true because you are in the kick of Ignorance. A drunkard says in the kick of the drink that "I am a king." And you say, "I am So-and-so." (pointing to a man who was given an Indian name.) To that which has no entity, why should many different names be given? What is the meaning of this? The one who understands says nothing has happened. So, nothing can do many things, because it is nothing. Reality is real, and doesn't do anything. It is not affected at all.

When you understand yourself, you can say with confidence that the world is nothing. When you see yourself as part and parcel of the world you say, "I am So-and-so," and "He is So-and-so." With understanding, you can erase everything just like writing a wrong word and then erasing it. Up to now whatever you have learned, forget it. What you say is all wrong things. You never speak the truth. The base is true, that is You without you. It is always there but it doesn't speak. So now nobody is a seer, nobody sees. But the base must be there otherwise how can the world remain? So don't be the seer and don't be the accused. It is the attraction to the mind's work such as virtue, love, good deeds and their opposites that creates the bondage. You keep duality as your companion, and when you die, the good and bad deeds remain and are reflected in your mind. When a Saint dies he doesn't worry because he doesn't exist and he doesn't carry these thoughts with him. He knows that nobody dies, and that birth and death are nothing but your thoughts.

Questioner: The other day you said that when the body is dead, and the mind is dead, only desire remains to be born again. Is there a relationship between Power and desire?

Maharaj: Without the Power how can you do anything? Desire cannot come without Power.

Questioner: Is desire and Power the same?

Maharaj: No. How can it be? Desire is a thought. Don't mix up these things. Unless the Power is there, the ego cannot come. How can you speak without the Power? In the "Final Understanding," the Power itself doesn't exist. It goes off. Everything gets absorbed in the Reality. Say that something comes upon you, you get a boil and you go to the doctor to cut it off. It's part of your body but still you want it removed. The Power works in you and then you say, "I do, I work, I feel pain." But it is the Power that does all these things. The body is just a contrivance. Without the Power what can you do? But the Power doesn't say anything, it doesn't even know it is the Power. It is the ego that says, "I want, I do," and it takes the responsibility for what is done. The ego is just your name, and all of your desires and fears come from it. The Power has nothing to do with all of this. All of your desires and fears are bodily affairs and the cause of your suffering and pain. And still you say, "I am this." This body is an abscess on you and you have to cut it away with understanding.

How many times have you cried in this life? For what! A young boy cries and cries and his father says that he is always crying for nothing. When you cry for nothing who will help you? Everyone cries for nothing. If it doesn't exist, they want it. Everyone wants happiness. How can you get it? Understand what joy, pain, and pleasure are. Unless you understand these things what's the use of it? After understanding nothing remains. That's the main point. When you examine your thoughts and your mind, nothing remains. You say this is a flowerpot. It can be broken in a second. It is nothing. That is what you must understand. People ask you, "What is your good name?" No name is good, but still they ask. You're no name. From where does everything start? Go to the source. If you go to the source, nothing remains. All of the Saints say to know thyself. Due to Ignorance you want to be somebody. If one has no name, what to say about him? He is just like the sky, nothing. If you go to the source of "I," the "I" goes off. When your mind becomes objective and says, "I am this," then all pleasures and pains are born.

Actions don't remain also. Action of what you do goes off in the moment. It dies. Actions become no action. Done is done. It only remains in the mind. The mind keeps everything which is not. The mind accumulates everything. All that you see and perceive, and what you understand is nothing. Nothing exists. So, the world is a shadow of Reality. Come on now! The shadow is not true. When you take it as true, you are lost. All worship God but they don't know what God is. By Ignorance you say God is there. God is not at all anywhere. That God, that Power that is in you, and works in you, will also go off. If you really understand God, you will not worship anybody. That same Power that is in you is in Krishna and Christ, but still it doesn't remain.

Questioner: That Power you are speaking of, is that the Reality? What is Power?

Maharaj: Power is Knowledge. Knowledge also gets absorbed in the end. There is no Knowledge and no Ignorance in the Final Reality. So, what starts from Zero, how can it be true? The sky is Zero. A big cyclone comes in the sky. Where does it come from? It makes havoc, and then it goes away. Where does it go? Back into the sky. The sky is nothing, and yet that nothing is so Powerful. Everything happens in the sky, but still it is nothing. So the Power and the Knowledge are also wrong. "I know," you say. That is the Power, and that is Knowledge. What comes up is always wrong, it's not true. Sky, or space, is nothing but Zero. Still, everything comes from it and it is so Powerful. When you are in Zero you get the dream. You can't get the dream if you're not sleeping. Power is Zero, and from that everything starts. This world is created from Zero. Then who is the doer of Zero? You cannot find the Creator of Zero. In the dream who is the Creator? You are sleeping, you do nothing, but the dream comes. When awakening comes, you can say "It's only a dream." The world is true for everybody, but not for the Saint.

Questioner: So what is real?

Maharaj: Final Reality, where Ignorance and Knowledge don't remain. What happens is nothing. It starts from nothing. It starts from Zero. You forget yourself, which means Zero, and then everything starts. Final Reality is forgotten and that which is not appears. The world is just a shadow of Reality as I said before. The reflection is not true.

Questioner: In the Final Reality, there is no Power, correct?

Maharaj: Yes, no Power, and no thought. Where there is a thought, the Power must be there. He is there. Your Self is true, but it has no name. Words come back from there. Words come from the sky. You must go beyond sky. If there is no sky or space, can you speak? Knowledge comes from the sky, from Zero. From nothing everything comes. So nothing can make anything. Zero has that much Power. All what you see and perceive comes from this Knowledge, and when you say it is real, then that is Ignorance. Knowledge is God. The Creator is Knowledge. This is both difficult and easy to understand. Forget yourself and everything is okay. The "I" doesn't allow you to grasp this.

Questioner: What is the experience of someone who has grasped the ultimate truth?

Maharaj: He understands that I without I is there. Self without self is there, that is his experience.

Questioner: So when there is no more Ignorance, where is the Power coming from?

Maharaj: Ignorance must be there. As long as the body is there, Ignorance must remain. Why talk of a realized person? First realize and then ask. The question doesn't arise then. When you wake up from a dream, you say it was nothing. Here, all are in Ignorance. What you see is nothing. A realized person says it's nothing. When a body dies, a realized person says that nothing has happened. From Zero all these things happen, so what is true? When all is nothing, then who am I now? You don't remain. "I" is not true.

Questioner: One plus one is two. It's logical. Is the understanding of the Reality as logical or as easy as one plus one?

Maharaj: It's easier. One plus one is a method. For understanding no method is required. You are He. When you are He, who will know whom? Duality is gone. One plus one is duality. There is no duality, only He exists, or Self without self.

Questioner: I cannot see that there is no duality. I have no proof.

Maharaj: It is because it is not. It doesn't exist. Oneness is there. There is only one. There is nothing in the world except Him. All are nothing but the bubbles in the ocean. Millions of bubbles and you are just one of them. You must break your bubble, nothing else. The Master helps to break your bubble by understanding, that's all. You are He. So, to know yourself, what you are, is more easy or not? You misrepresent yourself, what to do? Everybody is He. Everybody has the same name. So who to call, and who not to call? There is only Oneness. What to experience and what not to experience since everything is nothing? Why should the sky worry for anything? Things come and go, do they affect the sky? Sky remains sky. Be like the sky and say, "Nothing has happened." Everything comes upon the screen and goes off. If it were true it would have remained. If good thoughts come to you, you don't become good. If bad thoughts come you don't become bad. Thoughts just pass away. Past, present, and future are in the mind only. People want to help other people. Who are you to help anyone? When you don't exist how can you help anyone? For most people their existence is nothing but money. If one has no money, does he have mercy, or not? With money you say, "I've done something." With money you say, "I've done merciful things." What is mercy? It is just a wish. If you give five or ten lakhs, your mercy is limited. God's mercy is unlimited. So why should you have mercy on anyone? Who are you to do that? You don't exist. When you are not there who will be merciful, who will be bad and who will be good? All these things are nothing but the thoughts of your mind. The mind always takes on many colors. Knowledge always wants to grow more and more. But Knowledge is the greatest Ignorance. If you don't understand that, you will never be happy.

Questioner: The idea of being born or reborn means nothing, yes?

Maharaj: Nothing. Nobody is reborn, and nobody dies also. There is no birth and no death. Suppose a child is born to you in a dream, which birth date will you accept for it? This world is nothing but a long dream.

Questioner: The scriptures talk of rebirth and no rebirth. What is your understanding?

Maharaj: That depends on your wish. You take birth by your own wish. If one has no wish, what birth will you take? Wish for a body is the greatest desire. "I want a body," is the strongest wish. If a building is condemned and you are living in it, you want help to locate somewhere else. But a Saint doesn't worry. The sky is my home, I can sleep anywhere. You want a house or a body. The body is nothing. All these thoughts of birth and death are the mind's work. Understanding these things comes by thinking. Without thinking you can't get it. Nobody puts you in bondage. You take it on yourself. So it's not difficult to know yourself. You never forget yourself. You're always there. But you misrepresent the "I." Don't misrepresent! Say "Everything is nothing." That's the right way. If you say "It's something," you're lost, and troubles come. What is true? Self without self.

Questioner: What is grace?

Maharaj: Grace is understanding. The Master gives you understanding, that is the grace. So accept it! That is grace. The boy goes to school to learn and the teacher teaches him. If he doesn't accept whose fault is it? If he accepts he can become a teacher too, why not? Acceptance is required, nothing else. If you put your hand on someone's head can you learn? Is that grace? It's all nonsense. What a teacher says you must experience that. Be that. Nothing to become. You are He at this very moment. Master takes away your Ignorance. You gain nothing.

* * * * * * * * * * *

January 14, 1998

Questioner: All of my life I have been looking for this inner peace and serenity. Since I have met you, I wonder if the inner peace and serenity are an Illusion. Is this correct? Should I stop hoping to get this state?

Maharaj: A state is not the Reality because Final Reality is stateless. When you say, "I want peace," that is also a thought. When there is a peace some interference always comes, and then you lose your peace. What is lost cannot be true. Some Saints say that peace is the bliss of heaven. That's okay. But still you have to go beyond peace. Peace is of the mind. Something always happens to break the peace. There is no peace or its opposite in the Final Reality. On the screen someone speaks loudly. What does the screen have to do with it? The screen has nothing to do with all these things. Reality has nothing to do with the world that has come up. Many things happen, He, the Reality, has not lost or gained anything. On the basement (foundation) you may build fifty stories. The basement has nothing to do with this. When you sleep, peace is there. Does it remain? Peace can be broken. It doesn't remain, because whatever happens is nothing. It's an Illusion. You must understand that. A cyclone comes from the sky and causes many problems. Finally, it ends in the sky. What does the sky have to do with it? Still, you are subtler than the sky. This cannot be understood by experiencing. It is there, just like the screen is there. In the same way, many things come and go, the screen remains the screen. So you are just like a screen. Everything comes upon you and goes, and you are unaffected. In the beginning I agree you have to go for peace, but that is not the final state. Why? Because what happens and what you experience is nothing but an Illusion. So it is not. It doesn't exist, so how can it disturb you?

This world is nothing but a long dream. People are all in Ignorance. They have no understanding of the Reality. So they want some peace. So people like to go to a peaceful place where there is no distraction, but where is your mind at that time? Is it peaceful? You have to go beyond that. I don't say no, something is better than nothing. No harm. When you say everything is true, you chase it like anything. Everybody chases happiness. Many thoughts both good or bad come in the mind, still you are there, you never forget yourself. Self is always Self without self. Self is ego, there is no "I" there in the Final Reality. Forget the "I" and He is there. When nothing is true, then who remains? He remains. He is so natural. People make it so unnatural. When you say, "I'm in peace," you are not in peace. It's only your thought. How can the peace be He? He is thoughtless, no thoughts are there. The screen never says, "I've spoken loudly and sung," or "I killed someone." Nothing has happened to the screen. The screen doesn't take the touch of it. By understanding, one doesn't take the touch of it. When you do you are in Ignorance. How can nothing harm you? Peace is a concept or state. Understand that way. Swami Ramdas (Saint Samartha Ramdas of 17th century India) says "Doing everything, you do nothing." Understand that! By crying, you don't cry. You say, "I cry," that is the mistake. Crying is a state. Laughing is also a state. Nobody can cry forever and nobody can laugh forever. All these thoughts are nonsense. They don't remain and they are not true. Nothing is required of you, and there is nothing to acquire. Whatever happens, are you there or not? You never forget your Self. So I strongly say, "When you go to the graveyard, you never forget your Self" The body goes to the graveyard. All of these ideas come in your mind, and you take everything as true. In sleep there is peace, and when you get up, you say it's not true, it is nothing. You must have the complete conviction in the mind that nothing happens, and nothing is true. All the ornaments are nothing but gold. How can it be anything else. The name is wrong, but everyone accepts it. Shape is also wrong. The Reality in everybody pervades everywhere. So who will see Him and by which eyes can you look at Him? So, it is very simple to understand. Forget everything, and He is there.

January 16, 1998

Questioner: Today is my last day here. I know that I should feel close to you even when I am away, but I feel better when I am in your presence. So how can I reduce the gap?

Maharaj: There is no time and no gap also. He is everywhere and anywhere. You should not forget this. That is the main point. You are He, you are ever He, so what harms you? Only ignorance of the Self, nothing else. One should practice, "I am everywhere and nothing else is there at all." There is only Oneness so whatever you see and perceive is He. When you look at yourself in the looking glass you see your face only. So we call it a shadow or reflection. You feel it is true due to Ignorance. It is nothing. And as a result of this appearance you become something. The name you were given, you become that. So as you have forgotten yourself, you have to go to the Master. Otherwise there is no need. Body is ego, you have become the ego, but the ego has no existence at all. So, one should find out who is God or "Who am I?" God you cannot find. So find out who you are. You have to absorb that "I." The "I" doesn't exist. If you don't, then "God" and "you" will remain, and that is duality. As long as duality is there, no happiness is possible. Even with the best of minds there are mind differences and tensions. Where there is Oneness, no tensions remain. When the "I" goes off, then only He remains. He is so subtle, more subtle than the sky. Space and sky are Zero. He is beyond sky so how can you see Him? And who will see Him, and with what instrument can you see Him?

The Master can give you the understanding in words only, and words are pointers, nothing else. To say "I exist" is bondage; you become something. You are never bound by anything, but you say and think "I'm something." When you experience Oneness, then all that you see and perceive is He. Duality creates confusion in you, so first you should know, "Who am I?" You are nothing, but still you say, "I'm this." Can you give me a sample of yourself? Is it written anywhere on you? You say "I'm here," but the Master says, "You are nowhere." You say all these things, but he who says cannot be found. You have become a demon of Ravanna. (Maharaj recounts the story of Ravanna from the Ramayana and how Rama cuts off the devil's ten heads.) One drop of Ravanna and another devil comes up. So you're the Ravanna. By your thoughts everything has come up. Rama could not find out the death of Ravanna because Ravanna never existed. Rama himself became Ravanna so how can he kill him? Understand! His name is Bob, but he doesn't exist. When one doesn't exist, how to kill him? Hanuman was Ram's helper. Hanuman means mind, or monkey. If you give a ladder to a monkey he will just go up and down. So, the mind is just like a monkey, thinking of everything and then forgetting. You do that everyday. You do this and that everyday like the monkey. The scriptures give the understanding in a very nice way, otherwise it's just a story. You have forgotten yourself, and you are moving all the time just to support the belly. If no belly, who will care for whom? Tell me. So Rama has made many demons out of himself. By your eyes you have made so many demons. By hearing and tasting and thinking you create so many "I wants"! Ask your mind what you don't want. The mind wants everything, and mind is nothing but your thoughts. You say something is good or bad according to your thoughts. Only the "I" thought is bad, but even that doesn't exist. So don't be a Hanuman, a monkey. You do the same thing as him only in a more sophisticated way.

When understanding comes, there is neither good nor bad. Due to Ignorance you say, "I've got the birth and I will die." The body dies, you don't die. Then why should you worry? Everyone fears death, nobody wants to die. The ego doesn't want to die. So, you don't have to worry, you are always with the Master. You are never away from him. If you say that everything is true, then you must practice that "Nothing is true, including myself. I don't exist." The house doesn't say, "I'm a house," the flowerpot doesn't say, "I'm a pot." You give the names so you are the demon. You make many, many demons out of yourself. How can you get happiness? Ravanna (ego) should be killed by Rama. When you say "I am," then the demon remains there. The demon exists by your thought. If you don't exist then nobody exists. "I am everywhere and everyone," that should be your understanding. Even practicing is not necessary. Faith also is not necessary. You are He at this very moment. Why say more? The Master has to say these things because you have forgotten yourself and you don't know. The Master gives the address and you must follow it, or not? Then you get to the place. He never dies, is never born, and never comes and goes. Bondage and liberation do not exist. They are only thoughts.

The parrot catcher takes a hollow tube and string and makes a triangle and puts it on a tree. The parrot comes and sits on it. As his head is heavy he falls upside down. So he holds on tighter as he is afraid of falling. The next morning the parrot catcher comes. He picks up the triangle and the parrot is still holding on. The catcher then puts him in a cage. Then the parrot thinks he is free now while in the cage. I've got support now. Bondage is accepted, even though he knows how to fly.

In the West your food comes in stages, soup, salad, main course. In India we put everything out at the same time. It is a matter of custom. No need to change these things. What you like is often a question of custom, or fashion. In India it is the custom that when the wife dies, the husband must cut off his mustache. The people then know his wife is dead. When you are He you are never in mourning. But when there is nothing you mourn, what to do? Scientists say that matter never dies. I have spoken so many words, where are they now? Where have they gone? So many people have died, where have they gone? In a graveyard? Are they there? Before you die you say "Bury me beside my husband." All these nonsense thoughts are there. Where to find anything or anyone? Nothing exists. If you go to the market and say, "I want to sell myself," who will purchase you? The barren woman's son has no existence. What name can you give nothing? The body is nothing but a barren woman's son. You may be a hundred years old, but you never become old. You are ever fresh. In this way, you should understand that you are never away from anything. When you are He you are everywhere. Then, no question of separation comes. Separation is of the body only. As you have forgotten yourself, I have to say these things again and again for you. You are He.

(A man from Europe came into the room late. He has a spiritual name so Maharaj asks what is his original name.)

Maharaj: Both of your names are wrong. Why should Saints give more names? No need. One name is sufficient. Names are just names. The two names are both nothing. By two names you become more confused. You are the Final Reality. Why should names be given? You are nameless, you are thoughtless. Can you show me India? Is a map India? A name has no value. When you are born what was your name? You give names to that which has no existence.

* * * * * * * * * *

January 20, 1998

Questioner: Does the physical suffering of the body help us to realize faster that we're not the body?

Maharaj: Physical suffering is okay, and as a result you can understand faster. No harm. Swami Ramdas says, there are three kinds of suffering: 1) Things that come up in the world. You endure many worldly troubles. 2) When you consider yourself as the body, then bodily troubles come. Many diseases come. 3) When one dies without Knowledge, he goes through many, many troubles. God gives you troubles (cosmic or celestial troubles). When one experiences these three kinds of troubles or pains one asks "How can I get some happiness?" and there is a turn towards Reality. When one has a body, everyone experiences problems. Sometimes you inherit troubles from your parents. These are bodily troubles. Accidents like falling off a horse, these are worldly troubles that also brings you many troubles. "If I die what will happen to me?" The mind's troubles are from the worldly life. Your only son dies, and you feel bad. You say it is my son, so you have to suffer with the pain. If the neighbor's son dies you may feel sorry, but it's not the same pain. The wheel of suffering happens because you say that it's mine. It all comes from the mind. It's all the connection with worldly affairs. By your own wish, you have ridden the horse (taken birth). When you ride the horse you have to hold onto the reins, otherwise you fall down. You have to dance with the horse. What to do?

So it is, that the one who gets all of these three kinds of troubles has a real chance to go to the Reality. You may feel bad about these difficulties, but still it gives you incentive to find the right way. The bodily troubles are helpful to you. Once these body-mind troubles come upon you, you have a chance to get the nausea about the body. Otherwise you don't get the nausea. People feel bad because they don't understand. If you take the Illusion as true, then all these troubles come to you. But still you take this as true, what to do? It is automatic for you. When you say "I am this," then everything comes. If you say "I am not this," than everything goes off. If you come to a real Master then you get the understanding. I tell you, you can be happy with disease or anything. Take your body as a neighbor and not you. You say, "I am the body" and that brings ego, nothing else. And that ego doesn't want any troubles. It only wants good things, the best things. "My name should come first." The ego becomes stronger with the happiness of the world. If misery or troubles happen to you, take it for granted that it is for the good. So a realized person welcomes disease, let it come. "I am not this."

Worldly happiness is not true happiness. True happiness lies in forgetting the world. When you sleep you forget the world and you are happy. These worldly things are all bondage that you take as Reality. If you don't take it as Reality, no bondage for you. You are ever He. Let the bodily affairs come, why to worry? When a mother's son is sick she gets worried, but does she take the disease on herself? She gives only words, nothing else. Many people feel when there are sick that they want people to come and visit them. I disagree. You only remember your illness more. Why to come and see you? Always you see only your own interests everywhere. The interests of your body-mind come first. All people are of this type. Forget all of these things. What is there? One day you say the body will die. It is already dead at the moment, I say. People don't agree. Still, I say it.

The Self is so open, why to worry? If happiness or troubles come He is not concerned. "Let anything come, one and all. I'm unaffected like a rock." In that way, your worries go off and you go for the understanding very fast. One should not fear anything. Happiness or pleasure may be there, but don't be attached to it. Attachment should not be there. Suppose you are a king. Be on the throne, rule the country, but still understand that it is not true. There was a king. He was with a body but still without a body. So, he was always within his own Self. Body is there, but it is called bodiless (Videhi Mukti). Let the body be there, but still you are always free. Body is a bondage, but you are free if you understand you're not the body. Then you are the Power that is in you, you are everywhere. The Power is open and clear and you are always happy, and you never fear anything.

A saint who was a yogi came to see King Janaka. He knew the king was realized. So the king was told that Shukamuni wanted to see him. So the king sent him a message to leave all attachments and he would be happy. Shukamuni went home and thought about what the king had said. So the yogi decided to throw off his loincloth, and he went back to the king naked. The king then told him to leave all attachments. You are not the body, not a yogi and not a Saint. He left the palace and never came back. He understood the inner meaning of the king's words about attachments. You may be in pleasure also, but never forget yourself. Do things, do anything, no harm, but don't forget yourself. Don't get attached. Attachment is the worst because it is the wrong attachment. Be attached to the Reality and then you become the Reality. So when all these worldly bodily troubles come, take it for granted that it is for something good. At least you can get some nausea for this body and you can go on the real path. Don't say anything is bad, but when you say "I'm the body," it is the worst. Old age comes and you want some support. You say, "I can't do this." The Power that is in you gives life to you. One should understand that I am not the body, and that is the main point. Take the body as a neighbor. All these troubles mean that duality has come. If "I" is there, then "you" and "he" must be there. When you are not, who will be there? Then, automatically Oneness comes in the mind. Troubles must come afterwards, but it is nothing, so why to worry? You are He. You are He at this very moment. When you are not this, why to worry? All people worry for this body and fear death. When you are living, die by understanding. When you say "I am not the body" then you are He. Suppose you lose a leg then you become lame, why to worry? I am not lame, I am the Reality. When you understand what the Master says, that you are not the body and not the name, you are ever free. Be free in that way. Everything is for the good.

There was a king and he got a cut on his finger. The doctor put a bandage on it. He showed the finger to his counselor, and the counselor said "Everything is for the good." The king was astonished and said, "This is for the good? Put him in jail!" A few days later, the king went hunting and was captured by some jungle people. They wanted to make a sacrifice out of the king, but then they noticed that he had a bandage on his finger and decided he wasn't suitable for the sacrifice. So the king lived and thought to himself that what the counselor had said was correct, the cut had saved his life. He came home and went to the jail to see the counselor. The king said "Okay, I agree with you. The cut was for the good. But what about you? You have been in jail for over a week. Was that for the good?" So the counselor said, "If I hadn't been in jail I would have come with you, and I might have been sacrificed instead."

When you forget yourself, everything and everybody is yours. When you say, "I'm this" you become a small creature and suffer. What to do? You are not the body, one is sure to die. Let it die today. You say death is coming tomorrow, let it die today. In the same way, forget everything, forget the ego, and the body, and you get the greatest happiness. When you are sleeping you forget the body. Are you happy or not? From where does the freshness come after you wake up? It comes from your Self. There is a saying that when you get something good like money, whom do you remember? The goldsmith. When something bad happens to you, a disease for example, whom do you remember? Then you remember Ram (God). "Oh God, oh God, help me!" If troubles don't come I would say you are not lucky. Ego is the greatest troublemaker. When the ego goes off, you are He. Saint Tukaram said, "I gave all my money to Him. It is not mine. The body is given by God, I also give to Him. What is mine now? I've got nothing." When nothing is there, what remains? Your Self without self, the Reality. You are always free.

Questioner: Please explain the meaning of conviction.

Maharaj: Conviction means having a clear-cut understanding that I am not the body. That is conviction. Who am I then? I am the Power that is in the body. Finally, even the Power doesn't remain. Then you are He. The Power is also not true. It gives light then goes off. When you die nothing remains. So, first one should have the Knowledge, and then you throw off that Knowledge afterwards. Conviction means that this is all not true.

Questioner: Is conviction a concept?

Maharaj: Conviction is a concept, a very strong concept. Forget all this, and you are He. When you are there, He is not there. When He is there, you are not there. Two cannot remain there. Either you are there, or He is there. When you say "I am this," the ego, He keeps mum. But without "His" Power the ego cannot do anything. So, one should just be, and forget this or that. Forget the ego and you are there, and that is called conviction. All these thoughts come from Knowledge, and Knowledge is not true. All these worldly things, thoughts, and connections come as a result of the body. So when you say, "I am not the body," then these relations don't remain.

When you take the birth you come alone. When the body goes, it goes alone and nobody goes with you. In India, the son must be there. In India people are more fond of sons. Westerners are not so much for that. When someone dies, they say, "It's God's wish," and then they cry, but still nobody goes with the deceased. How can you? Who will go with him? He doesn't go anywhere. The five elements go to the five elements. The Power goes to the Power. Power itself is wrong, take it for granted. Then what remains? Only the wish for the body. So then you take another birth. That is the only thing. The ego is very fond of birth. It wants the birth to get happiness. "Without the birth, without the body I can't get happiness." So, when "you" are there, God is not there. If you say "I am not," then He is there. He does everything for you. Don't worry. He is in everybody. If you let the ego of the body go, then all is for you. You are everywhere and everybody. It is not easy and it is not difficult. Understanding should come and that is called conviction. When you are not, then what are you? Automatically the question comes. When one has gone to a Master he knows that "I am He. I am the Lord of the World." Don't be a small creature. Be He, and be the "Highest Power." You never change, circumstances change. You must change your understanding. That is all. He may be the poorest man in the world, in the most ordinary circumstances. Still he is great. He understands it's not true. All of the gods are nothing but Illusion. Then the fear of God doesn't remain in you. No fear for anybody because you are the Highest Power. You are the creating Power.

Suppose you are building a house. If you don't like it after it is finished, you can demolish it. Who can tell you "No"? In the same way, God has created, and if you understand that it is my creation, then why to worry. Anything that happens, it is by my order. Be That. That is the main point. Every Power is your Power. Everybody's Power is yourself only. Due to the "I" thought, nobody can understand. So, God is there and you are there. It's like two sides of one coin. Change the side, change the mind, and you are He. Why to worry for all this nonsense. For somebody's pleasure you take the birth and you have to suffer for the whole life. Say, "It is not mine, and I am not this body that is given by God." And when you say "I am not this," you are always happy.

Saint Tukaram never wanted to do anything. His wife always said. "Do something!" He never wanted money or anything. But one day his wife brought chilies from her father's house. She told him to go in the market and sell these chilies. He knew he should not be entrapped in all these worldly endeavors. So he went to the market and told everyone to take as many chilies as they wanted. "Don't pay for them," he said. So he went home and his wife said, "You have come home so early." He said, "All the chilies are gone," and she asked, "How much money did you get?" He said, "The money will come later." He knew that if you do business in this world and show worldly wisdom you will always be trapped. It's all an Illusion. And when you say, "I'm not this," nobody can trap you. All the fears come from the body only. So when there is nothing, where is the wisdom of the world?

People want to do something and they want to be somebody. Wisdom of the world puts you in the trap. In this way, one should try and avoid ego, nothing else. Only wisdom for Reality is good. Everyone is just running to fill up their bellies. What can money bring you? A good place to sleep. In sleep all are equal. If one sleeps in the street or one sleeps in a palace, they are both equal in sleep. The mind is never satisfied. It's like the tail of a dog. If you try to make it straight by putting it in a hollow tube, even after a hundred years it will still return to its original shape. The mind is never satisfied with what it gets. When you have more, you worry more. You always think something better will come. The best is to understand "Who am I?" first. "I am not the body, I am not the mind." Everybody wants to be so great. Reality is what is great. If you understand, you will be the greatest of the greatest. The mind is simply your thoughts, nothing else. There is no end to the mind. It thinks so much. Finally, even this Knowledge is to be absorbed. Ignorance has gone, agreed but now the

Master says to forget that Knowledge. Knowledge is dangerous. The wish of Knowledge cannot be fulfilled. It is not true. You are without Knowledge and Ignorance, and that is called "Thoughtless Reality."

In a dream, many things come and go, but the dreamer doesn't worry. He doesn't do anything, still many things happen. When he awakens, he knows nothing has happened. In the same way, see all of this as nothing but a long dream. So, the bondage of the body should be thrown out by understanding. Then the ego automatically goes off and nothing remains. The ego says, "I have no place to stay." Ego always wants something better, or the best. What to do? That which is best the ego doesn't understand. It is confused over what is true and not true. So it is always searching for happiness. Forget the ego first, and then forget everything else. When you say, "It is my house," all troubles remain for you. The one who understands Reality knows that every house is my house. It is the body that wants a separate place. When you are not the body, you can go anywhere. Ask, "What am I?" and "What I am not?" One should try to understand the ego in this way: When you get the bankruptcy of the world you are happy.

Questioner: When you are close to awakening do you face your own death at that time?

Maharaj: Why do you fear death? You don't want to die, so that fear comes to your mind. But when one says, "I am not that," then why to worry? He understands, "I am not the body." Suppose your neighbor's son dies, you don't feel so much. But when this body is going to die, you are so upset thinking about what to do and what not to do. When you are put on the gallows, what is your last wish? You wish that you should not die.

Questioner: When Ramana Maharshi was a young boy he went to his bedroom and faced his own death and realized.

Maharaj: These are all thoughts. This is a dead body. When you sleep you are dead. Saints say many things. It happened like this or that. It's all okay. Nothing has happened. That should be your understanding. But when you sleep, you are dead for the moment, and then you wake up. Didn't he also wake up? When death comes to the body what can you do? You call the best of the doctors but you can't do anything. So understand at the moment it is a dead body. Then you become the Power. Eyes cannot see, it is the Power that sees, but not even the Power exists. When electricity goes off no bulbs go on. So, understand now that "I am the Power." The Power works in everybody. When you die the ego and the Power must go off. And by understanding, the ego goes off automatically. The wish of the body is ego, nothing else. You can be out of the cycle of birth and death right now. Otherwise, you stay in the rotation. Birth and death come to the body and not you. You never die. That must be your understanding. The body must die even if you are Lord Krishna, Lord Ram, or Lord Christ. Why to worry? All of these experiences you should understand, and nothing else. The body is already dead. Disconnection comes, okay. Face it with Power. "I am not this."

When you are not this, you never worry. When someone dies you never worry. When you cry, you cry only for yourself. Everyone cries for his own happiness. "Now they are gone, what will happen to me?" A neighbor was there before, he was about fifty-seven. His mother died. "Now, who will call me Babu," he cries. For that he cries. Does he cry for her? So, you never cry for anybody, you cry for yourself. That is the main point. The world is such. If you understand the Self, then nothing remains for you. I am everywhere, the Self is everywhere. He always remains contented. But everyone wants somebody's support in life. And that is what makes all the trouble. Take off the support, the ego. Nothing is true. So what support can you get from that? It is only your mind that says it is true. When you are blind you want a stick, you want support. The one who understands says, "My eyes are gone, it's better not to see the world." Forget everything. In this way, one can get the satisfaction. Why not! Satisfaction should be there in the mind, nothing else. Wishes can never be fulfilled and the wishes are for the wrong things. How can the wish be fulfilled for that which is not? A realized man's wish is always fulfilled. He wants Reality. So he is never unhappy. He is always happy.

* * * * * * * * * *

March 5, 1998

Questioner: You have said that touching and hugging between Master and disciple has nothing to do with the understanding. What is the connection between the Master and student regarding thinking or thought?

Maharaj: Master changes your thoughts, nothing else. You've become identified with the mind, so he changes your mind. That connection is required. The boy is ignorant. Why does he go to the school? To learn something. Only putting a hand on his head can't do anything. The teacher has to teach him. He needs to understand the subject. So, what can embracing do for you? What is the meaning in it? If you embrace your child, does that make him literate? He has to go to school.

Questioner: But we have the feeling when we come to see you that something is alive in us.

Maharaj: That's okay. That feeling is why your thoughts get changed. The thoughts get some food here. The fly goes after the sweet things to eat. It doesn't sit on the bitter things. So, the thoughts which you've got, the Master gives some force against those thoughts, so you have to go and see him. At first the boy doesn't want to go to school. He cries at first, but later he wants to go. Why? His mind has changed, nothing else. The only reason the Master speaks is to change your mind. If your mind gets changed, then you can understand anything, why not? What the Master says is very subtle. You don't know yourself. You think as a body and say "I'm here." The Master says that you pervade everywhere, but you cannot understand that at the moment. You are everywhere, so where to embrace, and who to embrace? If a doctor puts his hand on your head will he cure your disease?

In India there is a custom that if you go in a temple and there are some ashes, by taking the ashes you can produce a child. Then nobody will want to marry, no need. The Master should take you out of the ignorance of all these wrong beliefs. To take you out of Illusion, he has to give you all these examples. Then you are out of Illusion. Otherwise, you can't get out. How can you? So thoughts are given to change your mind. If you change it's okay, if you don't, whose fault is it? The professor gives a lecture. Those who accept get a first class grade. Those that can't, get second or third class grades. What to do?

So, the Master can give you the understanding by thoughts only. You are the thoughtless Reality but to make you understand this, he has to give you words. All teachers teach differently. Each one produces thoughts in a different way. If you reproduce his thoughts correctly, it's okay. But if you reproduce his thoughts using your own words, in your own experience, will the professor be more happy or not? Not everything can change your thoughts. On the contrary, you often go more into Illusion. All of these so called experiences with teachers, what is the meaning in it? For what? It's just to impress the student with "Powers." Nothing else. To say "I can do anything by touching," that's the wrong way. If you don't eat, will your stomach get full? How is it possible? In a dream you have a very nice meal. And when you get up, you say to your wife, "Today I dreamt that I had a very nice lunch." Then she says, "In that case, I won't have to cook today because you've already eaten!" Also, attracting students by performing miracles is not correct. Why is it necessary? If you tell them the right things, they are sure to come. One who is thirsty is sure to go to water. Why should the water worry? When you try to attract students for any reason it's always ego. Does the wind care if you like it or not? It simply moves. When questions are asked, the teacher speaks. Whether or not you accept it, why should the teacher worry? First be out of ego and then teach. Some people came to my Master then left and never came back. So we disciples thought they are ignorant chaps that they should leave him. Our Master overheard us and said, "Why to worry? Everyone is Parabrahman!" Everyone is the Reality, everyone is He. My Master never looked on anyone as an aspirant or an ignorant person. The doctor gives the medicine to cure the disease, not to cure you. The doctor cannot cure you. Your habits cannot be changed this way. Only by understanding, by thinking can you change.

Questioner: You say changing the mind is very important. You say you can change the mind by mind, thought by thought. When my mother died I had this experience that is without words. I don't say it was good or bad, but it definitely changed me. It just happened and it transformed me. I was not the same thinking mind afterwards. So is there any other method besides changing your thoughts that can transform someone?

Maharaj: No. Ignorance came by hearing. It must go off by hearing. You didn't know your name, and then you say "I'm this." This information is given by your father and mother. Your mind accepts it, and in turn it gets confirmed by your mind. By hearing, no? In the beginning you didn't know if you were a boy or girl. The parents also say, "We're your parents." You again accept it by hearing. Ignorance has come by hearing. You were given a name at birth and you became that. Then the Master comes along and kills those thoughts. You are not the body, not the thoughts, not the name. You are something else. You are the Power that is in you. You are not even the subtle body, not the mind. Wrong information was poured into you, and you accepted it at the time. So new information is given and thoughts get changed. Would you ever say, "I am not the body," unless you heard it from a Master? When you say, "I'm the body," that is Ignorance. Since you don't know yourself Knowledge is given to take out your Ignorance. You say you are So-and-so. You'll have to prove it. Where is it written? You are not that, you understand wrongly. So the Knowledge that is in you is always wrong if it doesn't come from a sage. You have accepted everything. Without Knowledge, how can you accept? If I say this is a flower vase you accept it. It is not written on the vase. It is my thought now. But you can put water in it and drink from it, why not? Why only to put flowers in it? If your father and mother had given you another name, then you would have become that. There is nothing in a name. Everyone is just blood, flesh, and bones.

Some say that they are French, American, and so on. This is just written in your mind. What is the use of it? The mind takes you in the wrong direction. You were born in Ignorance and then more Ignorance is poured in you. So, you say the death of your mother changed you. No doubt, your thoughts have changed. Your mother died and you got some understanding that you may die tomorrow, or years later. So, you need to understand something. That change came in you. So she's dead and gone now, why to worry? So, her death was for the good. Others don't get that understanding, and then they only cry for the dead. A dead body says, "Why are you crying? You are on my same path. One day you're sure to die." The dead body says, "Don't cry for me,".

Questioner: I only meant to say that as a result of my mother's death, other dimensions opened up in my life and my search began, and now I am sitting here.

Maharaj: Okay, the death of the mother was good for you. Nothing is bad in the world. You have to accept it that way. Nobody dies, matter never dies, and thoughts can be changed by thoughts only.

Questioner: Ramana Maharshi was enlightened but he had no teacher. Can you explain that? Nobody changed his mind.

Maharaj: The mind has changed the mind. The mind is the Guru. The mind is your greatest friend and your greatest enemy. Maybe a mountain was his Guru. He had a Guru, otherwise you can't understand. The mind is the Guru. Make it the Guru! People always go to the wrong side. If you go to the right side, then the mind becomes your Master or not? How can you understand without a Master? A bodily Master is essential for understanding. Otherwise your ego won't go. You have to listen to your own mind. What I speak is your mind. You ask a question and I reply. So, is it your mind or not? Do I become your mind or not? Now tell me? The Master is required. You say he had no Master. He may have read books. The author of that book can be a Guru. (Pointing to the last questioner) His mother is his Guru now. Death of the mother gave him understanding. What is wrong with that? Any incident can happen, your life is changed, and you can take the turn, why not?

Questioner: Is life the Guru then?

Maharaj: Life is Power. The Master also has that same Power, that is the Guru's Power. Your mind is not able to accept some things so the Master's Power is necessary. You are ignorant; you don't know, so somebody has to tell you. Then your mind becomes your Guru, why not? But your mind can also take you to the wrong side, and for that you must be on the alert. Ego is always a factor. Perfection cannot come without the teacher. Knowledge itself is not true. The ego remains up to the last moment as long as Knowledge is there. Then that Knowledge is thrown off, and for that, the teacher is required. That is the most difficult point, and that is what I speak of. It is not a state, it is not peace. It is stateless. It is thoughtless. The Knowledge is to be absorbed. You have built castles in the air on that Knowledge. You have to go beyond that, where Knowledge ends, and that is where the Guru is needed. Knowledge is the medicine, not the disease. The disease is the ego, and that must go off. I don't like to comment on anybody but when you ask a question I have to say something.

Questioner: Many teachers I have known have talked about predestination. I would like some understanding of this. Where does our decision making come from? We have thoughts and we make decisions. If it is not destiny and things are not predetermined, what guides me and what helps me make my decisions?

Maharaj: It comes from the mind. From where does the wind come? From the sky. Castles in the air can be blown up by the Master. (He puckers his lips and makes a blowing sound.) Wrong thoughts can go off. Why to worry? If you make your mind strong you can blow off anything. The mind is the maker of all these things. Try to understand your own mind, that's the main point. Understand your own thoughts with the help of the Master. The wind comes and goes. It comes from the sky and returns to the sky. Sky is Zero. And our thoughts come from where? From Zero, from Ignorance. Zero is not true, and the Power is not true. He is He. Power always moves as thoughts. Electricity kills people and also gives light to people. Thought is Power but Power itself is wrong, and that is the lesson given by the Master. Destiny is nothing but a thought. It's nothing but Illusion. Knowledge, or thought, is the greatest Ignorance, and only the Master can tell you that. Knowledge is nothing but ego. So both Ignorance and Knowledge must go off, and that is the real meaning of what is referred to as no-mind. You have built castles in the air. Ignorance *and* Knowledge must go off, and that is the real meaning of what is referred to as no-mind. Everything comes from Zero, from Ignorance. You need a Master short, and sweet. Bodily or without body.

Questioner: In *Master Key to Self-Realization* (a book by Maharaj's Master) he talks about abandoning pride. How to get rid of pride?

Maharaj: The mind always takes the pride, it has this habit. It is simply Knowledge acquired by the mind. Still the mind knows nothing, I'll say that. Knowledge is wrong but to take out one thought, another is used. But the realized person knows that he knows nothing. So, what you know up to now is the source of your pride. You think that what you know is true. When you say, "I don't exist, He exists," then all the pride goes. As long as the ego remains, pride remains. So when you are full of Knowledge and say, "I am everything, I can do everything, I am the Creator of the world," you are still in Illusion. Everyone says God is great. God makes more Illusion. If you say that what he has created is true, then you become a dog (God backwards). Dog becomes God when there is understanding. But in the Final Reality there is nothing to understand. Suppose you give something to a poor person. Then you think "I've done something good," that's pride. You say "I've done something," and that makes it true in your mind. Who are you to help anybody? So, the Master says he never helps anybody. I only speak, and if they accept it's okay. Pride always remains as long as Knowledge is there.

Does the Power in you ever say, "I do it?" It does everything, and still you say, "I do it." If the hands move, it's the Power that does it. So Power never speaks although it does everything. It runs the whole world. Electricity never says, "I give the light." It doesn't even know it's the light. Knowledge is the greatest demon. It wants to know more and more. It is never satisfied. The mind becomes no-mind when you understand that nothing is true. That is the end of pride. "I do nothing." That should be your understanding.

* * * * * * * * * * *

March 16, 1998

Questioner: How do we know we are moving in the right direction? Some people get stretched one way, others another. How do we know what's best for us?

Maharaj: Suppose someone gives the address and says to go this way. Then you are going in the right direction. If you try to understand what the Master says and if you experience it, your mind can take you there. Your mind can tell you if you've understood correctly.

Questioner: So we just know?

Maharaj: Yes, why not? When you eat you know how much more you want. Same way, if you experience what the Master says, you've understood rightly. The mind always goes here and there, but still it eventually brings you to the right point. If you understand that this is all Illusion, the body, mind, and all that you see and perceive, then I can say you are on the right path, and you've understood yourself. What to understand? You are He. Who will understand whom? Only the Ignorance should go off, nothing else. If you say this is true, my body is true, and my name is true, that is ego. So one should know one's ego. If you know your ego, it goes off. It doesn't remain. You don't have to search for anything. Who will search for whom? That is the fundamental base. You are He. But the ego says, "I'm this." The ego will never leave you. You will have to leave it. If you understand that the ego is just a thought, then it can't touch you. Otherwise it stays in the mind. Suppose you have glasses and you don't put them on and then say, "I can't see anything." What to do? Put on your glasses! The Master is there to cut your ego. You have the power to accept what the Master says. You automatically can feel that you are the creator of the world, come on! You have made the world due to the body. Don't be so small.

Questioner: You can avoid being the Creator, can't you?

Maharaj: In the beginning you must make the balloon big since you say, "I have no Power, I'm the body, and I'm the mind." Be unlimited first. Don't try to do anything. When you sleep, you do nothing, you forget the world. Do many things happen or not? Who is the Creator? Nobody is the Creator. A thought came from Ignorance and it created the whole dream. You say, "I created the dream," but that's wrong. The Creator never existed. The barren woman's son never existed. So, since you have become smaller by mind, and limited, you have to expand your thinking. Make the mind unlimited. The Master makes you bigger and bigger. You are "All." Then you feel you've become enlightened, and you feel joy. Then, the Master says then you have not understood. Nothing is true.

Questioner: Before you have said Sat-Chit-Ananda could be avoided.

Maharaj: In the beginning you have to be that big. You have to open your mind. But, Sat-Chit-Ananda is still a thought, a very big thought. First you must understand, "I am not a small creature." The mind doesn't want to accept "I am everywhere." So be the Creator of the world yourself. Say, "I've created it." One small piece of salt will never say, "I'm the ocean." But when it dissolves, does it become ocean or not? Make Knowledge more and more expansive for understanding. Then the ego comes in there, "I know everything." Then, the Master says, "You still don't know. Forget this also, you are still dreaming." As long as "I" is there, it's a dream. Then the Master cuts the ego. Just like cutting a birthday cake. Each year you say, "I'm such and such age." The Master says that you were never born. So the Master cuts your mind to eliminate the kick of the dream. Eat it! You must get the Knowledge, then you can cut and eat it.

Questioner: Is it necessary to go through this process as you've described or can you shortcut it?

Maharaj: Your mind won't accept it! That's the main point. The mind won't accept "I am He." Sat-Chit-Ananda is everywhere. It's the original seed. Sat means Being, Chit means Knowledge, and Ananda means Pleasure (Joy; Bliss). First understand Ignorance, and then you get Sat-Chit-Ananda. Sat-Chit-Ananda is not the final understanding, but if you want to go to the fortieth floor you have to go up to the thirty-ninth. Even if you know the final destination, do you still have to go through some states, or not? Your mind in Ignorance fears everything, even a tiny mosquito. Due to the body, you've become so small. The mind has made you smaller. All is Illusion, but you take it as true. Even Sat-Chit-Ananda is Illusion, it's just a thought. And that thought has created the whole world. If that thought wouldn't have come, then no dream. If you are sleeping and no thought comes, then no dream. If one man sleeps, he gets many dreams. The one who doesn't sleep, he doesn't get any. How can he get the dreams? So unless you sleep, how can you get the dream? So unless you forget yourself, how can the world be produced? So you have to say, "I'm the Creator of the world." The whole world is one thought. Thought means Knowledge. Everybody in the world has got Knowledge and nothing else. Even if you say, "I'm ignorant," do you say it with Knowledge or not? Unless you see both sides, Ignorance and Knowledge, you can't go to the Reality.

People are all in Ignorance. They say I'm a doctor, lawyer or whatever. They are just murmuring in the dream. In Sat-Chit-Ananda you become the Creator of the world. "What happens is my choice. Everything is by my order." First you forgot yourself, and then Sat-Chit-Ananda came up, nothing else. It is the original dream. A dream is always a dream. A king becomes a beggar in the dream and vice-versa. You are not a king or a beggar. The Creator has created nothing. "I am the Creator of Zero." Reality is beyond all of this. There is no Creator, and nothing created. It is just a thought. Knowledge and Ignorance are just two sides of one coin. The coin is not true, and only emerges when the Self is forgotten. It has come up, what to do?

Questioner: How does the aspirant move ahead with the investigation of the "I" and the four bodies? * (See Endnotes for Volume 1)

Maharaj: By thinking (Vichara; enquiry) you have to go ahead. By non-thinking you have become a body, or a demon. By understanding, you have to prove that it's not true. You must think again and again. All people put Ignorance in you. The Master says that you are the Reality and what you see is not true. He pours Knowledge in you. So, with that Knowledge understand everything. Then automatically you will say that "I am the Creator of the world." Why not? By Knowledge you can understand this. Some Saints stop at this point only. For final understanding you have to go beyond this. Knowledge is very powerful, but it's still dreaming. Knowledge is the greatest Ignorance.

Questioner: I guess what I'm asking is how to proceed, not to think I am the body?

Maharaj: You have to think about it. Since you take it as true, to make it not true you have to think again and again. If you make a mistake on something you have to find out where the mistake was made. Come on and find out your mistake. The Master clarifies your mistakes, but if you continue to make them who is responsible? You have forgotten yourself and all this was created, what to do? You take the touch of everything and you create the whole dream. Follow me?

In a dream, if a thought becomes objective, do you get the dream or not? Sometimes you are sleeping and a thought comes, but you are a little bit awake so the dream doesn't come. But when you take the touch of the thought then the dream comes, and you become Knowledge. So you have to say, "I'm not this," then who are you? "I don't exist." This you have to say. As long as Sat-Chit-Ananda is there, the body must work. When Knowledge is there, you have to act accordingly. For a Saint or realized person it's the same. He works in the world also. If someone comes to my door, I'll tell them to come in. Should I not say something? But the Saint is like the lotus leaf in the water. He lives in the water but doesn't take the touch of it. It's not true. You must think again and again to teach the mind up until non-thinking (no-mind) comes. Then there is nothing to think, everything is over. Then your Self remains or not? So there is a saying, "To be or not to be is the question." All people think or not? To do this ,or not to do it. As long as Knowledge is there the question remains. If you understand that Knowledge comes from Ignorance, then you have to kill that Knowledge. Master tells you to forget it, that it is nothing but a dream. Ignorance and Knowledge are both in the dream. To be or not to be is the question now. Take it as true and then it has to be. Don't take it as true, then the question doesn't arise.

If someone says, "Take this road," and then someone else says, "No take this road." Then the mind enters duality. What to do? This or that, to go one way or the other. On one side the whole world is there, on the other side Final Reality. Nothing else. Cut it through understanding. The Master gives you the understanding to cut it. As long as you are connected with the Knowledge, to be or not to be must be there. Otherwise, how can you understand also? As long as Illusion is there, you have to think of the Final Reality. If no Illusion, what to think? What Reality? Then Reality and unreality both go off. Without thinking you can't understand this. People say to understand and be That. But what to be, or not to be? Don't be like a bee and buzz around. By thinking everything can go off now.

Questioner: I understand that movement in thought creates something physical or emotional. I've also experienced dropping off of that when there is nothing going on. And now you are speaking of something beyond the nothing going on.

Maharaj: I agree. What is going on is in the dream. Why should you worry? It's not true. When you worry you take it to be true.

Questioner: Then what's left when everything falls away, when there is nothing?

Maharaj: You are left without you! A dream comes and you do many things. The dream goes off, then are you still there or not? Do you remain or not? A dream comes, but what harms you? You are sleeping and you've done nothing. And if you understand that here? Let the dream go off, nothing has happened. Then no question remains. While doing also, say "I'm not doing." That understanding should come. In a dream you do many things, but you didn't do anything. Suppose you kill a person. When you awake, you say how is that possible? You only experienced that in the dream, so when you awake it becomes nothing. It's null and void. It doesn't remain. If it doesn't remain what value has it got? He knows that nothing has happened, so he says that he's the "Creator of the World." So, when you awake, you know that nothing has happened, and this is how you stay in the world.

As long as the body is there, even when doing, I do nothing. When I eat, I don't eat. Body or mind eats, I don't eat. If a man has a meal in a dream, and he tells his wife, she says, "I won't have to cook now." He objects and says he's hungry. In the same way, what you do in the world has no value. Otherwise, bondage comes to your mind or not? Why should the body-mind concern you? If you say, "I do," you become the smallest creature. So, if you understand what the Master says, you will automatically say, "It's not true." So go ahead with Knowledge, and make the balloon (of mind) bigger and bigger. But how can what starts from Ignorance be Knowledge, or True? The mind gives the understanding and then goes off. Once you've reached the destination where is the need for understanding? You're at the fortieth floor. What is left to understand?

Questioner: At the same time we say we are all *and* nothing. It is that correct?

Maharaj: Yes, yes. Say at first "I am All," Then say "I am nothing, and I do nothing." Unless you pass through the thirty-ninth floor you can't say I'm on the fortieth floor. When you reach the fortieth floor, then nothing remains to go further ahead. Then you can understand it's not true. Then the "I" doesn't remain.

Questioner: What exactly do you mean by being the Creator?

Maharaj: You are part and parcel of the world. Knowledge has created the world. If you put a piece of salt in the ocean, in a fraction of second it becomes ocean. So when you say, "I'm this," in order to take out that thought you have to say, "I'm the Creator of the world." From Knowledge everything happens. Knowledge is the Creator. So the Creator of what is wrong, is also wrong and not true. But still you say, "I created it." When you awake from the dream still you say, "I got a dream." You don't forget it, but still it's only a dream. Unless you say that, how can you be out of the dream? Once awake you say, "It's not true," but first did you take it to be true or not? First you say yes, then Knowledge comes, and then you say no. So, to be or not to be is the question. That's the meaning in it. First you say yes, then you have to say no. The mind needs to be very subtle. Otherwise many questions arise in it.

Suppose a man plays a double role, a hero and a villain. At one moment, the villain troubles the heroine. In the next moment, he cherishes her. Who did it? So which role is true? Duality is the question now. When you're in duality you have to act accordingly. But the actor is only one person. Duality is nothing but your own role. Everyone is nothing but myself, one understands this. All the bubbles are nothing but the ocean. They break and what happens? They become ocean. Here everybody has to break himself and then he's He. Then no one remains and Oneness comes in the mind. Good or bad, everyone is myself. You must have that much courage to understand. The player of the roles is only one, but he plays dual roles. Is he bad or is he good? He's not bad and not good. He's apart from that. He says, "I took the roles and I played them. I must play the villain's role, and when I take the hero's role, I play that." This is the same thing here. It's a dual role you are playing. But people are afraid to understand. "How can it be so?" Suppose you kill somebody in a dream, when you awake you say, "I've not killed." This waking state is your dream. It's a dream in the dream of the Creator, and you are part and parcel of it. You killed somebody and then you have to say, "I've not killed." How much strength is required to say that? "When doing, I don't do anything. By killing, I've not killed anybody."

All people here have different names. If you kill the names, are all one or not? If everyone has no name, is Oneness there or not? If a father has four children and no names are given, all of them will come when he calls. So names are given only to understand. Body and mind does everything, you don't do it. The world is nothing but the connection of two wires, positive and negative. When you sleep the whole world goes off. Nothing remains. You awake and you see the world. When the body dies, the disconnection comes completely and you can't see the world again. Your thought is the world. So you are the Creator of the world. I want to say this again and again. Be the Creator, and then understand. Then automatically it goes off and you're out of it. No doubt should remain. Doubt is Ignorance, nothing else. Electricity doesn't know it gives the light. Final Reality has no Knowledge and no Ignorance. When disconnection comes, nothing remains. Where has it gone? As it was not, it disappears. If you touch electricity you die. If you touch the Knowledge it goes off. If you understand the Knowledge, it goes off. So Knowledge and Ignorance are both not true. So, my Self is without Knowledge and Ignorance. Let thoughts be there, but I have no thoughts. You can say that. One should die oneself, and then live.

Questioner: You said this morning, "Become He and then worship." Is there value in our worshipping now when we go home? Should we do puja (worship) and bhajans (devotional singing) at home, or only when we are here?

Maharaj: If we go home should we eat or not? Do it, why not? The question doesn't arise, should I eat or not? Put the recorder on and sing. You don't have to be realized to worship. Master has given you the Knowledge, why not praise him? To not worship is ego. "I have become great now, so why should I worship?" Ego is the dirtiest thing. It comes in at any time in the mind. It's true that there is a difference between worship with understanding and without understanding, but now you have the understanding. If a student becomes a professor himself, maybe even a better professor than his teacher, still he acknowledges the one who has taught him. As long as the body is there, you do many, many things. If someone comes in, you say welcome, come in. So why not worship the one who has given you this understanding?

Questioner: There are many ways to worship besides puja and bhajans, isn't there?

Maharaj: Like what?

Questioner: You can think about your Master. You can be thankful about your Master, but not necessarily do bhajans.

Maharaj: That is ego.

Questioner: Are you sure?

Maharaj: You can worship in your own way, I don't say no. But if you say, "Why should I worship?" That is ego. You eat and drink, so where is the harm in worship? But, it's also not necessary to make a show of it. Be faithful to the Master, that's why you do it. You need to remember what the Master has told. Out of sight is out of mind. Keep the touch of what the teacher says. That is what you keep the touch of. You and the Master are one, but still as long as you are in body you must worship. If you have full faith in the Master, he will take you to the right place. The Master is everywhere. He is never away from you. You and He are one.

* * * * * * * * * *

May 3, 1998

Questioner: When you initiate people with a mantra (sacred word or phrase given by Master for meditation) is that enough to take someone to the Reality.

Maharaj: There are two ways to realize. There is "The Bird's Way," and "The Ant's Way." By meditation (The Ant's Way) one can realize. The word or name has so much power. The name you were given by your parents has done so many things. Mantra is given by the Master, but the path of meditation is a very long way to gain the understanding. By chanting or saying the mantra you can go to the Final Reality. There is nothing in the world but words. The whole universe is nothing but words. There are only two things; one is Reality, the other is Illusion. One word can wipe out Illusion.

Suppose you have an enemy and you think about him. In a fraction of a second, with a change of your thoughts he can be your friend. So one thought from the Master who has realized is sufficient to help you realize. It is a very lengthy way, that's the only thing. So, my Master found the shortest way, by thinking (Vichara). Because of a lack of thinking, you have become the smallest creature, and by thinking you can become the greatest of the great. Why not? If you don't have the capacity to understand by thinking using the Bird's Way, then you can go by way of meditation. But, it is the long way, and you have to meditate for many hours a day. People say that they meditate, but most don't know how to meditate. They say that God is one and myself is another, but that is duality. Duality will never end that way.

So, one word from the Master is sufficient. Words can cut words, and thoughts can cut thoughts in a fraction of a second. It can take you beyond the words, to your Self. In meditation you have to eventually submerge your ego. The one who meditates, the action of the meditation, and the object of meditation become one. It is a long way, and in this world today, people have no time to do that. They have no time to die also. They say, "Wait, I have some work, then I'll come to you." The world is going so fast now. So my Master found the shortest way. You have taken all this as true in the world because of words. There are only words in this life. If there are no words, then where is the world? If you have no name, then where is the ego?

Your father and mother have given you one word, and you have become that, and you have become so powerful in your acceptance of that. If what is wrong is accepted, it cannot be made right. What to do? All of your teachers have said that this world is true, and you have accepted it. You had no name when you took birth, and when the name was given, you accepted it and said, "I'm this." So if the Master gives you one word you can meditate on, you can go ahead and realize, but it's a long way with many obstacles. And in the end, you must submerge the mantra and the meditator, which is yourself, and then be

That. It is a long process. The ant moves slowly, and if he climbs a tree he may die before he reaches the destination so he will need more births.

The bird, on the other hand, can fly from tree to tree in no time. My Master found the Bird's Way. He was taught the Ant's Way by his Master, Bhausaheb Maharaj. My Master's Master founded the lineage in the meditative tradition. He left his body in 1914 and people at that time were not so keen on understanding. There were four disciples with my Master and my Master wanted to find a shorter way, but his co-disciples said the meditative way was the way that was given and no other way was necessary.

So, my Master went to Bijapur alone and was determined to find another way for the Final Understanding. He sat for nine months in meditation without getting up. He said, "I may die, but I want to find out the easiest way." He was not a learned person but the caliber of his mind was so great that nothing could stop him. Before meeting his Master, he was a body builder and could do a thousand sit-ups without stopping. Then, a friend told him about Bhausaheb Maharaj and suggested he come to learn something about philosophy. He was with Bhausaheb Maharaj for 6 years, but after only four years he decided to renounce the world, and became a disciple and began spreading the teaching of meditation. He did that for two years and then decided to leave and find another alternative to meditation. Even though his Master had only taught meditation, his mind and faith was so strong that he decided to go forward. He had a faith with eyes (seeing), not a blind faith. Finally, after nine months of sitting Bhausaheb appeared to him and said, "Okay you understand, and I agree with you, so now you can get up!"

Meditation is okay, but by thinking one can go faster. So he decided to teach the Bird's Way. In the scriptures it is said that you should first renounce the world, and then Knowledge will be given. But he said no, first give explanations to the people and give understanding, then if they renounce the world it will have some meaning. To renounce without understanding is meaningless. But when you understand that what you see and perceive is not true, then if you renounce, it will have some meaning. When the world is not true and all is Illusion, what alternative do you have but to renounce?

So, he gave the understanding, and then he told his disciples to go and beg. The whole world is your home now. And after some time, when the disciples came back to the Master, he told them now to renounce the renunciation! When nothing is true, what is there to renounce? What to renounce when it is nothing? Renouncing is ego. Stay as a simple person in the world. Then he gave the final teaching that Knowledge is also wrong, and that finally the Knowledge must be submerged, then you are He. Then there is nothing to fear.

Be fearless. Roar like a tiger. Don't be a mouse always running away. People worry and fear so much. What to do and what not to do in this world? Even in worshipping they fear. "I've committed a mistake, I must confess," what to do? People sometimes ask me if what they are doing is okay or not. You people worry so much over some little thing. So I tell my disciples that everything is okay. You are also so afraid of the Master and of God. When everything is nothing what is a mistake and what is not a mistake? When you understand, then the Power is there and then everything you do is correct. Come on now, have that much courage to say this. Say anything, it's okay, Wherever you put your finger is the Reality. The Power you get should be that strong in your mind. No need to fear anybody or anything. The mind accepts everything as true, and then it fears. That fear is taken out by the Master. He makes you roar like a lion. You take everything as true, because the mind has accepted everything. You accept the name given by your father and mother, and you die with that word. If you make your mind strong, whether you do meditation, or go by the path of understanding, you can go to the Final Reality. If an ant concentrates on a bee, one day it's sure to fly. So without wings you have to fly. I say you that are not to question why, but do your duty and die. Duty does not mean helping an old lady across the street. It means to do your duty to the Self by understanding yourself. "Who am I?"

When you misrepresent yourself, then everything you do is wrong. You are He, and whatever you do is correct, I can dare say that! Why? Because it is all an Illusion. You must have a strong understanding. But your will-power is weakened by your thoughts and doubts. Thoughts make the difference in the caliber of the mind. He means He, and I means I. Understand that way. When you don't exist, only He is there. There is no need to say anything, either. When I is there, He is not there. As long as you remain I, He says, "I am sleeping." He keeps mum. So the Master nourishes the aspirant like a mother nourishes the child by, giving understanding, nothing else. If the understanding is given in the right way, you can understand at this very moment. If you have a log, the mind must have the ability to cut that log in two. But the mind has become a chicken-hearted thing. Don't be chicken-hearted, have a Master's heart.

Don't be afraid to give bad news. Use your Power in the right way. It has produced everything, but still you must have the ability to say that it is not true. That is the caliber, that is the Power you must have. You make many things and your Power is so strong. But you have forgotten your Power. Be strong and say, "If I die, I don't care." You say, "I am this," so you care. When you say, "I'm not this," why should you care? Why care or feel for anything? If an ant is there, you pinch it. Do you feel anything? But if you want to kill a person like yourself, you have to think again and again about what to do, and what not to do. So don't be chicken-hearted. Say that what is true is true, and that what is not true is always not true. Ignorant people often say, "God is great," and then they say, "but, I have to do this." Both are wrong. Let God do what he has to do, why should you care? Why to worry?

So be the aspirant of the real Master. I don't say that I'm the real Master, otherwise you will say I'm a real Master and that is ego for me. (Pointing to a picture of his Master.) He is the real Master, and he gave that understanding to me and an ant became a bee. An ant became fearless, and can run anywhere without any fear. So, always be fearless.

Meditation and thinking are the same. Both require thinking. Mantra is given by thinking, and during sermons you can meditate. Both require thinking. Master then says, "It's your choice now." One way is towards happiness and joy, the other way towards troubles and misery. Where you want to go, you go. The Master is a pointer only. He takes you up to door and he's finished. He doesn't remain there. Be strong in the mind and have the caliber to accept what he says. If you put faith in the Master, the caliber becomes stronger. If you go to the doctor and you take medicine or vitamins you become stronger. The Master is a vitamin, nothing else. Be strong and forget your body. It's a dead body at the moment.

Questioner: Is there more to the thinking process than the mantra?

Maharaj: Both are the same, I told you that already. Why are you asking? One is a longer way, the other is a shorter way. Come on now! Now they have email and you can receive mail instantly. Before it took months before you got mail to and from India. You could be dead before you got your letter. So, be a little faster, and have the caliber to understand and accept what the Master says. What harms you? In the beginning the mantra makes the mind more subtle, I agree.

Questioner: The mind is built on fear. And heart and mind are one you say. Is the heart also built on fear?

Maharaj: No, heart doesn't fear, mind does. Heart gives the impulses to have thoughts. Heart and mind are like twin brothers. A thought comes in your mind and the heart gives force, or Power to it. Without heart you can't do anything. What does electricity have to fear? It gives power to the bulb. They are two but they act as one. Can a dead body have a thought? So heart is Power, it is life. The mind discriminates and makes differences. It fears about what to do and what not to do. All this is the mind's work. Power is force, and everything comes up in the mind. Heart is your soul, agree?

Questioner: Are you saying the Power of the heart is love, and that it makes things happen?

Maharaj: You say it's the love. The Power doesn't make love to anyone. Love comes to the mind: "I like this, I don't like this."

Questioner: By love I mean relatedness or communion.

Maharaj: Okay, I agree, but love is not true. So, now what do you want to say? If mixing comes, then love comes. When nobody is there, whom to love? Tell me. Something should be there; a man, a woman, a tree, something has to be there. Where is love? Saints also say nonsense things. What to do? They say to love everybody. If am everybody then whom to love? If you love a snake it will bite you and you will die. If you worship a lion and you touch him, he will eat you. So worship at a distance. Electricity is the Power, and if you touch it you will die. Knowledge has come, and it is so Powerful, but if you touch it the Knowledge dies, you don't die. Knowledge goes away. Then Final Reality remains. The understanding should be there, and it all depends upon your mind and your caliber. I don't say that you are wrong. But when there is only one, whom to love and whom not to love? When there are two, then love comes. When there is one, where is the love? How should I embrace myself? Or how shall I love myself, tell me. You love yourself, yes? Do you love the body, the mind, the heart, or the Reality?

Questioner: But when you love the Self...?

Maharaj: Then no love remains. Self is the Self. Then the question of love doesn't remain. He never dies. He never goes away. He is always there. When the body dies everybody cries. Power doesn't die. So Saints don't cry. Nothing has happened. The Power brings life and everything. You can't see it but still it is there. How can you love what you can't see? Understanding should be given in this way. Break the things and understand what is there. The five elements and Power are there, all mixed up. All the different parts are there, and they're assembled in such a way that everything works. When the disconnection happens, then the parts separate. So whom to love? Love means love yourself. Love means no duality. Love is understanding, is it true or not true? If you understand this, then this is the love. Okay?

Questioner: Is "He" love?

Maharaj: Who? Where is God? Self is Self. Whom to love, and whom not to love? When love comes, then thought comes. Love of what? When there is Oneness whom to love? Since you don't agree I'll be blunt; love is Illusion. You can love something else. How can you love yourself?

Who will love? There is no entity there. Who can electricity love? Who does the Power love? The Power doesn't know it's the Power. As you are in Ignorance, the Master says make love to the Reality. Then when you understand that you are He, no question of love comes. Everybody loves themselves. Nobody loves anybody else. You love your body first. Love for others is secondary. It is not primary. What is most lovable? The Self. The body is not the Self, mind is not the Self, Knowledge is not the Self. Final Reality is Self.

In Final Reality there is no you, no I, no-mind, and no thought. That is your state. You are He. So whom to love, and whom not to love? Understand what the Saints say, "Everyone is myself." Those that are the Self don't love. If you have a dream, a good dream, and then your wife awakens you, you complain that she awoke you from such a good dream. But when you awake where did the dream go? It's just a memory now. What is there to remember, of that which is not? Where is the love? All these examples are given by the Master for the purpose of understanding, but there is nothing you can do to get Him. Since you are all in the habit of doing something, the Master gives these things for understanding. You can't get "Him." Forget everything. Forget meditation and sit in your Self. Only when there is Beingness, can love be there. In sleep, whom do you love? Can you say? A child sees the moon in the water and says to the mother, "I want this." How can the mother give it? It's a shadow, so you love the shadow, and you don't love yourself. Forget the shadow, and you are He, and there is no question of love. Love is nothing but duality!

Questioner: In the Christian tradition it is said that God is love, and Ramana Maharshi would say that God is the essence of all religions. Not the love of objects but true love is the essence of all things.

Maharaj: What is true love and what is false love? You have to discriminate that first. When discrimination comes, the mind comes. When the mind is there you can't reach the Reality. Love is a state, Reality is stateless and thoughtless. Love is a thought. Love is nothing but love for others. When there are others, how can you be He? The duality should go off, and that is the understanding the Master gives you. Then there is no God, and no love, also. Where is God, tell me? Where is the love?

Questioner: But you could ask where is He? That could be duality too.

Maharaj: In "I am He," the "I" doesn't remain, the "He" doesn't remain and the "am" doesn't remain. Am is also Beingness, then you become something. "I" is the ego. If I am here, then another is here. That "I" makes duality. This is a very subtle understanding. I don't say you are wrong, but this, what you speak of, is not the final understanding. In the Reality there is no love, there is nothing: You say you are something, the love. If everything is Oneness, whom to love? If everything you see and perceive is He, then where is the Love? So whom to love, and whom not to love? My right hand has five fingers, some bigger and some smaller. Tell me, which ones are the best? The whole world has started from Sat-Chit-Ananda, it is called the root of the world. It is the "Joy" (Ananda). But Sat-Chit-Ananda is not true, it is a thought. It is your Beingness. "I am Knowledge, I am Joy, and I understand." This is all the mind's work. You have to go beyond the mind. The mind gives the wrong understanding. If He, the Reality is not there, then nothing can come up. The screen, Reality, is there so the pictures come up, but the screen doesn't love or disregard anything or anybody. So don't hate anybody, or love anybody. The screen doesn't discriminate, the mind does. The five fingers are different but still you say it's my hand. That is Oneness.

Questioner: I was walking by some cliffs and I had a fear of falling. You said earlier that the Master can take away your fear. In that situation how can you do that?

Maharaj: You are not the body. Why should you care? Let the body die, you're not the body. Take the body as your neighbor. If your neighbor dies, you say, "Oh, the poor chap," but you really don't care so much. Understand that when the Power goes off or disconnects, you don't die. When you understand that "I am not the body," then you can ask, "What am I then?" Otherwise not. If you give a boy a rubber snake he will be afraid until he realizes that it can't bite him. Then he plays with it. What is the difference? When he understands, then the fear goes off, that's the difference. How can I take out everybody's fear? I don't have the time to take out everybody's fear. Understanding takes out your fears. If you were not He, then there would be no chance to remove your fears. But He is fearless. Due to your mind, in Ignorance you say, "I am going to die." Saints say, "I was never born, how can I die?" There is no death for you, and no bondage or liberation either. Who is He to give you liberation? You are ever free. Since you say, "I am the body," the Master says that he can make you free. You create monsters for yourself and then you fear them. The Master gives you understanding. He gives the injection (the cure) that is all.

* * * * * * * * * *

May 5, 1998

Questioner: When I think of letting go of the sense of my personal self, great fear comes up, and I wish you could help me to have courage to face it.

Maharaj: The mind always fears. What to do? It doesn't want to go off. Even though everything is Illusion and not true, still the mind takes it as true. First mind takes the body to be true, the most true. The mind says, "I am the body," and that thought always makes you fear. When you take an airplane and go high in the sky you pray that nothing should happen. The mind always worries: "What will happen to me?" The mind always fears its own death. With rich people, the ego is even stronger, and the fear is more. So, one goes to the Master to get rid of that fear. If you go on an airplane it may fall down, why to fear? What is the meaning of that fear? Let it happen, there's nothing to fear.

The body is going to die, you are not going to die. With this understanding, you become fearless. There is nothing, all is Illusion, yet still you fear. Your fear is due to Ignorance. The Master takes out your Ignorance, that's all.

At this moment, this is a dead body. If the Power is there, it works. Can the Power say how long the bulb will last? Some bulbs last two days, some longer, not even the Power can know. There are no guarantees. And when it breaks, you all cry. The realized person says to break it beforehand, and not to cry. It's a dead body right now, I tell you! The Power is there, so it works. Understand the Power. You are the Power. You are He. But people don't want to leave Ignorance. You people worry about what will happen if the body is not there. Understand, "I am not the body." If you break this table what will happen to it? Nothing will happen. You all want happiness from the outside. There is no happiness outside. When you go to a store you see many things. What to choose and what not to choose? You get confused and ask, "From all of these things where can I get happiness?" The mind has created so many things you feel that you can't get out of it. If you understand, "The mind is my thought," you can forget the mind.

If someone dies what do people say? They say to forget about it and go on with your life. Same way here, forget the mind. The mind has the habit to make many things out of nothing. Out of one point, one thought, the whole world has been created. What to do? You have become the mind and created many things. When you sleep you become no-mind, no? What remains? Nothing remains. When you try to go to sleep, if you hold on to even just one thought, you can't sleep. You must break the mind. Cut it. Cut it means to understand "Who am I?" Know yourself!

(To the person who asked the question.) Why fear? What do you fear? (She hesitates.) You have love for the body, and wonder, "what will happen to me?" The mind always fears. Let it all go, and say it's not true. With the mind you give value to it. Like doctors give the medicine, the realized person says "Take this medicine. Say that it's not true, and you are okay." You have taken many bodies and they have all gone. Now, understand first, and then leave the body. When you say that you are not the body, that is the first condition, the first step. Otherwise, how can you go on? Once one hurdle is broken, then you can go ahead.

Another hurdle is the mind. At this point, the mind feels a loss of support and looks for something to hold on to. The Master then gives the support, "Everything is false, only you are true. You are true and all supports are wrong." Is that the greatest support, or not! Let everything go to the dogs, or to hell, why to worry? You should not fear the mind. Now, the mind is riding you, but you should ride the mind. You are the "Highest Power," the Reality. Unless you ride the mind, it makes you a slave. The mind wants everything, so the king has to beg for things. The king has all the power, but still the king cannot get all things, so he has to beg from Illusion. You are the king, you have the Power, but due to the love for the body, you beg from God, you beg from the Illusion. But "He" keeps mum, because He knows that happiness does not come from the body. Happiness is yourself. You have forgotten that, what to do? Does water get thirsty? Water should understand, "I'm the water, I have no need to drink." Understand, "I am the root of happiness, and the ego is the root of unhappiness." Be the master of the mind, not its slave. Because of the mind you have become so small that you fear even an ant. You produce (create) the bug, and then you fear it.

In the end, both happiness and unhappiness go off, and nothing remains for you. That is the Final Reality. He is He, and that is your Self. The ego is such a dirty nonsensical thing. It makes all of the trouble and confusion in the world. Say to the ego, "You are in my service, I am not in yours." The Master gives this to you, this power to command your ego. To kill the ego or to not kill the ego is your choice. Due to your fears and love for Illusion, you don't kill it. The hammer is given to you, but if you don't beat the ego, whose fault is it? Be strong enough to accept what the Master says. Be out of Illusion and you are He!

The mind is such a selfish thing. It always wants good things for itself. When you understand yourself, you are everywhere, and there is only Oneness. There is no need to be selfish then. Then you can give blessings to all. Let it come in the mind: "Let whatever happens to me happen, let any troubles or confusion come to me, but I should try to make everyone happy." Don't be shy to accept anything. The Master says accept everything with love and gratitude, not just the good things. Say that there is nothing bad in the world. That is love. Why should love be for one person. Why not for everything? When you love like that, no bad comes to anyone. In love there should be no bargaining. In Oneness there is no bargaining, as Reality is always aloof. You people always want to bargain for things. The mind is always a beggar, what to do? The mind always wants. The mind needs a good slap! Why should you want anything when you are the happiness itself? You are the fountain of happiness. An ordinary fountain only gives water, not happiness. This fountain gives happiness.

So don't fear anything. Do not fear death. Your body is a dead body at this very moment. The mind fears, and that is its support. Take out that support. If a horse is lame and it can't run, they kill it. So make the mind lame. Forget the mind, how much time does it take? The Master says that the whole world is going that way, so come with me to my side. If you are feeling you are going to lose something, don't worry. What you will gain will be your Self, the Reality. Illusion can never be true.

Questioner: How to prevent the loss of pure knowingness? After the understanding, how to prevent the loss of "I am That?"

Maharaj: You want to keep the "I am That." That is not a correct understanding. In "I am That" the "I" doesn't exist, and the "That" doesn't exist. You want to be that which doesn't exist. How can you be that? First be the king. You have all become beggars, and then you want to be a king. Who will accept you as a king? Forget the begging, and all must accept you as a king. Be the master of the Illusion, and then give understanding to all in the Illusion. Don't put yourself back in Illusion. Teachers often put students back in Illusion because they fear that students may become greater than they are, or if your son does better than you, you feel proud of him. Why should the Master feel anything? Give everything to the students, and then it is in the students' hands whether to accept it or not. If God comes to you in a dream and asks you what you want, first you have to think about it. Many people are afraid to ask for what they want and what they do not want. You may ask for money, and all types of other nonsense things. If God comes to me, I should not want to think that he is God. I am God, why should I take anything from him? Will anyone say that? You are all slaves of the mind. Everyone wants something that is not true. What to do?

There is a story in the mythological books about a demon who came to a village and promised to give two of the same items in return for every item given to him. So, everyone came and gave the demon their possessions to get the two-for-one offer. Then, he went away after giving everyone what he promised. But he was playing a trick on them, and the trick lasted only for as long as he stayed in the village. After he left, nothing of what he gave remained. So, the villagers lost all that they had given. It's the same thing here. Everyone runs only after Illusion. You always want more and more. Should more have some limit, or not? Everyone wants better and better, but where does better come from? The mind is always that way, so don't go after what the mind wants. The mind takes you on the wrong path. When you follow your mind you lose yourself, and that is the greatest loss. If you have a strong understanding you cannot lose it. Either the Master is wrong or your mind is wrong.

If there is a little rust left in the mind, take it out completely. If you have the correct understanding, the rust will not come back. Love can bring you back. If the boy is naughty, his parents send him outside and then he cries. Then they feel guilty, so they bring him back. Their love doesn't go off. What to do? The understanding should be so strong that it should not be broken by any thought. The Master says that all of this is nothing but a long dream. Don't worry for it. But the mind has the habit to worry. You are always the Truth. Clouds may come and go, thoughts may come and go, but the host is always the host. So let the guests come and go. Be the host. You are always there, so say bye-bye to what comes and goes. The mind always wants to accumulate things, and then everything troubles it.

Questioner: I have a question about happiness and sorrow. Why do we feel that other people are happier than we are? Is this only an illusion, or should we try to be happier ourselves?

Maharaj: This is all Illusion. If you want happiness there is still a "but" in the mind. The mind is the "but." The mind always wants something that it has not got. The mind is only happy when it gets what it doesn't have. Whatever it gets does not make it happy. If you ask a businessman, "How is business?" he will say, "So, so." He says that even if it's good. Why? He is afraid that if he says, "Everything is okay," then the limit of prosperity will come. He wants to be limitless. He wants more and more, so he says "so, so." It's not because he fears the envy of others, it is due to his desire for more and more. The mind is never satisfied. Why? Because what the mind asks for is Illusion, and the mind itself is Illusion.

In our mythological books, there is the story of Rama and Ravanna. Sita, who is Rama's wife, was taken by Ravanna. So Hanuman, Rama's right hand man, went in search of this ten-headed demon in order to kill him. Hanuman then asked a seer to help him find and kill Ravanna. He asked him how to point the arrow and kill the demon? So, the seer told him to fill this bucket of water and take it to a particular place. He filled the bucket, but it had a hole in it, so he could never get it filled. What is the meaning in all of this? Ravanna is nothing. Rama had himself become Ravanna. When he does not really exist, how can you kill him? If Ravanna was an entity, you could kill him. Ravanna had ten heads which represent the ten senses. You are He, but since you become identified with your ten senses, you enter Illusion. So, you can only kill Ravanna with understanding. An arrow can never kill Ravanna because there is really nothing in the world. The world is nothing, Zero. How can you kill Zero? Rama and Ravanna are one, but Rama doesn't know this. So, with understanding you get Sita, which means that you get the peace (Sita means peace). You have lost your peace, and by killing yourself through understanding you get it back. The ten senses represent the love of Illusion that prevents you from knowing yourself.

Books of Knowledge must be understood according to their inner meaning. When it is said that Christ will take you to heaven, it doesn't mean that the body will arise, and that you will be taken there. It means that when you understand that Christ is within you, that is the heaven. Then, you know that you, yourself are "The King of Kings." It is said that all that glitters is not gold, but still, you take all of this to be true. If you go to the source of it, it doesn't remain. It's not true. Go to the source. You can kill the body, but can you kill thoughts? Only by understanding your soul, and the Power, can you kill the thoughts. If you understand that Power, the ego automatically goes off. Thought starts from Ignorance, and if understanding comes, then everything is nullified. "I am not this, I am not that." "That" which is there, is always there. Don't be anything. If you want to be something, it's a stamp of the ego and you remain in a state. Be nothing and Reality remains.

In order for the ego to remain, it needs a state. If you remain in Knowledge then ego has a place, a support. But without Knowledge, the ego doesn't remain and you are He. If the house is demolished then what remains? The base, the foundation remains. When the coverings go off, then Reality remains. When one becomes old, only the body becomes old. The Power doesn't become old. You never die. "You" are always True, and "You" always remain. For You, there is no birth, no death, no sin, no virtue, no joy, and no displeasure. God and his creation are not true when Knowledge goes off. So if it is not true, then just let it be. Why try to harm or demolish that which is not? Don't worry for anything, just say "I'm not the body."

There is nothing to renounce when nothing is true. Then, "nothing" can't touch you. Let everything be there, but don't take the touch of it. If you touch it, attachment remains. Take the body as "my neighbor and not myself." You are the Power. You are not lame. The whole body exists on the Power. The Power doesn't need crutches from the mind. Why to cry for the body? Does the Power care if one bulb goes off? Be like the rich man who says when something breaks, "Don't worry, I'll get another one." With understanding you won't fear anything. When nothing ever happens, what is there to fear? If you rent a house and something happens to it, is it your responsibility? It's the owner's responsibility. When you say, "It's my house," then all of the troubles come on you. Say, "I'm not the body, I don't exist," and there is no me and mine. The boy asks, "what is this?" He is ignorant of what this thing is, so he asks. Does he ask with knowledge or not, tell me? He accepts the reply because prior to the knowledge, he was in ignorance.

Questioner: When the screen is all white and there is nothing left, what then?

Maharaj: Yes, there is nothing left now. Now, what do you want to know? Knowledge is also wrong. Whatever you saw, everything there disappears. Why did it disappear? Because it was not! If it had been something, it would have remained. When you sleep, does everything go off or not? And when you awake, from where does it come? Knowledge brings everything. So go a little beyond Knowledge, and you are there. It is so easy, but you don't want to cross the line. The mind cannot cross it, so how can it cross it? The mind always wants something to understand. If when a young boy sees the ocean he says, "That is water papa," the father will say, "It's not water, it is the ocean." Who is right? You give it the name. You are in the habit to give yourself a name, and to give many names. Afterwards, you create many, many names.

When you were born you didn't know anything. You got a name, and then you start giving names such as mama, papa, etc. All this comes from you. Where is papa and mama? Where are they? They are only your thoughts! So understand that Knowledge itself is wrong. Knowledge has made all confusion. So, Adam told Eve that when the world was created, "Don't touch it. If you touch it, you create all of the confusion." The mind has this habit to always touch. If a boy sees fire, he will want to touch it. Even if you say don't touch it or go near it, he will, and then he burns himself, and then experiences it. Due to Ignorance all these things have come up. Knowledge accepts all things as true, what to do? Both Knowledge and Ignorance are one, and Knowledge accepts everything as true. So first the Master always increases the Knowledge more and more. Knowledge should be increased so that it can understand that "Myself is wrong." So, the Master gives more and more Knowledge to you. He tells you many, many things.

It is written in the scriptures,"I am He, You are He, and then everything is He," and finally, it is said that "Knowledge is He." But still, the scriptures say that nothing is true, so you have to go ahead a little farther. Where Knowledge ends, at the end of Knowledge, "He" is there. What you see and perceive with the mind and the eyes, the scriptures say "neti, neti" (not this, not this). This means that what you see is not there. Everything that you see is not there, it is space, it is Zero. But still you say, "space." What to do? You are in the habit to take on your name first. You have no name. Your father and mother gave you the name, and you took it on and started giving names to others. You gave good names, bad names, whatever you liked. You say, "He's a bad person." The mind has the habit that what it likes is good, and what it doesn't like is bad. Really, he's not bad. It is understanding that is given by the Master, nothing else. He gives you Knowledge, so take more and more. If a boy fills up a balloon too much, he cries when it bursts. When death comes, everybody cries, what to do?

You have accumulated Knowledge. Money is Knowledge, everything is Knowledge. Without Knowledge, what is there? Suppose you have ten million in the bank, can you take it with you? No, it is only in your mind. Knowledge shows many things that are not true. You see a rainbow, the seven colors, are there really any colors there? Is it true? In a fraction of a second it goes off. The world is the same. As long as the eyes are open you see everything. When the eyes are closed, everything goes off, and that is called death, nothing else. So, the Power is there and everything works, but still, it's not true. It starts from Zero. So, go beyond Zero now. So, how to do what the Master teaches you? You can't know. How can you know? You, yourself are Zero. Knowledge is Zero, and "I am" also is Zero. It all starts and ends in Zero. Everything ends in Zero.

You see the dream, and you say, "It's not true." It all starts from Ignorance. Knowledge comes from Ignorance. So then, who will know what? There is nothing to know. Where Knowledge ends, you are there. You don't go to see the Reality. Who are you to see the Reality? How can you see the Reality? It is so subtle. It is more subtle than space. You feel the wind, but can you see the wind? And where does the wind come from? It comes from the space. You feel space, but there is no color there. You say, "the blue sky," but it really has no color. It's colored only in your vision. So, your question was about Knowledge?

Questioner: I think you answered it. Is that Knowledge a capital K?

Maharaj: How can it be capital K? When Knowledge ends, how can it be capital K? It is not there. Capital (assets or wealth) always ends. What to do? When you sleep, your capital ends. Capital means what you've gathered. When one dies, everything goes off. Nothing remains, because it is not true. When you take the birth you don't bring anything. Do you bring anything?

Questioner: Some say you bring karma.

Maharaj: What is karma? Karma is a thought only. I agree with you. You only bring thoughts when you take the birth. Where do thoughts start from? They start from Ignorance. You come with that Knowledge, but that Knowledge you don't know. People talk of karma, but do you know your karma (actions) from the last birth? Can anybody say? Even with a great Saint who knows your mind and everything, can you ask him what karmas you have done? If you don't know, how can he know? It's a foolish and wrong thing people say. If you really don't know, don't give out wrong ideas. Say, "I don't know." Teachers often put bundles on people, bundles mean wrong things, wrong ideas. Know first, and then tell. Okay? If you know, you can speak, no need to be silent. But if you don't know, don't give the address. So it is told, "Give thy ears to all, but to few thy tongue."

Questioner: Is this your advice to me?

Maharaj: It's your choice to accept or not.

Questioner: Thank you, I'll do my best. Are these teachings good for children?

Maharaj: Why not?

Questioner: Should children not learn?

Maharaj: Learn it, but understand it's not true. Children's brains are very mild, so if you put these things in their mind they can become the greatest of the great. But you teach them the wrong things. Still, the mind doesn't want to go to the Self. A young boy can learn very fast, but his mind is not as strong as your mind, or others around him. You give him names for everything, so strong impressions are given that are difficult to break. You people pour more and more ignorance in the child. He says "water," you say "ocean." Who is right? Your minds are so objective, and his is not. You make more and more trouble. A boy draws a picture, but you want to make the finishing touches. "Be like me," you say, but differences are there, minds differ. The mind is thought. Thought differs, nothing else. There are two brothers from one father. One becomes knowledgeable, the other illiterate. What is the reason? The mind doesn't accept, nothing else. Sharp minds can accept very fast. Once the mind accepts one side, it's difficult for it to go to the other side.

Your question was very good. People are grown up, but the mind is still in Ignorance. What to do? You can earn many degrees, no harm. But you don't know what Reality is. You don't know your Self. The Knowledge that you have accumulated is nothing but Ignorance. Who says? The realized person says. Say like Socrates, "I know that I know nothing." What you know is nothing. If it is true, you cannot know it. The eyes see everything that is not true. That which is "True," you can't see. Knowledge is Power, but it is also Zero if you understand. Call it a table, no harm, but know it is not true. As long as you've taken the part, you have to play it. If the hero dies in the picture, the heroine cries like hell, but she knows that her real husband is asleep in his bed at home. If you understand that everything starts from Zero, then you are beyond Zero. Otherwise, you are in Knowledge only. Then you want fame, name and many, many things. Knowledge takes you to death because it's not true. Ignorance takes you to hell. Knowledge also takes you there. What I speak is all wrong, I tell you! Words are wrong, but I speak *for* the Truth, the Reality. Words cannot go there. Forget everything, and you are there. Where are you not? You don't want to forget all of this. Forgetting brings you to the right place.

So, teach the children. This is not a fable. It's the Reality. Reality is difficult to understand. Fables can be understood by children. Big children don't agree with what we say, so how can small children agree with me? It's not a fable, it is a true thing. Truth always remains the Truth. That which is not true never existed. Make your mind that way. The mind can take you to hell or heaven. Think and think, and then finally forget everything. You can give Knowledge to children. Because of mind, all are children. They don't know the Truth, what to do? Okay?

Questioner: I counsel about twenty children in high school. I'm confused, and they are confused. Sometimes I try to share with them the principles and teachings of a priest from Bombay. He died about ten years ago. His teaching is very simple and you can use it with children. Sometimes I walk out of the sessions thinking maybe I've added more confusion. You have given the example of the poisonous snake. My question is: Do you set the work aside and first take out the tooth of the poisonous snake, and then do your work? Or do your work and try to take the poisonous tooth out at the same time?

Maharaj: Both at the same time. As long as the body is there you have to work. The body always wants something. There are five senses of knowledge and five senses of action in everyone. The senses of action have to do their work. They are the laborers. Suppose you want to see something, so you tell the legs,

"Come on, let's go." The legs have to obey. So with these ten things, everything is going on. You've taken a part, so play your part, but say, "It's not true, I'm not the part." You were a priest, now you're not a priest, so do your job, but understand, "I'm not this." When you were a priest, you were not a priest, I tell you. Whatever you are, say "I'm not this." Do no harm in doing. Why take out the poisonous tooth first? If you give a boy a rubber snake, he is afraid at first, but later on he knows that it can't bite. Then he will play with it. So do everything, but don't take the touch of it. The screen shows all of the pictures, but it doesn't accept them (as real). Be the screen yourself. Don't accept anything. If you accept, you become the smallest creature. Many things come and go, why to worry when they are not true?

Questioner: Sometimes I teach things that are contrary to what we are saying here.

Maharaj: Teach that everything is wrong. Understand that what you say is wrong. Just now I told you that my words are wrong. Words cannot be true, what to do? Why do you worry for that?

Questioner: Habit

Maharaj: Leave the habit. Habit is mind. You are untouchable. Habits may be many, but can one change habits or not? Understand, "I am doing all wrong things, but I make money." In fact, I even told someone to be more dishonest and make more money, no harm. Understand, "I don't do this, I am the Reality, I've taken on a part." Act well on your part, and therein the honor lies. All are He. Do all play their parts or not? If you don't take the touch of the part, you are always free. So it is told: "You are not to question why, you are not to make a reply. Don't ask anything, carry on, but do your duty and die." Your duty is death, so do your duty. What is there? Why should you take the touch of anything? Be a thief, but don't commit a theft. You are He, you produce the world, so why to worry? If you take something from your own house, have you committed a theft? It's all mine. When you understand you are He, everything is yours. The world is yours. Commit a theft, no harm. So I told him to be dishonest, and to do more wrong things. But know that both are wrong. Money is wrong, and your body is also doing wrong things. Why to worry? Understand that it's all wrong. It's not true. But who can do this? Only one who understands, otherwise not. You always fear you are cheating people, but say, "It's my money that I take from them." Do your duty, but don't say, "I'm a priest," or "So-and-so." Say, "I am He." You show many things to others. Ignorant people are tricked and they come, follow me? They pay money, and finally they go away. Everything happens on the screen. Many, many troubles happen, and the screen shows it all, but it doesn't worry. Be the screen. Don't worry for anything.

I always say don't worry. Why? Because it's not true. Everything is my choice. Everything is your choice. You are the Power. The king does what he wants, so he has no law. There is no law for you, if you understand. Be out of the law. Law means the society that has been created by people, ignorant people. How can laws be true? Ministers, prime ministers, all of these people are all ignorant. They make the wrong things. Don't tell them, there is no need to tell them. Why to tell a mad person that they are mad? If you tell a mad person he's mad, he'll tell you, "Your father is mad." Nobody will agree with you, especially if they are mad. Do everything, but don't agree that it's true in the mind. Know that you do wrong things, but say that you do right things. You have to put your fingerprint on it. The mind is the fingerprint. It can solve anything in any way, because it's not true. If you know that it's not true, you can do anything. You can do any trick there. Why don't I mind to say these things? Because I know everything is wrong. It's your choice whether you are dishonest or not. So do everything, but be out of it, nothing else. Be in it but be out of it. You take the touch of everything and you create confusion. Do your duty with the body, but you are not the body, so why to worry? The body does its job, but know, "I'm not the body. Knowledge does, the Power does, but I'm beyond the Power." Then what harms you? Because of Ignorance you accumulate everything, and with understanding you throw it off. Understanding is realizing.

Questioner: I was thinking that this teaching was true, but what I hear you say is that even this teaching is not true. But now I am thinking that none of this is true.

Maharaj: I told you that the words are wrong. Words cannot reach Him. But you have to point Reality out with words. Somebody asked me last year in San Francisco: "If everything is Illusion, you are Illusion too?" I said, "Yes, I am a first class Illusion." What I say is wrong, what I speak is also wrong, but for *whom* I speak is true. That's the difference. How can I show the Truth? You are He. How can I show you? I point it out to you. Forget everything, and you are He. Everything is not true, Illusion is not true, so how can I be true?

So, don't be a Master also. In order to take out wrong ideas, I say what I say. The Master is just a pointer, just like an arrow pointing you in a certain direction. He takes you to the door of Reality, and then he says, "You know yourself now, I don't know anything. I don't exist here." He, the Master, is not there at all. If the Master says, "I'm the Master," he is the most ignorant person. How can you give Reality to anybody? Reality is yourself. Show them the way, nothing else. You can give the address, and then you become the owner of the house. Always think this way. Don't be a Master. My Master always said, "Twenty-three hours of the day I'm in myself, for one hour, I step down and take you as an ignorant person, my disciple, and I teach you." The Master sacrifices himself by coming down, what to do? Coming down is a sacrifice or not? But whom to tell, and whom not to tell, if it is all Illusion?

By words you have become bound, and by words you can be free. By thoughts you have become bound. Your mind or your thoughts result in bondage or liberation. You're never in bondage, so how can I liberate you? You have forgotten your liberation, so I say I give it to you. If you lose your purse, and I give it back to you, what have I done? Nothing! So why should you be a Master? Say, "I know nothing." If you know, then all troubles come to you. Don't know anything. I don't know anything, I know Him only. So understand with your mind. The mind takes you to church, or to the bar, what to do? Both ways it takes you, it's your choice. You are the Master, you are He, don't forget that. There is no bondage on you, you are always free.

Questioner: Now that I have found you, I wonder if I should wrap up all my affairs here and go and be with you in India. What to do?

Maharaj: If you feel like that, it's okay. Keep in your mind what I've said and accept it. What I have told you, accept it. Then, wherever you may be, whether India or America, what harms you? Don't worry for that. Understanding is given. Understand and stay like that. Wherever you may be, you are He. If you want to come, come, I don't say no. I live in one room, ten by ten. You can come and stay in India, I don't mind. Experience what I say. Then you are ever free. The mind always thinks about what to do. The mind always thinks wrong things. If you are serious about this, we can discuss it afterwards, not here. This is a personal question, and not all are interested in this question.

Questioner: You have spoken before that the Master can only take you so far, and the rest is our responsibility. What is our responsibility?

Maharaj: He takes you to the place, then you open the lock. That is your responsibility. Open your mind which is locked. He gives the key, you open the lock. You fear to open the door wondering, "What will happen?" Don't fear. Nothing will happen. The world is not going to change, because it doesn't exist. So what I say is the key. Open the door, and you're the owner of it. Why should the Master come with you? Who is he to come with you? He doesn't exist. Why should the Master come with you? You are He. He makes you He. He makes you what he is. Don't think that you have to go somewhere. Understanding is required. Wherever you are, you can understand. Wherever you stay is heaven. Open your mind, nothing else. The mind should be changed, nothing else.

So I told her that I stay in a ten by ten room. I don't feel anything. When I go to India in June, I won't feel anything. Why should I feel anything? There are many, many things here. There are no different things than what is in India. There is a kitchen, and a toilet. My ten by ten room in Bombay has everything.

Everything is there, except my bathroom is outside. Where I eat is my dining table. My arati (worship) is Maharaj's arati. What to do? Whatever is there is okay.

One should not feel anything. So, the Master takes you up to that point and then he leaves you. Understand for yourself now. Make your mind understand, nothing else. When the mind accepts, everything is yours, and nothing is yours. Both things come in your mind. Everything is mine, and everything is not mine. You can become so big, but your mind makes you small. Break the walls of your mind, and you are ever free. You're a free bird. Why to worry? Be prepared for anything. So, in this way the Master gives you the key, nothing else. Why should he come there with you? You are the owner, how can he come with you? Your Self is He. There is no duality at all. So keep in mind what the Master says and act accordingly. Worldly bondage, and society's bondage doesn't allow you to accept. Forget them, and try to understand that you are He. Any more questions?

Questioner: Why not, "I am She?"

Maharaj: Why is He not She? "He" is gender, "she" is gender, nothing is there. What you call a rose smells the same by any other name. Now I say, "She is He." Come on! You are She. What harms you? In the body of a woman you become She. It's a cage, so she says, "I am She," but she is He when she's out of the cage. What to do? Leave the body. You stay in the cage, so you say, "I'm She." Be out of it. Understand yourself, and you are He. He is the Power, nothing else. The Power is always He. Everyone has the same Power. You say, "I'm she" What to do? Forget yourself, and you are He. Why to worry when there is only Oneness. Whether to say he or she is all nonsense. Forget those thoughts, forget your mind. The Power in woman is not woman. The Power in man is not man. Both are nothing. Forget your body and say, "I am He." You are always He. This is just fighting over words only. Don't worry for the words. I refer to the Reality as He, that's my choice.

Questioner: There are certain Saints who have attained Knowledge, but they don't go further. Why do they get stuck at Knowledge?

Maharaj: Ask them, why ask me? It's not my concern. There is nobody there but Him. Whom to tell and whom not to tell? To go beyond Knowledge is your choice. Who am I to ask anybody? It is my duty to tell what I know. To do or not to do is your choice. In the military they say, "Not to question why, not to make a reply, but do your duty and die." So, here also, do your duty. Death is your duty. You have to die when you are living, then you get the heaven. Don't die, and then you are in hell. Die and then you are in heaven, how much time does it take? Right here is heaven or hell. It depends on your thoughts: To be or not to be is always the question for the mind. So don't be, and also don't not be, and you are He. Okay?

Questioner: I am unclear about what is honest and what is dishonest. What is right? I don't understand

Maharaj: When the world is not true, what is honest and what is dishonest? Everybody is dishonest. I can prove it. That which you say you are is not true. Are you honest? When you say your name, is it anywhere written? Is that honest or dishonest? The one who says, "I'm not this, and I am not anything else," is the only true person in the world. All are dishonest. It's only a question of a small dishonesty or big dishonesty. How does someone become rich? Only at the expense of others. Money is not more, it is just a matter of circulation. When you yourself are not true, how can you be honest? Understand "I am He." That is honesty. Then everybody is He, and there is nothing to worry about. Then the question of honesty or dishonesty doesn't remain.

In a dream you were dishonest, are you dishonest? This is also nothing but a long dream. Try to understand this point, nothing else. Understand what is at the bottom of all this. It is Zero. In Zero there is nothing, no honesty or dishonesty. Both are the same. You say this is a table, I say that in a moment it can become ashes. Are you right or am I? Go to the root of it. What is there when everything is Zero? What is true? When you say it is true, you are in bondage. Honesty and dishonesty are taught to satisfy a child's mind, that's all. Reality is always true, it never changes. How can it be honest or dishonest? When all are dishonest, why to worry about being honest? That honesty is also dishonesty. You cannot prove that honesty is true. It is not there, so then, how can you say that it is true? Both are wrong.

I don't say to be dishonest. Just understand that honesty is not there, and then do whatever you like, it's your choice. To be or not to be is always the question. The mind is always that way. This is all the mind's work. Understand that it's all okay. In this world you can make more money by dishonesty. An honest man says he's poor because of his honesty. There is more profit in being dishonest. An honest man says. "I am an honest person so I can't do anything. I can't fill my belly." So, is honesty or dishonesty right? Both are wrong! Forget everything. Nobody is honest and nobody is dishonest. When you pay for something, it's your choice. It's just a trick to make money. Some people have the trick.

My uncle had a clothing store and just when he was closing for the day, a rich man came in. My uncle showed him the best cloth as requested by the rich man, but the cloth wasn't good enough. The man was of that type, so he asked for even more expensive material. So, my uncle went to the back room and brought out the cheapest fabric, and told the man that this was his finest cloth, and the man bought it. So my uncle got the highest price for the cheapest cloth. Whose fault was it? Was it honesty or dishonesty? If my uncle had said that he had no better quality then he wouldn't have done business, so he did the trick. Can you prove whose fault it was? Was it the purchaser or my uncle? The world is not true, so anything can happen. Don't be honest and don't be dishonest. Understand yourself.

* * * * * * * * * *

May 14, 1998

Questioner: When I am in your presence, I am very touched and moved, and I feel less attached to the world. But that brings me some sadness, and then I feel like I know something, and I sense the ego.

Maharaj: So when you forget everything you feel sadness because you don't know yet what you have to do. Everyone feels this emptiness, this sadness. They go up to Zero and then they come back. You have to go beyond Zero. You have to go beyond the space. Your Self is so subtle. When you don't understand, you feel the emptiness, a sadness. When you understand that all is Illusion, then everything goes off. You feel, "What should I do?" You want to know something there. The mind is always in the habit of wanting to know something. But who is there that will know? So, sadness comes in the mind.

It requires a Master at this point to take you to the right place. You should not feel the emptiness or sadness. It is due to Ignorance or the Zero state. You have forgotten yourself, what to do? So you have to take yourself beyond Zero. Zero is nothing and yet you feel sadness over it. You are afraid because you want something there. The mind is dying and it naturally feels some danger. At this point, there is no entity at all. As long as the mind is there, duality is there. So you have to understand without the mind. The mind wants something objective, but the Master points you towards understanding, not to objective knowledge. In this understanding there is neither joy nor sadness. Your Self alone is there and nothing else is required. That is called Oneness. No duality is there and that means no sadness and no emptiness. When you awake from sleep, you feel a freshness and you can do many things. That freshness comes from forgetting all this, and then real joy comes in your mind. The sadness does not remain.

It is natural to feel okay in the presence of the Master and ask, "How I can manage without him?" The Master takes you to the right place and your mind must do the same. Then when you are away from the Master, everything is okay. The mind does not want to die, so it goes towards worldly objects. The mind wants. It wants something tangible. If you understand that everything you have done is nothing, then what can more give you? So, the Master cannot give you anything, because everything is nothing. You are He.

You have forgotten yourself so the Master says these things. The Reality is that you and the Master are one. When nothing is there, what remains? You yourself remain. Forget the ego, the "I," and you won't ever feel any sadness. Everything is the Reality, nothing else. It is called the "Stateless State" or the "Thoughtless Reality." You want joy and pleasure but nothing remains there. Joy and sadness is only the mind's work. Forget the mind. Unless you leave the mind, you can never be happy. You don't have to achieve anything. You just have to know yourself. So Knowledge brings all these states, but Knowledge itself is only a thought. When you feel something it means that the mind has not yet completely gone. Illusion must be eliminated. What is not must go off, and then it is very easy to understand.

Everything has come up on Him, the Reality. The whole world is nothing but His shadow. If you understand this, then what to achieve and what to get? The shadow is not true, the host is true. Sadness comes from the love of Illusion. When you want something more you have forgotten yourself. Nothing is to be acquired. At this very moment, everyone is He. Once the wrong thoughts are taken out, a clear-cut understanding remains. A strong Master is required to take you to this place. When you go away from your home for a long time and then you return, you feel happy. Same way, over many lifetimes you have forgotten yourself, and when you return to yourself, do you feel happiness or not? Say "I am not this. I am not that. I am He." Then there is nothing to worry about. When you are working you want to be retired, and when you are retired you worry about how to fill up the time. The mind always wants another state, and what the mind does not have is what it wants. Death of the mind or ego is what is required.

Questioner: What do you mean when you say that you are the Creator?

Maharaj: You say, "I am the body," and make yourself into a small creature. So in the beginning the Master says you are the Creator, and you have created the universe. The Power in you is the same Power that has created the world. For example, a fifty-watt bulb gives less light than a 100 watt bulb, but the electricity is the same. The Power has come into the body, and then you say, "I am this." That makes you a very small creature. Lord Krishna says that the Power has entered the body so I call it a part of me, and that part is my original Self. You are He, but due to the body you say, "I am this." Instead, you should feel that I have created the world when that Power or Knowledge comes to you.

When you are sleeping and forget the body, you create many worlds with just your thoughts. You are so Powerful that a plane can come into your room. The Power can do anything. The whole world is your dream, nothing else. This Power has no limit. Your wish makes everything. Yet everything you see and feel is not true. You say that yourself after you awake from the dream. So this world is created by the Creator and you have created it yourself, understand that. You have taken a part as an actor in this dream. It is a dream in a dream. Reality has been forgotten and the whole world has been created by God. Now you have taken a birth and become an actor in this play, and you have created your own world in the world.

This world is nothing but a long dream. So, you must understand "Who am I?" first. Then you can feel the joy. But the understanding that "I understand" is still only a thought, and although the Master makes you bigger and bigger, finally he says that the Creator and his creation is not true, and that you are beyond even that. Everything starts from Zero and therefore cannot be true. The Master makes you the greatest of the greatest, and then he tells you that what you know is all wrong. Then when one dies what remains for him? Everything is there but what is the use of it? The whole world is just moving on the breath. When that stops where is the world? Breathing is just the wind and you have made all these castles from that wind. If you understand this, that all is Illusion, then you will be out of the clutch of Ignorance.

* * * * * * * * * *

June 12, 1998

Questioner: If I understood correctly yesterday, you said that heaven and hell are equal in the Illusion. I was under the impression that a sattvic mind (pure and harmonious) was a requirement for attaining Reality.

Maharaj: You need a subtle mind, but what is pure and what is impure? Purity and impurity are concepts of the mind. When all is Illusion, what is pure and what is impure? So I say they are equal. Suppose you have bad thoughts in a dream, does that make you bad, and can you not get the Reality? If you think that only purity can take you to God, that is a nasty blockage. If a man says, "I don't believe in God," does that make him unfit for the Reality? The one who says that is himself God. You people in foreign countries where it is cold wear your shoes in church, and Indian people never wear shoes in the temple. So who is impure and who is pure? Does God accept the prayers of one and not the other?

There is a story of a Maulvi. A Maulvi is a Mohammedan priest, a realized person. He refused to wash his hands and feet in the mosque before he prayed, so the people in the village threw him out. They refused him water and fire to cook with. After a few days he became hungry and went into the jungle and caught a deer, but he had nothing to cook it with. What to do? So he asked the sun to come down and cook the deer so he could eat. The sun came down and everything became extremely hot, so the villagers prayed to God to make the sun go back in the sky. But God told them that the Maulvi had ordered it and they would have to ask the Maulvi to do it. He said, "I can't do anything." (It is said in Marathi that even God has troubles.) So the villagers had to go to the Maulvi for help. The Maulvi said, "Okay, but first accept that God will accept your prayers even if you don't wash your hands and feet." Everyone has the Reality in him. To be pure or impure refers to the body and mind. You are quite separate from that. Now, I don't say be impure, but just don't say that only certain people can get the Reality.

When it comes to the body how can it be pure? The body produces shit and piss. It is nothing but a shit factory. It's a dirty thing and as long as the Power is there you worship it, but when the Power goes off you want to get rid of it as soon as possible. The body is the dirtiest thing and yet you say, "I'm this!" You people think these nonsense things. Suppose you are on a plane and you are in tourist class, and someone else is in first class. You both are going the same way and can reach the destination. The difference is in your thoughts. So God doesn't know purity or impurity. This is nothing but a long dream, and purity and impurity are part of it. Reality is quite different. So whatever state you are in, it is nothing but a dream.

Lord Rama was the eighth incarnation of God. His motto was, "One word, one woman, one arrow." He always spoke the truth. Lord Krishna was the ninth incarnation and he had many queens, and he always told lies. Lord Krishna is considered the perfect incarnation of God, and Lord Rama is considered a half incarnation. People say to always have good thoughts, like compassion and mercy. Good and bad thoughts come and they go, why to worry? Forget the thoughts. They are nothing but the mind's concepts. The Power is neither good nor bad, right nor wrong, pure nor impure. I don't say to be corrupted, or to be bad. But everyone is He and due to the attributes (gunas) everyone is in a dream, and nothing is true.

＊＊＊＊＊＊＊＊＊＊＊

December 14, 1998

Questioner: Last year in Sedona you said, "Do your duty and die." How can I know my duty in this life?

Maharaj: You have taken the birth, you have taken a body. The body has to do many, many things. The body requires many actions and you have to do it. You have to eat, sleep, see, hear, smell. One day this body is sure to die. This is a mortal body. It is not immortal. Reality has no duty. Electricity, the Power, has no duty. If you push a button it gives the light. This body has a mind, and mind has to do its duty. The mind brings duties and everything. She is a young girl (referring to someone in the room) but she knows she has to go to school and learn and get through. If you become a soldier, they say you are not to question why, and not make a reply, you are to do your duty and die. Everyone is sure to die one day. There is no alternative for anybody.

Whether you are a king or a beggar this is sure to happen. Both are beggars, one begs for taxes, the other for alms. Duty is the same for both. Everyone begs for food to fill their bellies. The body is such a rascal. It eats every day, but still gets empty. If you eat a big lunch you say, "I won't eat in the evening." When evening comes you want something more. So to fill up the belly one has to do his work, his duty. If your mother makes your lunch, you have to put it in your mouth. Suppose she puts it in your mouth, you still have to chew it. You have to do these things. Everyone wants that this body should be immortal. The Power that is in you is immortal. Without the connection of the Power the body cannot work. When you take the birth and the Power is connected, duty is always there. One should do one's duty and die.

Questioner: Duty of the body is easy to understand, but what about social duties? Sometimes people want me to do something and I want to do something else. This is a conflict for me. These are my conflicts in ordinary life.

Maharaj: The mind always creates conflict. The boy wants to touch the fire. His parents say no, but he touches it anyway and he gets burned. Let people say anything. Why should you worry about other people? The world is always fighting. Realized people never care for what people say. Let the dogs bark, the Saints are not afraid. The minds always differ, so conflict is sure to come. If you understand your own Power and say, "I am He," then you'll never be defeated by anyone. Your Self is immortal. So the body dies, you don't die. That which works in you is immortal. That is the Power. When you go to the Master you ask many, many things. Otherwise you can't understand. That is your duty here. If you say that you are the body and death is the end of everything, that is Ignorance. And in that Ignorance you take another body or birth. Understanding should come. When you know everyone is myself, then whatever you do, whether you eat nice food or stale bread it's all the same to you. What is there? Nothing is there. To die means to forget everything. So, when you are living, die in that way. Say, "I don't exist." That is the death. To die doesn't refer to the body. When you are living, die and see what happens. "Do your duty and die" means to die here.

What does the Master do? He puts the knowledge in you so you can understand that you are He. Knowing is your duty. You do everything. but you don't know yourself. You don't know "Who am I?" You are the Power, that Power makes a dead body speak, and sleep etc. Know yourself as that Power, not as a body. To have a body is a mistake. Say, "I am not true, to say that 'I am,' is wrong." Have that much courage to say this. Denial of oneself is not easy, but duty belongs to the body and not to you. When your body goes, what duties do you have? You say these are my duties. It is the body's and the mind's duties. You are beyond Knowledge and Ignorance. Knowledge must know, and that is the duty of Knowledge. But you are beyond that. You are nameless and formless. The beginning of the world is Aum. When Knowledge comes you say, "I am there." When you take the body, Aum comes in it. Forget that Aum also. Then what is your duty? Then nothing is your duty now. Agree? There is no duty for you when you understand yourself.

Saints never care for the body. My Master's Master, Bhausaheb, wanted to leave his body, so he stopped eating and stopped drinking water. He did his duty to make people understand, and then he wanted to die. One day he clapped his hands and said "Narayana," and he died. Say that you are Narayana, and that you are not going to die. The body goes off. Why to worry? People worry for the body. Think in this way. Right thinking is your duty. Then you are He.

The Master takes you to the right side. He says everything is Illusion and everything is a dream. Forget everything. Let everything be there, still forget it. Have the understanding in the mind that you are He. Say, "I don't do anything, the body does it." Do everything but say, "I don't do it." Okay?

Questioner: Is He beyond Zero?

Maharaj: He is the father of Zero. He is beyond Zero.

Questioner: That is difficult.

Maharaj: The one who says that's difficult is He. You don't want to say that Zero is Zero. That is ego. Nothing is yours. Be bankrupt in the mind. No need to throw off anything. That way you will feel rich in the mind. Have that much courage in the mind. Don't care for anything or for what will happen. Say, "Nothing is mine, because I don't exist." Nobody wants to go to Zero. Be Zero and then act. When you sleep what do you do? Nothing remains for you. Be He and remain. Be rich and not have a single coin in your pocket. Who can stop you? Don't worry for anything because it is Zero, nothing. When you are Zero that is the real bankruptcy, and then you are He. Be naked while you are living and say, "I am not this." Then you are the Reality.

* * * * * * * * * *

December 29, 1998

Questioner: Could you speak about the relationship of guru and disciple?

Maharaj: If you are an aspirant then you must have the faith in the Master, that is the first thing. If there is no faith then it's all useless. When there is no faith then doubt always remains in the mind. When the doubt is there, how can you be He? Anything may happen to the aspirant, but still you must have the complete understanding that everything is for the good. One should not worry about the Illusion. The Illusion always troubles you. Illusion always comes in the way to break your faith. Many things happen against your wish, but you should say that whatever happens it is all for the good. Whatever happens, happens to the body, but the Master says that you are not the body. That much faith you must have. You have to submit to the Master. Why to worry for the Illusion?

You have taken yourself to be a body, and that ego always goes against the teaching of the Master. The ego doesn't allow you to keep the faith. Faith means full faith! Suppose the Master says to a disciple, "Tell that dog outside to go away," and he goes outside and finds only a cow there. Still he tells the cow to go. Why? It is because of faith only. The Master tests your ego there. You must be faithful to the Master, but he must be a real Master. If he is realized then whatever happens, let it happen. After all, it is only an Illusion. Nothing has happened, that should be your understanding. In a dream many things happen, do you worry about that? Because you know after awakening that it was only a dream. So when awakening comes here, by the grace of the Master, then what is there? Don't worry for anything.

The mind always requires support. The mind has got the curse not to hear the Master. The Master says, "You are He," but the mind doesn't accept, so the mind always makes that mistake. The mind always worries and has the dilemma of what to do and what not to do. The mind fears, and that is the nature of mind. It thinks of both good and bad. It has got that habit. It thinks bad first, and then good. If someone's husband is late the wife thinks "Oh, what has happened? Maybe an accident." One thinks bad things, one never thinks that something good has happened. The disciple of the Master doesn't worry for anything! Anything can happen, let it happen. Why to worry, say it's something always for the good. But the mind is short-sighted and cannot think this way. When you have the understanding in the mind then it goes to the right place. Whether the Master is with you or not, the faith you have in him takes you to the right level, and then you do the right things.

When I was in Rishikesh at a young age, I was very sick, passing 150 stools a day. I wrote a letter to my Master that I wanted to come home. As I was walking to the post office I remembered what my Master had said. He said, "If death comes, it comes to the body not to you, so don't worry for that!" I tore up the letter. Why? That is the faith. If death comes, let it come, the body has to die, I'm not going to die. The Master makes you understand that. That is what you should feel in the mind, and that is the relationship between the Master and the disciple. I finished staying four months in Rishikesh and then came home. If I had feared death, then I would have died and gone.

The body-mind is such a dirty, and a fantastic thing. It doesn't allow you go to the Reality because its death is there. So, one should try to understand what the Master says. Even if he says anything wrong to you, accept it. Sometimes he can test your faith, why not? With that faith your problems will be solved without doing anything. The Master does everything for you, but faith is required, nothing else. So you have to kill your mind and say, "I don't exist, He exists in me now," and that brings everything to the right point. Tell me, what can a disciple do? But if a Master has the final understanding, then he can give the correct advice to the disciple. Try to understand the Master first.

The Master must also understand that he is not the Master. Then he is the real Master. He is everywhere. Why to say that I am a Master? You have forgotten your things and I give them back to you. Have I done anything? You all have forgotten your own liberation. He liberates you. How can he liberate you? Only if you have faith in him. Otherwise you are more and more in Illusion, take it for granted. He never says anything to you. He says, "Who am I to tell anything to anybody?" My own Master was giving discourses, and some people came to ask him questions. He said, "I don't say to them, do this or do that. It's always their choice."

Don't blame anybody when things go wrong. The mind has got the habit to blame others. Those who have understood don't say to anybody "It's your fault." Say "It's my fault." If you can know your own thoughts, then you can know everything. Put the blame on your mind. It is your mistake. If anything happens, say nothing, or that "It is my mistake." Be able to say that everyone is myself. Then you have the right understanding.

A woman committed some mischief with somebody and they asked Saint Tukaram who had done it, and he said, "Vitthal" (a name for God). They asked him if he had not done this, and he said, "Vitthal." Saint Tukaram understood that everyone is He. What to say and what not to say when everyone is He? Nobody is at fault. Why should you find fault with others? He, the Reality, has not done anything. He is always free. Vitthal means He, nothing else. So, everybody is nothing but He, and there is nothing else in the world but He. Always say, "I do not know anything. Everything is He." Then, if you see it that way, He protects you everywhere and anywhere.

You worry because you take the entity of this body as true, and say "I am this." The mind makes all this mischief and then it puts the blame on others. There your faith is needed in the Master. He says everybody is myself. So I say, when a realized person sees someone killed he says, "I don't know anything because the killer is He, and the one who is killed is also He. So who to blame?" That should be your understanding, and there will be no quarrel with anybody.

If a madman comes to a Master, he never says that he is mad. He says, "Okay, come with me and have understanding." When the understanding comes that all are myself, the ego doesn't remain. Who is bad and who is good? So, one should not say anything about anybody. Everybody is okay in his own way. If doubts come in the mind ask the Master. If you don't, then doubts will remain. Be doubtless, no doubts. And if you still don't understand, then ask him again. So what is the relationship between the Master and the disciple? They both become one. There is neither disciple nor Master in the final understanding.

Saint Tukaram went with some thieves to a house, but he didn't know they were thieves. He went with them with the attitude that everybody is He. They all went through a window and entered the house and he went with them. He saw an idol of Vitthal and he began praying. At that time the woman of the house got up and said, "Oh! Thieves are in my house!" But then all the thieves began to sing bhajans with Tukaram. Her husband woke and said, "Oh, no it's only Tukaram here, there are no thieves here, so don't worry, he is just praying to God." So, can a Saint change many many things or not? Tukaram was a simpleton. He says everyone is okay. Whoever you are, you are always He.

For those who come to the Masters feet, he gives them understanding. He doesn't say, "I can do this or that." No advertisement is required. Water never says, "I am water." When you are thirsty you go to water. So, the realized person should not have any ego or fame or anything. Who should bow down to you? When everyone is He, who remains? There is only Oneness. My Master always told us that if anybody bows down to you, say that he bows down to my Master and not to me. Otherwise, ego comes in the mind. And finally, faith is not required, because you and the Master are one. There is no need for faith afterwards. When you sit on a throne you are a king, no? Why should you doubt you are a king? So we called Maharaj the "King of Kings." Why are these words used, "King of Kings?" If you have that faith and understanding, you yourself are He. How much time does it take? Don't worry for all this nonsense. The body is nonsense, mind is nonsense, Ignorance is nonsense, and Illusion is also nonsense. All these things come in your way.

People often make offerings and sacrifices to God. God doesn't want any sacrifice. What is God lacking? So, why should he worry? In one thought he can prepare the world. So what would he want from the world, tell me? He doesn't want anything. He wants your ego to go. Ego means that I am, and that I know everything. Let your ego go to hell. Indian people put prasad before God, and we bow down to him. But God doesn't eat. You eat! What to do? He doesn't want anything. Be like that! Your mind should be like that, "I don't want anything. I am not this body, I am something separate from that." If that understanding comes, then you're He always. It is the faith in the Master that brings you there. One is ignorant and doesn't know the way, so the address should be given by the Master. If the aspirant doesn't go to the address, then whose fault is it? If he goes to the address he says, "I am the owner now of this." He opens the door and enters the room and says, "I am He." It is very difficult to accept. "How can I be He?" The mind always brings in objections.

The mind always creates problems for you. If you win the lottery, or a win a big case if you are a lawyer, and you get a large sum of money, you offer only a small amount to God. Are you cheating God or not? Offer Him everything! Say, "Nothing is mine. By His grace I got it." So offer the Master everything. He doesn't want anything from anybody, but by His grace you have understood. He makes you He. What can you give the Master when everything is nothing? Ignorance prevails in you, so take out that Ignorance by accepting what the Master says. That is the grace. Only by full faith in the Master can you get the understanding in the mind. Without this faith the ego won't go off.

Questioner: In the book, Amrut Laya, it mentions that God has fear. (The questioner then reads a passage from the book.) "It is true that God has created the world, but the world exists only as long as this perishable body exists. God exists only as long as the devotee exists and vice-versa. So long as the dream lasts, the dreamer is present However, the basis of all of this is Parabrahman, the Reality. God has intense fear of getting destroyed. Only whatever is without fear is Parabrahman."

Maharaj: Yes, God does have this fear. When the body dies, God goes off. The connection with God is gone. Where does it go? Nobody knows because it is nothing. God says, "Oh, I bless you, and I do this," but everything goes back to Zero when you awake, what to do? If God comes to you, say "Why have you come? I don't want you!" God may say, "But I am happy with you." And you can say, "But I am not happy with you." The creator of the false, or Illusion, how can he be true? He has created and his curses and blessings are on you. But you are also not true, and God is not true. Both are untrue.

When both who are cheaters meet, how can they cheat each other? When two cheaters meet, then nothing happens. Both are wrong. So God has the fear. Where does the Power go? It goes to Zero. Power comes from Zero and ends in Zero. The body dies and everything goes off. What remains? Nothing remains, and this is the understanding you must have. You, yourself have become God. You have become something, then the fear is there. When you understand that you are He, then you don't remain and neither does the fear. Now, nothing can touch you. You see with the eyes, and then say that everything is true. Close your eyes and what remains? For a blind person the world is not true. Understand this way. Reality has nothing to do with all these things. If one or two floors fall down on the basement (foundation), the basement remains the basement. Reality is just like that. Everything comes upon Him, and then goes off, including God. In complete darkness and Ignorance the world has been created by Him. How can it be true? All that you see and perceive is nothing but God's dream. It is the magic of God, and it's all wrong. But the magic of God does not work on a Saint. Saints don't take the touch of anything. So, Saints have more Power than God or not? God is perishable. If God is perishable how much Power can he have?

* * * * * * * * * *

January 26, 1999

Questioner: You have told us that will is necessary. What is will? How can I find it when my ego is so strong? How can I strengthen my will for the Reality?

Maharaj: What is will? Will means desire. Whatever is your desire, that is your will. When desire becomes stronger, then will is stronger. If it's for worldly things, then the ego is there. It must be there. When the desire is for Reality, the ego goes off. Ego doesn't remain. It is the death of the ego. If a real king comes, the false king will be found out, no? Will is yours and it comes from Knowledge. The wish for the "Knowledge of Reality" is a good wish, then the ego doesn't come. Ego means nothing. It is just the shape of the Self. It takes the place of the Self. What is ego? It is nothing. It has no entity at all. As long as the Reality is hidden, the wrong king can sit on the throne. If your desire is strong for the Illusion, then the ego comes. But when your wish is for the Reality, it is not called ego. If you understand the Reality the ego can't stay, and won't remain.

Everything is will, nothing else. Desire, wish, and will are all one. It all depends on you and how you tackle the problem. Some desire for worldly things, and others say that the world is an Illusion and don't care to know anything. What to know and what not to know, when it is nothing? If you understand that everything starts from Zero, then the ego doesn't remain. When you are sleeping everything goes off, the body, mind, and thoughts. But the Power is still working in you. You are breathing, you are not dead. That breathing is ego, breathing is Knowledge, and Knowledge is ego. It is the ego of the Knowledge. You are sleeping no, and you forget everything, but still Knowledge remains in a very subtle form. Follow me? From that Knowledge, Ignorance comes, and you see the whole dream. Here in the waking state, it is the same. Knowledge comes and you see the whole world. Reality is forgotten, and the dream of the world comes. Otherwise, there is nothing. Everything was Zero when you were sleeping, but you were near the Reality. You were Reality at that time, but you didn't know it. But, even knowingness is in the mind. The mind is a thought. The mind sleeps, I agree, but subtle mind remains there. When that subtle thought takes on objectivity, then you see the dream. Sometimes when you are a little awake from sleep a thought comes, but if it doesn't materialize you go back to sleep. If it materializes then the dream comes. Many times that happens, then awakening comes, but you are not attached to the thought, so ego doesn't come.

Pure Knowledge is not ego. Pure Knowledge is He. Pure Knowledge means no Knowledge. When a flower dies, the scent remains, and the essence has nothing to do with the flower now. Same way here also. Ego remains there. You say "I am sleeping," and that is ego. But you forget that in sleep, and then when no one is sleeping, you go to the Reality. There is a very subtle difference there. So the realized person's sleep is called samadhi, because they don't go to Zero. They go to themselves. Everyone goes there, but they don't know it.

When we went to Pathri on the pilgrimage, Nandu asked, "Where is Pathri?" We were three minutes away. We were there, but he didn't know, so he asked for it. So, knowingness lasts up till the last moment. Forget that knowingness and you are He. Knowingness is so strong, Knowledge is so strong that it has made the whole world. Animals, birds, even ants all have Knowledge. Everything is nothing but Knowledge, but only humans have the power of discrimination to know what is real and what is ego. "Where there is a will there is a way," it is said. It applies to the Reality also. The will and way is there. Forget this, and you are there.

It is just like if I am in America and I say, "Where is America?" You are He always, but you don't know due to Ignorance. What to do! The will is there but you don't know the way. You are stopped because everything is Zero. How to find out when all is Zero? All of the scientists have failed. They have discovered the black hole. Where there is no sunshine, and nothing is there. No mechanism can go there, because it all starts from Zero. They can only go to Zero, they can't go beyond. Many Saints have also failed for the same reason. Zero is Knowledge now. From Zero, Knowledge comes. Knowledge has no entity at all, because it comes from Zero. No Zero, no Knowledge. So you are always in Zero, and that is Ignorance. Everything is nothing so how to find the way? You must know the final stage. My Master has taught this. "Go beyond Zero." When you understand that thought is wrong, that is the thoughtless Reality.

Without a real Master, you can't find the way. Suppose her name is Ann. If her name is not there, then who is she? She is He. Follow me? All have got the names, and all are fond of names. Let Ann go, and the Reality remains. How much time does it take? Forget yourself. First though, you must know yourself and then you go a little ahead, and then forget yourself. Knowledge makes everything true. Has that which you are not become true or not? Does Ann have any entity? Tell me. If you understand that Ann is only a thought, and that thought is wrong, are you the "Thoughtless Reality" or not? It is so easy but you all make it so difficult. The Master must have the final understanding otherwise he can't give you the address. Some Masters give their disciples Indian names. What is the use of it? They only pour more ignorance in them. Why give names to anybody? Is one name not sufficient? It is accepted with love and it is given with love, what to do! People just don't understand. People should know themselves, "Who am I?" How can you know yourself when you have two names?

All is wrong, nothing is true. Everyone is running in the wrong direction. The ego is so cunning. It works here and there. Cunning people are difficult to be with. They say one thing and do another. The ego says, "I am Brahman, I am He." So try to understand your ego. The ego brings will or desire. If the ego, or mind, goes to the wrong side, it brings the world. If it goes to the Reality, then everything goes off, and Reality opens up. There the cleverness doesn't remain. How can you be cunning when there is no duality? Only Oneness is there, and you remain He.

Questioner: Sometimes my wish for Reality is strong, and sometimes it isn't strong. Is it in my control?

Maharaj: Why not! If you drive a car you have the power to stop it. You can go fast or slow, that depends on you. And you have brakes as well. When you ride a horse, you hold onto the reins, and you can stop the horse at once. Ride the mind. But you are always ridden by the mind, what to do? The mind means wish or thought. In the same way, have the brake on your thoughts. It is said, "For the Illusion always be carefree, but the wish for Reality should be great." Then you can ride the mind. As long as the body is there, eyes must see, ears must hear. But when you hear a song, understand that "I am writer and the singer." You are everywhere and in everything. Have that much power in the mind to say that. But you don't use your Power correctly, you use it in the wrong way. Nobody is right, and nobody is wrong. Nobody is good, and nobody is bad. All this nonsense comes in your mind. Nobody dies, but you say "He's dead and gone." What to do? Who dies? No death is called death.

Questioner: Yesterday I lost a very good friend, and I went into a very deep pain. I understand what you say, but still I feel all these things.

Maharaj: Illusion always remains in the mind. Your love for Illusion doesn't go.

Questioner: I understand, but it doesn't go.

Maharaj: You may understand, but you don't follow. What to do? You understand that there is a right and wrong way, but you take the wrong way. "Nobody dies," I tell you. Five elements go to the five elements, and the Power goes to the Power. What has gone? Only the name. On the record it is put that "So-and-so" has died. The strong wish for the Reality has not come in your mind. Reality is always true. Somebody dies on the screen, do you cry for them? He may be the most lovable character, hero or heroine. You don't cry because you know he is not dead. Only the picture shows that he is dead. Same way here, the picture shows that she is dead, and she is dead and gone now. Breathing has stopped, why to worry for that? Why feel for that? So if death comes to you, then you'll cry again and forget the Reality. Have the courage to oppose all of these things. Nothing is true! Once you understand that correctly you'll never cry for anything. Someone told me earlier that she had died. A thought came to me, and a thought went away. That's all! You should feel that nothing has happened. Why to care or cry for anything? Everything comes and goes. So, you are not posted in Reality when you react.

Nothing is bad, nothing is good, because it is not. This is a long dream, there is nothing to worry for. If you are killed in a dream, when you awake, do you cry for that? When we were with Siddharameshwar, a dead body passed us on the way to the crematorium. He asked us, "What do you feel?" We answered, "A dead body is taken away, that is all." He said, "If your dearest dies and you feel nothing, be assured that you are realized." The dearest is your body, the most dearest, no? When someone dies, you don't die with them. Don't feel sorrow or anything. Be brave enough to accept whatever happens.

You worry and think like this because you're only on the way, and you don't have the address up to now. When your mind is stronger the address is there. You are He, you are always He. Every minute three people die and five are born. What is God to do? Does he cry or laugh? God knows that he can create or destroy a life with just one thought. Accept what happens. There is no need to worry for anything. I can die in five minutes. Don't worry for that either.

Love for the body and mind is so strong that you forget the Reality. Reality never worries for anything. Be the screen. The screen never worries for anything. When the Master dies you may feel something. But understand that in the mind and in the body you are limited, and without the body you are unlimited, you are everywhere. The problem is that all you see is the figure and shape. If golden bangles are broken, the shape goes. Does the gold worry for that? Many other shapes can be made, why to worry? Understanding should be of that type. Don't worry for anyone's death. Death has no value. The body has come from Zero, and it returns to Zero. Many names and figures have gone, where have they gone? Has anyone sent a letter from there? You don't exist so how can a letter be sent? Nobody dies, and nobody is born. What is never born and never dies, is the Reality.

Everything is null and void. Nothing is true. This is all for fun only. The foreigners say, "Eat, drink, and be merry." So, if someone dies they drink, just to forget the death, that's all. But when the kick wears off, they remember again and then cry. When the understanding comes from the Master, that kick is everlasting. Nothing comes, and nothing goes, Zero has gone to Zero.

Questioner: What did you feel when your Master died?

Maharaj: At the moment I felt it. He is gone now. I did everything for his body. I was very young at that time. He gave the Reality, so his death should be felt. My elder brother and younger sister died. I went to their funeral and I didn't cry. Everyone else was crying. Why to cry? Accept what happens, but when it is nothing, what to accept? My brother was nothing, and my sister was nothing. So nothing always gives you a cry. Forget nothing and then are you happy or not? How can you get to sleep otherwise? Forgetting must always be there. Dust has gone to dust. Only what is true remains. Reality is always there. When you praise the Reality, you become the Reality. Reality is here at this very moment. The body goes, you don't go. So, never worry for anyone. And don't worry for your body either. You worry, and then all troubles come.

Whether one dies in a good or bad way it is only thoughts. Forget all these thoughts. Suppose one says at the moment of death, "Christ, Christ." Does he go to heaven? No! Or, at the moment of death if someone says bad words, does he go to hell? A realized person can say anything at the time of death, but his final understanding is "I am not this." It all depends on the final understanding in your mind. If your understanding is "I am not this," then you don't go anywhere. The body is a combination of things as long as the Power is connected. At the moment of disconnection, does the Power cry? It doesn't care! Understanding should be like this.

When my Master died, at that moment I felt something. One should feel something, but the next moment I changed myself. He put the Reality in our hands, "This is the Reality, so go." It is not wrong to feel something but he made us the Reality. So why to cry? You are He. Your friend died and now she is in you. Before there was some duality there and now there is not. Change your mind. The mind is such a nonsense thing. It makes all mischief. Your friend is dead now, Zero went to Zero. Don't be affected by the circumstances. Understand and be out of it.

Questioner: Maharaj, on the way here today I saw an accident and someone died. I was affected by it.

Maharaj: Because you took the accident as true. A dead body died, that's all. What was dead has died now. This is a dead body at the moment I say. If the connection is there it speaks. Unless you leave the body-mind, you can't be He. You are not the body. An accident happened, so what was not, is gone now. Don't be affected in the mind.

Questioner: What do I do now that I am affected?

Maharaj: Don't be affected, he has become Reality now. If this pot breaks, do you worry for it? It is earth now. It was earth before. Nothing has happened, dust became dust. There is no entity at all in the mind. You don't die with the person who is dead. Nobody dies with anybody. If a package weighing ten kilos is there and if you disperse the contents, does the package remain? In the same way this package, the body-mind is opened by the Master. The package doesn't remain a package. It is no entity at all right now. This understanding should come in the mind.

Whatever happens, let it happen. The realized person says it is my choice. When you understand your own Power, you will say that everything is your choice. If a plane is late say it is my choice, it is my order. Then unhappiness does not come in the mind. If someone dies say it is by my order that they should die. When the judge gives the death sentence, does he cry? If you have no-mind then what has happened? What happens is only your thought. Everyone is He, the Reality, so what is there to cry about?

Reality doesn't worry for all these things. All things happen due to what you see and perceive. That is mind. As long as the body is there, things are sure to come, good and bad. Be out of it. You are all affected by Ignorance, what to do? Forget that! Nothing is happening. Understand that! What happened yesterday? Can you repeat that? Gone is gone. That which is not, must go. Only Reality remains. Forget the picture and you can see the screen. Then you become the screen yourself.

Questioner: Does the mind have to be fully convinced that nothing is happening before the understanding comes?

Maharaj : Yes. The mind should be convinced that I am He, the Reality, then the mind goes off. The mind remains only as long as you say, "I am this." The mind is your thought so you have to erase your thought. Be out of your thoughts, then you can understand the Reality. The mind will never allow you to go to the Reality because its death is there.

Questioner: Do you have to check your mind all the time?

Maharaj: Yes. Check your mind, and that habit will be developed and you will be okay. If you get engrossed in the world it will overpower you and there is no limit to it. But if you turn your back on it, you become the highest Power and then you can understand. Why to worry for anything? Everyone worries for today, tomorrow, and what has happened before. Someone came to my apartment and wanted to sell me life insurance. But the money comes after death! What is the use of it! Be worry free. If someone has died, say that no one has died. Why worry for this body? Say that whatever happens is for the good, and don't know anything. Be out of knowingness. Then, you are always with yourself. So, you don't care for anybody after understanding. That is the Master's teaching. You should be That. One has to carry on with with things that don't suit him. Otherwise, does the ego go off, or not?

Questioner: Why are we sitting here with you Maharaj?

Maharaj: Greed for the Reality. When one hears the understanding of Reality one should be very greedy for that. He should leave all his comforts. Suppose you have a fever. Don't worry about that. Come and sit here. Say, "I want to know something." Forget everything else. (Pointing to the body), "It's such a dirty thing. Leave the body and be greedy for the Reality, no harm." If anybody says there's a good show say, "Oh, I'm sick, I don't want to come." They want you to do that, but they don't want you to go to the Master. The mind is of that type. People say "Oh, you're sick! Why are you going there? You'll get more sickness." But he has the greed for that, so he goes. Nothing happens. What will happen? Nothing will happen! The body is a dead body at this very moment. Why worry about it more? In this way be out of the "Circle of Ignorance." People are very ignorant. The one who comes here I dare say his fever goes off. Nothing happens, why worry? If your mind has the greed for Reality that makes you okay. But mind stops you there. Tell the mind "enough!" The Master is responsible. He know that he doesn't do anything. The Power in him knows these things.

* * * * * * * * * *

End of Volume I of Illusion vs. Reality

Endnotes to Volume 1 of Illusion vs. Reality

The four bodies are:
1) The Gross Body
2) The Subtle Body
3) The Causal Body
4) The Great Causal Body

The Gross Body is the physical gross form that is seen on the physical level. The Subtle Body includes the components of the mind, the senses and the objects of the senses, the organs of action, and vital breath or Prana. The Causal Body is represented by "Forgetfulness" or Ignorance. In the Causal Body, there is no thought of either the Gross or Subtle bodies. In the Causal Body, there is no knowledge of anything objective. The Great Causal Body or "Mahakarana" is the state of Pure Knowledge. This state is also called Turya or SatChitAnanda. The reader is advised to read the book "Master Key to Self-Realization" for an in-depth explanation of the four bodies given by Shri Siddharameshwar Maharaj.

The three pains or tortures are:
1) Adhyatmik 2) Adhibhutik 3) Adhidevik. Adhyatmik refers to bodily tortures or troubles affecting the body. Adhibhutik refers to external difficulties, accidents, life's pitfalls, mental anguish, etc. Adhidevik refers to divine tortures, problems that go beyond the earthly realm. It is similar in Christian ideology regarding to the tortures associated with hell based on actions committed in one's lifetime.
There is an extensive discussion on this subject in the book "Dasbodh" authored by Shri Samartha Ramdas of the 17th Century.

The three karmas are:
1) Karma 2) Akarma 3) Vikarma
Karma refers to all action. Akarma refers to action, which when completed, leaves no residue in the mind. Vikarma refers to action, which when completed, leaves traces in the mind. The mind dwells on it and keeps the memory of it.
Each karma is associated with one of the three gunas:
1) Karma is associated with rajas.
2) Akarma is associated with sattva.
3) Vikarma is associated with tamas.
Rajas refers to agitation or worldly activity. Sattva refers to purity or spiritual inclination. Tamas refers to anger and lethargy, or Ignorance.

Illusion vs. Reality

Illusion vs. Reality
Volume II

Dialogues with Shri Ranjit Maharaj
From 1999 – 2000

Preface to Volume II of Illusion vs. Reality

During the later part of finishing this book Shri Ranjit Maharaj left his body. Maharaj, a great Master, took Maha-Samadhi on November 15th, 2000. He first took ill on October 3rd, 2000 when he had a stroke. His last official Satsang occurred on October 2nd, 2000. His birthday was January 4th, 1913 so he was 87. I discussed the book with him in September, and he was happy that it was progressing. The book is a continuation of the one published in 1998 so we decided to call it Part-II. The format is the same. Audio tapes were used and a transcription was made from each tape. Some editing has been done for ease of reading and clarity, but has been kept to a minimum. For those wanting verbatim transcripts, they can be made available upon request as many disciples have recorded his talks.

Presently, the small room on Dubash Lane, off of V.P Road, in the Girgaum section of Mumbai that he lived in for over 58 years is still being used for singing bhajans and performing devotional practices. Westerners are still going to Mumbai, and it is hoped that the room will remain open indefinitely as bhajans and worship are an important part of the teaching. Also, for those interested the pilgrimages to Bhagewadi and Pathri, they will continue and all are welcome to attend.

The first volume has been translated into Marathi and French, and recently I was told it is now in German and Spanish, and it is hoped that this second volume will be equally well received.

Robert Wolff

Introduction to Illusion vs. Reality Volume II

Master Chi Hsien met his Master and the following exchange occurred: "Master Hsien, you have a very high intelligence and have a mastery of all the literature due to your high thinking and discrimination, but all this is the cause of birth and death. Now try and tell me in a sentence about your real face before you were born."

Master Hsien went home and searched his books, but failed to find an answer to this question. He sighed and wrote on a piece of paper, "A cake drawn on paper can never satisfy hunger."
He went back to his Master and asked him to disclose the truth to him. His Master said, "If I tell you about it now, you will curse me afterwards. Whatever I tell you will always be mine and will never concern you."

Master Hsien left the monastery, burned his books and became a wandering monk. He made a decision to leave all feeling and discrimination behind and live as a simple monk. The following is a statement of Master Chi Hsien, a Ch'an monk, over 1200 years ago about his own awakening some time later:

Oh Venerable Master! You (indeed) have great compassion.
Your grace exceeds that of my parents.
Had you then disclosed to me (the truth),
How could this today have happened to me?

The sound of a blow causes all Knowledge to cease,
Gone is my need of further practice and observance.
Casting away old habits, I tread the Ancient Path.
To avoid falling back into (a state of) dull potentiality.
That path leaves no traces anywhere
Being beyond both sound and form.
Those who on it achieve success
Say that this is the highest (state of) potentiality.

Last year my poverty was not poor enough,
But this year it is real.
Last year, though poor, I still had ground in which to stick an awl,*
This year my poverty is real for I do not even own an awl.

I possess potentiality;
It is seen in a blink.
He who does not understand
Cannot be called a monk.

---

* *An awl is a pointed instrument for piercing small holes in leather and wood.*

It is useful to put this vignette or story in the framework of Maharaj's teaching. You have the Master and you have the disciple, both are needed. The Master gives the teaching and eliminates the disciple's doubts when he has them. Maharaj is very clear in saying that the Master must be a real Master or else it is useless. He must be a complete Master otherwise he cannot give the correct address.

In the story the Master asks the disciple, "Who are you, what is your self-nature?" The disciple is of high intelligence and knowledgeable, but he only has knowledge of what other people say so he has not understood himself. Through words, this knowledge is transmitted by the Master. Maharaj says that the Master must speak, otherwise how can the disciple know? The Master who does not speak is nothing but a statue or an idol in a temple. The Master directs his comments to the disciple's mind in an effort to get rid of Illusion or Ignorance. The mind or thinking was created in Ignorance by words, so to gain Knowledge, words must be used to rid the mind of its wrong thinking.

The disciple must listen and churn what the Master says and accept it. So this disciple went home and understood how futile his was search for true understanding from books. He asked the Master for more knowledge but the Master said that he was only a pointer. The Master had given the correct address, so the disciple had to go by himself and let the knowledge unfold in himself. Maharaj is clear that the disciple must go there by himself, the Master cannot come there. When you get the address and enter, the Master doesn't remain Master there, and the disciple doesn't remain disciple.

Only Oneness is there, so neither remain. Maharaj states that a Master who says that he can give you the Reality, is not a real Master. You must enter the door yourself so the understanding is yours. If you don't go to the address or don't enter the room, whose fault? It is only your fault. So, the disciple put into practice what the Master had said, and changed his way of life and left knowledge behind. Maharaj says that what you understand must be put into practice. If you want to know what a mango tastes like, "Put it in your mouth, short and sweet!" Understanding is practice, without practice there is no real understanding. Habits must be changed otherwise you remain in Ignorance.

The first stanza honors the Master. Maharaj says that understanding without worship is ego. If you don't honor the Master, the one who has given you this priceless understanding, the ego is sure to come back. Yes, you and the Master are one at this point, but still you worship for your own pleasure and without expectation. What to do after understanding anyway? Nothing is to be done, but still, for complete understanding, you say that the Master does everything and that all bow down to him and not to me, then your ego doesn't remain, only He remains.

The next stanza shows the disciple's own Self-Knowledge unfolding and his sense of "I am something," or "I am this" or "I am that" has gone. He is no longer identified with the body consciousness and is in his own Power. Maharaj is very clear that the body is the main obstacle to understanding and that you are the Power and Knowledge only, not the name and form. You are beyond space and time but you misrepresent yourself by saying you are something. You are not the body, not the mind, not Ignorance and not Knowledge.

Knowledge is still ego, no matter how subtle it becomes. Knowledge itself is not true and must be absorbed (laya), so nothing remains there. That happens when the mind understands that nothing is true. Then there is nothing to understand, nobody to understand and then understanding itself goes off. There is nothing to do also. Doing and not doing is of the mind. What to do when everything is nothing? The one who understands that nothing is true, is himself true. Self without self is your real nature. Forget everything and you are He.

The next stanza is his final renunciation. He realized that something was still in his mind. He was not poor enough, he still wanted something. Maharaj says that there is no need to renounce either. When nothing is, what to renounce? If it were something, then you could let it go, but it is nothing. Maharaj says to be a pauper in the mind. "Have the conviction that nothing is true. Be supportless. Be wishless. The mind is always looking for support but you are supportless. You don't even exist, He exists. Nothing is there, still something remains without saying. It is not a void because You without you are there. That is the final understanding, the Stateless State."

In the last stanza the disciple has reached the destination. Maharaj says that you are He, the Reality, at this very moment. "How much time does it take," he says. "No time, not even a blink. Bondage and liberation. are of the mind only. You were never born, so how can you die? You are eternal and ever free. You are everywhere and nowhere." Maharaj has this saw that cuts both ways. Everything is true and nothing is true. So he says, "Try and understand the Master, it is not easy and not difficult also. Everyone is He. There is nothing but the Reality, all else is Illusion. Be He and stay. Lead a simple life, no need to say anything. You have been given the Master's Power, use it in the right way for the Reality and protect it. Now go!"

I am grateful for the opportunity to have done this book and to those that helped in its preparation. Many people helped in different ways. Some did transcriptions, some did proof-reading, and some did readings. I appreciate everyone's time and effort. Whatever mistakes there are belong to me. I didn't expect to do another book, but when you are with Maharaj anything can happen. Most of these talks took place in Mumbai. I was present for all but two.

To me Maharaj was like the sun, ever shinning. I say "was," but to his disciples he is still present in their hearts and minds. He had no concern about his body and was always available to anyone who needed his time, even at the expense of his own health. He welcomed all to his little room and treated all the same, no matter if they were rich or poor, and no matter what their social position.

One day I said to him that he was the most impartial person I had ever met; that he was the same with everyone. He said, "I have no choice. I couldn't do what I do if I didn't see things that way." What an answer! The whole of his teaching seemed to be contained in those two sentences. When Oneness comes in the mind who will choose and what to choose. He didn't see differences or separation, and he saw equally in all. For him no one was good or bad, pure or impure, right or wrong. Choice is of the mind and mind is in duality. Everyone was He, whether they understood or not, so how could differences be there. And when everything is nothing what to say about anybody.

Maharaj had both Western and Indian disciples. Over the last five years he went to the West for a few months each year at the request of his Western disciples. In each culture, certain concepts are more dominant than others. In the West both the questions of love and compassion were often raised. Last July someone in Paris asked Maharaj why he never talked of love. (Whatever concepts you brought to him, he would look at from the highest point and make his comments. Again like the sun, when an object approaches it, it can't remain, it burns up. In the same way, no concept could remain when he looked at it.) For him love comes from Ignorance, from duality, and when Oneness comes in the mind, whom to love, and who will love?

Not everyone was prepared for his answers and during the same talk someone mentioned compassion. The questioner gave the example of a mother who sacrifices her life for her child. Maharaj said, "No, that is ego! When you say 'It is my child, I have sacrificed,' that is ego." Desire is selective, love is all inclusive and when you say mine and yours, you are in choice in the mind. No matter how noble your actions were, no matter how lofty your concepts were Maharaj always saw the subtle ego. So when you give, does one person deserve more than another? For Maharaj all were equal no matter who they were. "Who will be worthy and who won't be when all are myself. Judgment comes from the ego and when you don't exist, who will say!" Maharaj once said, "To give is ego, and not to give is also ego, you are beyond both." Beyond means everyone is myself so the question of giving or not giving doesn't remain.

But if someone asked, "What should I do Maharaj?" Maharaj would say, "Do whatever you want, who can stop you?" He would say to do what you want, but then he would say, "Do, but don't take the touch of it." He always said that virtue and goodness were a "nasty" blockage, so don't be good and don't be bad.

Christ said in the Bible, "Let the left hand not know what the right hand is doing." When you know something, the pride of Knowledge comes, the ego comes and then you take yourself as something. When the "I" remains, then you remain in Knowledge and you can't be He. Maharaj's Master, Shri Siddharameshwar Maharaj, always said, "Knowledge is the greatest Ignorance."

Maharaj was a model of both devotion and understanding for his disciples. Maharaj gave everything to his Master, so if someone bowed down to Maharaj he would say, "They bow down to my Master." He never took credit for anything. When Part I of "Illusion vs. Reality" was finished in time so that he was able to take the books to the West, he said that it was a miracle of his Master. He said worship with understanding was the best and even if you make duality, you and the Master are still one. "Never forget your Master!" And most recently, some of his last few words were, "Never forget Siddharameshwar," his own Master.

Even in his casual talk Maharaj taught. A few months ago we decided to change the time of Satsang so we discussed it with Maharaj. Three times were recommended and finally 6pm was chosen. One of the disciples said, 'That is a good time." Maharaj said, "You mean it is a good time for you!" Another disciple said, "Now Maharaj, you have more time in the afternoon to sleep, so you should rest in the afternoon." Maharaj hesitated and then said, "That's my choice." He never cared for his body so why should anyone else. He was always the Master and he never missed an opportunity to give to his disciples.

Once after Satsang, I said asked him what time Bhajans would be, which I sometimes did, but this time I said, "What time would you like Bhajans?" He said, "It is not what I like or want, it is what is best for everyone as some people work, so let's make it for 8pm. He never said these things in a critical or judgmental way, he just wanted you to hear what you said.

Maharaj always raised you up to his level, and in each Satsang, or whenever coming into contact with him, he gave you courage to be what he knew you were. In his own quiet way he "roared like a lion" and when he said that nothing was true, all is Illusion, you knew he had accomplished what few have ever done. He gave us his Power, and just as his Master had said, he also said, "I give you my Power, preserve it and use it in the right way."

Nothing you can do or say can begin to express your gratitude for your Master. He leaves imprints on your mind that sustain you no matter what circumstances you find yourself in. He opens your mind in a way that no one else can. And when you were with Maharaj during bhajans, you could feel the pure, innocent devotion he had for his Master. It touched your heart in a way that can never be expressed. He gave us everything we needed as aspirants and devotees and He revealed to us the "Final Understanding."

A quote from Siddharameshwar Maharaj ends this introduction to second volume of Illusion vs. Reality: "Spiritual Knowledge unsupported by worship is baseless. If there is no devotion there is no Knowledge. Devotion is the mother of Knowledge. Without the Master's grace there is no Knowledge. When will the Master's grace flow? Only through steadfast devotion. Then even mud will turn to gold. The Sadguru is your protector. Why bother about others, when the Sadguru is your guardian? Worship with understanding, and without expectation, that is the best."

Robert Wolff

February 15, 1999

Questioner: I have a lot of energy inside. I don't know how to use it, so how to use it? I feel I am very impatient inside.

Maharaj: Energy is Power, it grows and becomes more. If you understand that "Energy is myself," then you can use it. You have a hand, you use your hand, no? To take something or to give something; you use it that way. It's the same way when the energy becomes more inside. Use it for the right things, not for the worldly things, because they are all nothing but Zero, or Illusion. So why should you use your energy for that nothing! Understand that energy. It is nothing but the Power. When a boy is small he doesn't have much thinking Power, but when he grows up he has lots of energy in his mind. But he thinks wrong things always. He never thinks the right things. He is always thinking about worldly things or worldly affairs.

All these things bring more and more troubles or problems. When you sleep, is the energy free or not? So, that energy should be used. Try to go beyond Zero, but there is no energy there also. Energy is Knowledge, and Knowledge has the Power to know more and more. Is the world moving ahead more and more or not? Now they have invented the computer, email, and fax. So now, no matter what the distance, you can get the answer from someone in a moment. And when that Power is disconnected in the body, what remains? Everything goes to Zero. As long as the body is working it is okay, but it is sure to die one day. One who takes the birth must die one day.

One should understand that the body is not myself. That energy, or Power, that is inside should be used for the right purpose, then you are happy. Try to understand your energy. In the beginning one has to increase that energy. That means Knowledge, energy is Knowledge. So, why to increase Knowledge? In order to know what is right and wrong; that this is not true, and that this *is* true. All people try to know by physical mechanisms, but they can only go up to Zero. They cannot find out anything more than that. So the scientists have proved that the world is a "black hole," they can only go to Zero. They can't go beyond Zero.

In Indian mythology they showed that also. In all that darkness or blackness God has created the world. He does everything in nothing. When you sleep many dreams come to you, but the one who doesn't sleep doesn't get the dream. If you don't sleep, no dreams can come to you. When you sleep many dreams come to you, they must come. You want something, that is Knowledge. The breathing is also Knowledge, nothing else. That is going on even when you are sleeping, otherwise you would be dead. So that is all energy, nothing else.

Energy is inside and outside, this you can understand. See that it is also outside, and understand that it is everywhere. Use the energy in that way.

Everyone is myself, everyone has the breathing. You all breathe and sleep, but you take yourself as a separate entity. That is ego. Then some problems come, and you think, "Oh, what has happened, what to do?" A realized person gets many problems. Don't think he doesn't get problems, but he throws off the problems and doesn't worry for them. Everything is finally Zero, so why to worry. When death comes to the body he doesn't worry. It is Zero, it has started from Zero.

One drop of the father's semen has started this. Many drops go out and nobody cares about them. But when a form comes you say, "Oh, he is my son, she is my daughter, these are my people." You take all as "mine," and by Ignorance you make the world so small, because your understanding is limited by the identification with your body. No body, then what remains? Everything is just space. What does space have to worry about? Many things come in the space and go. The wind comes and goes, does the space worry? You are subtler than the space. You can feel the wind, you can sense the space due to Knowledge, but still you have the power, or understanding, to say that it is not true. That is the beauty of it. See everything, but say it's not true. Who can say that? Only one who is a brave man. He sees everything. Many things happen, but he says, "Nothing is true."

When you sleep where does the world go? It is not there, you forget your name, body, and everything. The mind also sleeps, what to do. When a bug stings you in sleep, you scratch, and if someone were to ask you what you are doing, you will say, "I don't know." He does it, but he says he doesn't know it. He murmurs in his sleep and if you ask him what he is saying, he will say, "I never said anything." He denies everything there. Why? Because he is in negation.

When the mind is in Zero, you can go beyond Zero, if you understand it is Zero. Why not! The Master teaches how to go beyond Zero. Do nothing, but understand it is Zero, then you can go beyond it. Do nothing. There is nothing to do, and the Reality is there. Reality has nothing to do with all these things. Many things happen. Experiences come and go, no? Thoughts come and go, bad or good ones, whatever they may be. You still don't worry because you never loose yourself. So I always say, "You may be in heaven or hell, always say that I am He."

The man who dies, does anything remain for him? Does he ever say that I am dead? If he feels I am dead, he didn't die. One thought won't allow you to sleep. When you sleep all the thoughts go off, Knowledge goes off. There is no knowledge of anything at the moment, just the breathing and that is only Knowledge. In our language they say he is throwing out the breath when one is out of breath. The final breath is there and he throws it out. He has no sense perceptions at that moment, and no understanding also. If someone comes and says, "I've come, I'm your friend." He again closes his eyes. He is worry free. No Knowledge, no worries.

Suppose you want to go to the airport and some friend comes just as you are leaving. You will say, "Yes, yes, I am very sorry, but I have to go." You forget him also. Whoever comes you say, "I'm very sorry." You say that the most. I am very sorry is a very good word in English. Do everything, slap someone, and say "I'm sorry." He can't reply at that moment. You may be doing it purposely, but you say sorry, and what can the other person do. Sorry is a very good word, I tell you. Do every fun and then say "I'm sorry." (Laughs.)

So when energy is more, use that energy in such a way that everything becomes Zero. Have that much Power to cut everything. Say "Nothing is true. Death is not true, birth is not true. I never take the birth, and have no sin, and no virtue." Everything should go off. This is all the mind's work, sin and virtue. Body gets death and birth. That is jiva, or the smallest creature, in our language. When you identify with the body you become the smallest, otherwise you are so open. When you break the wall down you become space, you are so open. But you don't want to break the wall of the body, and that is ego. Break the wall of the ego, then you can easily say, "Ah, I am everywhere."

Doing bad or good things, why should I worry. Slap somebody, no harm, but if four slaps come back, take it. Just don't say "I've gotten the slap." People don't experience what I say. Instead anger comes, one becomes angry always. Swallow that anger also. Say, "I don't want it" and don't care for anything or for anybody. I tell you don't take the touch, but still you take the touch. You give value to your mind, to your thoughts. Tell your mind, I don't care for you. Try to understand your mind. The mind is the greatest factor. The mind is your thought only. It takes you to heaven and it also takes you to hell. The mind is your greatest friend and your greatest enemy. You use your mind in the right way when you say, "It's not true."

Why do people become angry? You ask the boy, "What are you doing?" But you do the same when you say, "I'm right, he is wrong." The realized person says, "I'm never right, I'm always wrong." You keep your "I." Say that "I don't exist." If you experience it that way, then what remains for you? If someone brings 10,000 rupees and offers it to a realized person, he doesn't feel anything. He doesn't care for that. Don't worry for anything. In a football game you kick the ball and get a goal. If you kick the Illusion by understanding, nothing else is required. You get the goal and you become He. You are He always, but you always want the wrong things.

Rama and Sita were together. Sita saw a golden deer, and she wanted its skin. She wanted it for a blouse. How can a deer's skin be golden, tell me? But it is written that way and Rama was induced to catch it. Rama went after it, and Sita left alone, was then abducted by the demon Ravanna. What to do? Who is Rama? He is the one who plays in everyone. And when Rama enters in the ten senses, he becomes Ravanna. Rama becomes Ravanna. Nobody will say that in public. Your tongue will be cut if you say that, I dare say. So when you enter the ten senses then your peace, Sita, is lost. Sita means peace.

It is written that Ravanna has ten heads. In ten ways he was acting. You also act in that way. If one eye is gone, you can still see with the other. If one drop of Ravanna's blood comes out, then another demon comes out. If one eye is gone, the other one works, no? It works more powerfully when one eye is lost.

For what purpose was the Ramayana written? People don't know the inner meaning. The inner meaning should be understood. Lord Krishna was a King's son. Arjuna was his disciple, as were the five Pandavas. Krishna goes on the battlefield and teaches Arjuna about Knowledge. Has Krishna no other place to teach? Both are kings, as Arjuna was also a king's son. Was it that they had no other place to go? Also, Krishna was driving Arjuna's chariot. Impossible! I should drive my disciple's chariot and they should enjoy! There is meaning inside this. Everyone has got that power to understand. Krishna told Arjuna that these people on the battlefield weren't his relatives as he thought, so he could go ahead and kill them. Arjuna says, "How can I kill them?" Killing does not mean killing with a gun, but with understanding. There were laws at that time also.

Understanding should come. He's not my father, and she is not my mother, because I am not this! I am the Power that is in me. Otherwise in the story Krishna becomes the driver and Arjuna sits inside. Is that ever possible? Impossible! He, that Power drives everyone's body. Krishna says, "Everyone is myself and all thoughts are my thoughts." Whatever thoughts come, good or bad, let them be. Understand from where thoughts come. They come from Knowledge. Knowledge itself is also wrong when you have a complete understanding.

After that understanding nothing comes in your way. Nothing can trouble you then, your energy is so strong. You can take on anybody but you must use the energy in the right way. You become so "Powerful" with the understanding. You say the world is true and that I experience everything, but when you use your Power in the right way you can say that it is not true. Go on the understanding side, the Master's side, then you can beat anybody. Say everything is Zero, nothing is there. The world itself is a battlefield, no? You take birth and you do so many wrong things. You fight with your wife, what to do? And what do the Westerners do? They divorce. In India, there is no divorce.

Always you think that something or someone else is better. If you don't understand each other, what is the use of living together? All is nonsense. Understand your mind and know yourself. You are not a woman and he is not a man. You are He. There is no woman and no man. The same Power works in everybody. All are just bulbs with the electricity there. What is woman and what is man? Power is one. Man and woman are just your thoughts. When you say you are a woman and he says he is a man, conflicts must come. If you understand that the Power is the same, then what conflicts can come? Do according to your wish, I don't mind. Someone in America asked me if someone takes your wife, what should you do? Take someone else's wife. What can you say? Tit for tat.

The world is wrong. Say it is wrong. It is not true. Anytime be happy, don't worry for anything. If someone takes your money, be happy at that time also. I have two pockets. If I put the money in one pocket it is mine and if I put it the other (someone else's) it is still mine. Understand that way. Say, "It has gone to my pocket, why to worry." Realized people don't worry. They understand that Power and use it in the right way. All is mine, nothing is mine. This understanding should come.

If someone becomes rich, it doesn't mean that there is more money, others just have less. You have taken from other's pockets, what to do? If someone takes from your pocket, be happy with that also. Don't say "what's mine is mine." What you have got you have to share. When understanding comes the Power is used in this way. If you use it that way you will always be happy. If someone gives ten lakhs of rupees to a Saint, he says, "Okay." If someone takes it away, what does he say? "It was never mine, why should I worry?" If I take it as "mine," I have to worry. Don't say mine. Nothing is yours, because you don't exist. Say with conviction that you don't exist. I am not. Forget that ego. If you forget that ego, you are always happy.

If you are walking and you see someone in a Rolls Royce, you say that he is a very lucky man, no? When understanding comes you won't feel anything. Everything is okay as it is. Walking is fine, and it is your duty to walk when the body is there. The mind should be tackled in this way. You can easily say that it is not true. When you say that, no worry comes to you. People worry for what is not, always for what is not. You are always there, but do you worry for yourself? You don't know yourself. You say, "I'm this. My name is this," and if someone asks you your name, you say it so strongly, "I am Mr. So-and-so." This is all nothing. It is just like accumulating wind only. Wind is sure to pass away from you, no? How can you accumulate it? Nothing is true, so nothing remains to be accumulated.

If someone gives you food, ask all to eat. Be happy in that way. I am eating everywhere. Why should you worry for this bloody body only? But you say, "I want this." You take your share first and then give to others. Give to all and say, "I eat in everyone." If someone does something bad say, "I've done it." Nobody can beat you. In this way you can't be an enemy to anybody. Tukaram was accused of doing a wrong thing which he hadn't done. When he was asked if he had done it he said, "Vitthal" (A name for God). And then they asked him if he hadn't done it, and again he said, "Vitthal." If you say that you haven't done it, that is also ego. Vitthal is everywhere; in the good and also the bad things. So Tuka said, "Vitthal." Think in this way.

Nobody does bad and nobody does good, but you say, "bad," no? Everyone is myself. Christ is everywhere, no? So what is bad and what is good. That is how your mind should work. (Pointing to his heart area) You always say Christ is here. He is not the body. That's impossible. He is the Power that is in you that does everything for everybody. Don't put blame on anybody. If someone does wrong things or good things, say that everything is okay. Always say that nothing is good and nothing is bad in the world. If you do that you can achieve the Reality easily. When the world becomes Zero for you, you can cross Zero and go to the Reality without any trouble. Understanding should come. You can sit right here and cross it without doing anything. With wrong understanding you become wrong, with right understanding you become right. The mind is very great and it can take you to heaven or hell. Both ways are there.

You should know how to tackle your mind. The mind is just your thought, nothing else. If you say that it is just your thought, what remains for you? You go beyond Zero automatically. Do nothing and you are there. Nothing is good, nothing is bad, nothing is sinful and nothing is virtuous. Virtue is also ego. A big industrialist went to an astrologer and asked about his next birth. The astrologer told the man that it was better not to know. The man was insistent so the astrologer told the man he would be a dog in his next birth. The man complained that it couldn't be because he had given so much to charity and had done many good deeds. "How can this be?" he said astonished. "Okay," the astrologer said, "You will live as a dog in an air conditioned house."

Why should the Saint know everyone's birth? What does the Saint need to say or do? That rich man always wanted money, so what to tell him? What does a dog do? He begs! And when he sees his master, he wags his tail. And when you get money, are you happy or not? Is your tail wagging or not? What is the use of knowing anyone's previous or next birth? Your mind takes birth, nothing else. If it is after money, then you become that. When you are after money, you become it.

The final understanding is that you don't exist, and He is always there. There is nothing to worry about. Okay! So use your energy in this way and not for all these Zero things. What are the Zero things going to give you? They will make you cry. Someone gives you a nice thing and it breaks, what to do? Be out of all this Zero, be out of Ignorance and Knowledge both and you will go to the Reality automatically.

Questioner: How does thought begin?

Maharaj: You think, so thought begins. If you don't think then thoughts cannot come. The mind is only a thought. Every thought comes from the mind, and mind means Knowledge. From Knowledge everything comes. When you go beyond Knowledge then there is nothing to worry. How does thought come? You think, so it comes. If you don't think, then...? When you sleep, does any thought come to you? You throw off the thoughts at the moment. You are bored by many, many things in this world. The whole day you think and think, and then you get tired and bored. I am never bored. Why? Because I don't think. If I think at all, it is for Zero which is not true. Why to worry for that?

If I don't sleep I don't mind. You run to the doctor if you don't get sleep. Insomnia has happened to me! He gives you this pill, and that pill and it gives you more trouble. Medicines are nothing. Natural things must be there always. Don't think! Let thoughts come and go, it happens but it is all Zero. If you think for something it always troubles you. Thinking comes when you think of something; should I do this or that, and the result should always be good for you. What to do? If some bad result comes, let it come! Thought is the mind's work, why to worry for that? Say, "I do no wrong." A king does no wrong. Follow me? Your bad thoughts do not make you bad.

In this way tackle your mind. Don't think, but if you do, don't worry for that. Thoughts just come and go. Do thoughts sit on your body? Good or bad, many different kinds of thoughts happen. You don't become good or bad with thinking, that is the main point. But you don't like bad thoughts and then you think bad of yourself, what to do? Don't think good also, that is also a obstruction. Many things come to you; riches may also come. That is troublesome because then you worry for the income tax. You think that no tax should be there, so you run to the tax experts. You want them to worry for you, and if they think of a wrong way to fix your taxes, you will do it. "Carry on," you say. You have fifty lakhs profit, but you only want to give two lakhs. (One Lakh is equal to ten-thousand.) The mind is of that type.

Try to understand your mind. Here there is only nothing, so what is profit and what is deficit? No deficit and no profit. Thinking brings deficit and profit. Forget everything and then what remains? Who can tell you, "My value is *this*"? It costs 500, 1000, or 2000 rupees, but the one who says it is false, what is the cost for him? He, the Reality, has no care for that. You make money and then like to make a show of it. To show that you are rich, nothing else. Nobody wants to say that he is poor. Don't show your riches. Your riches are only worldly riches. You can make many, many worlds just by your thoughts. That much Power you have. In a dream you can have a plane come into your home. Can a plane ever come there? You board a plane and go.

Understanding should come. A thought comes from where? From Zero. Where there is nothing, thoughts come. You always think of Zero, what to do. The mind is Zero. Everything starts from Zero and ends in Zero. Let thoughts come and go, but don't touch them. That is the main point, nothing else. You touch Zero and then many problems come in your life. Tell your thoughts, "I don't care for you. Everything is nothing." A poor chap dreams of being a King and thinks I will do this or that as King. What happens when he wakes up? He is still a beggar and he has to beg. Don't say that a rich man is rich! They are the poorest people. Why? They always want. You always want something. If you throw a ten rupee note to a dog what will he do?

Questioner: Does Zero come from Reality?

Maharaj: When you forget the Reality, Zero comes. When you sleep a dream comes, otherwise not. In the same way, you forget the Reality and automatically the whole world starts from that. All problems start from that. Go to the Self, rest in the Self, then nothing remains. Let everything be there, don't destroy anything. As long as you have a body, you have to use it. You are not to kill anything. It is simply not true; that should be your understanding. Suppose you are used to sleeping in a palace and hard times come, you may have to sleep on the pavement, but don't worry for that. Always the mind wants the better things. The realized person sees the lower things always. The mind always wants the palace. My room is ten by ten and everything is here. My kitchen, my bathroom. bedroom, living room, praying room. Is it all here or not! It depends on the mind now. The ordinary mind wants and wants. It wants many rooms. So, the mind brings in all of these things. Knowledge is mind, nothing else. When you were born what thoughts did you have? No thoughts, you were in the Zero state. You saw the whole world, and you cried. Then your mother and father put some honey on your lips, or in the West I heard you use brandy and you stop crying. You say, "Ah, I've got some support now." Everybody wants support in life.

Questioner: I have the feeling that as long as there is a kind of attachment to something, there is a fear of losing something. Like being on a diving board and we must give up everything. But there is the fear of losing something. To lose what, I don't know. Unless we really dive into the void or nothingness, we can't get the Reality, but there is always some kind of attachment or fear to dive with no guarantee. We always want some guarantee, and then we can dive.

Maharaj: I give the guarantee, no? Die yourself, and you won't be lost. That is a guarantee. Forget everything and you are He, or not? You remember everything, and forget yourself. What to do? You have got that habit. Somebody tells you to go and see who is in that room. "Nobody is there," you say, but were you there or not? You forget yourself. You forget yourself and count everything. There is a story of ten men who were travelling and they crossed a river. Once they reached the other side they decided to count and see if all had made it safely. They all counted up to nine, so they thought that the tenth was lost. All of them counted and all came to the conclusion that the tenth man was lost. A wise man was passing by and asked them why they were all crying? "We were ten men and now we are nine. We lost a man when we crossed the river." The wise man saw that there were ten men there, so he started counting and when he came to the 10th man he gave the tenth man a good slap, so the tenth was found. It all depends upon your mind. The mind always counts others, not oneself.

Questioner: Referring to the last question, when you come to the silence and there is a strong feeling that he describes as wanting to dive, you have said before that there is a trick there, but we don't know it.

Maharaj: That is the trick. What does the Master do? He proves your Self with a trick. You are always there, but you have forgotten yourself. The slap is the trick. Follow me?

Questioner: No, say you are sitting there in silence, and in that moment what is the trick? There is nothing to think about and nothing to do.

Maharaj: The trick is that it is all wrong. Come on! Nothing is true.

Questioner: But you can't think about that at that moment.

Maharaj: Why not! If you think that I'm there then...? If the tenth man is there, he got the slap and understood. Otherwise he'd still be crying. Same way, if you say, "Is anybody there?" and you answer, "Nobody is there." But you were there! That is understanding, and that is the trick. To know oneself is a trick. How can I make you know yourself, tell me? It must be a trick, nothing else. One slap is a trick. If everything is wrong, then what is true? How to convince you? Forget all, and do you remain or not? You are there but you have forgotten yourself, and then you say that you are "So-and-so."

Maharaj: What is your name?

Questioner: Claude.

Maharaj: You say that you are Claude. I say to forget Claude. Claude has got a mind and intellect, and then everything comes. Knowledge is there, and everything comes. I say to forget everything. Then who will remain? Will Claude remain? He is not true. Only Reality remains, no?

If all the floors of a building fall down, does the basement remain or not? If you want to see the basement, you have to fall down yourself. If you are on the 21st story and you want to see the basement, you have to break yourself down. If a bubble wants to know what the ocean is, then it has to break itself. It becomes the ocean at that moment. If you put one piece of salt in the ocean, does it become the ocean or not? Understanding should come, nothing else. You yourself will say it's a trick now. You have to prove yourself by a trick only. That which is not, you take it true, so a trick should be done. All of this is wrong, and you are true. Then you can understand, otherwise not. That is the trick.

A fact always remains a fact. In geometry you have to prove the theorem. Then you can understand it is correct. Here everything is Zero. The world is a theorem. It is the problem to be solved. You have to solve it. Solve it and only you remain. There is nothing except you. There is also no you there; no "I." If you put all the gold ornaments in the fire, they all become nothing but gold. Everything is gold, no? These are just examples I give. You say bangles or ear rings and then everything comes. If you say it's all gold, what to say then? If you take the ornaments to the jeweler and you ask him what is the weight of the bangles, what does he have to say? (He gives the weight of the gold.)

So if you ask, "Who am I?" then what do you have to say? Tell me! Nothing to say! Forget all these things and you are He. With the mind you make many, many differences. Everything is Oneness, nothing is there except yourself, or God, or Reality, or whatever you want to say. There is no name for it. All names are wrong. Words are wrong. You cannot reach there. When you get the address and then reach the place, the address becomes wrong at the moment. How much time does it take? No need to keep that address, you throw it off. To give that address is a trick. So one should reach there, nothing else. The address is a trick. The trick doesn't remain when you get to the place. The trick goes off. If someone asks you to take a playing card and he tells you what the card is without seeing it, it is a trick or not?

Why are tricks required? Because, all is Zero and you say all is true. So to prove it is Zero tricks are necessary. So the Master proves first that all is Zero, that all comes from Zero. Then, in "Who am I?" the "I" is also Zero. The one who knows this is He. That is the trick. Finally you have to say that everything is a shadow of Reality. The world is a shadow of Reality. Can a shadow be true? No! These are all tricks nothing else to make you understand that you are He. Okay?

So Christ says, "Know yourself and you will know the world." This is also a trick, no? Christ said that he was God. He understood the trick, and then his disciples killed him. You can't help it. People's minds weren't so open at that time. Nowadays the intellect has come up so nicely. So I can say very freely, "Don't worry you are God." You ask, "How can 'I' be God?" Okay, you are right, but the one who speaks is God. Even the one who doesn't believe in God is himself God, what to do?

These are the tricks, nothing else. The earlier questioner asks why mind brings thoughts. Understand your mind and thoughts will never come to you. Understand your mind means what? The mind is a thought. Bad or good thoughts come, they come and go on you. They don't remain. They have no entity at all. Whatever thoughts come, they are sure to go. A dream comes and goes away. Thoughts are like the wind.

Questioner: Is mind and memory the same?

Maharaj: Yes, stories that come in the mind is memory.

Questioner: Memory is needed, isn't that so?

Maharaj: Memory means what? If you have more intellect you remember many things. Understanding makes memory less, then your memory becomes short. I forget in a fraction of a second.

Questioner: If I want to come back to some place memory is required.

Maharaj: Memory is required. But you know the roads are all wrong. Roads are not true. Once you know the way, they don't remain. There is memory in you, but you can change that with your own thought.

What does a doctor do? You get some medicine and then you are okay. You say "Oh, he is a very good doctor," but finally do you have to die or not? My Master said that no doctor makes you eternal, only a Master can give you the understanding that you were never born and that you never die. That is a real Master. The others are so-called doctors. They give you medicines, but still you die sooner or later. A doctor for death is not required. If you understand your Self the question of death does not come in your mind. You never die, you never take birth. Then you always feel that your Self is free. Why to worry?

Everyone worries about death. "What will happen, what will happen?" So, I say that it is a dead body at the moment. If the current or connection is there, it speaks. If the current is there it gives the light, if disconnection comes, it goes off. Gone. Then you all cry. He doesn't cry. The one who dies never cries. Does he cry? Death never comes to you. You can understand that. They say, "Oh, he succumbed to his injuries." After death he doesn't know if any injury was there. Everything is gone. Memory is there only up to what point? When you take it true, memory remains. If you say it's wrong, then...? What memory do you have to keep? When you know yourself, then no memory is required. Memory is a part of the mind, nothing else.

If you are a poor man, you think only of today and you purchase for one day with your dollar. You don't worry for the next. When the next dollar comes you buy again. You worry more by accumulating more. Memory makes life more troublesome. When you sleep, you close the door and windows so no thief should come inside. So you put yourself in a jail or not? No watchman is required there. You never go out of it, you stay in the jail just to keep the memory of your money in your box.

I never close my windows. A thief may come. Let him take what is there. He cannot take anything from me. He can take many things, no harm. I am not those things. Nobody can steal me? Can you steal anybody? Impossible! Know your mind and you are He. That is the "Final Understanding." We will meet tomorrow.

* * * * * * * * * *

August 6, 1999

Questioner: If there is no right and no wrong, then are there any mistakes from your point of view, or is everything always correct?

Maharaj: When everything is nothing, what will be correct? There is nothing, so what is correct? What is real exists. It is called the Reality. One thing is real, but it is not even a thing also, so we say everything is He. Knowledge starts from where? From Zero. It starts from Zero, so how can it be true? Nothing is true. When nothing is true, then nothing can never be correct also. It is the mind's work, or thought, when you say this is good and this is bad, or this is true or this is a lie. So, anything that happens can never be true. But your mind says true, what to do?

In a dream you are in complete Ignorance, your eyes are closed, and you are in the Zero state. Then thoughts come and you see the dream. Who made the dream? It has come from Zero. You see yourself in the dream. There you eat, sleep and do everything, just like you are doing when awake. Anything can happen there. You marry, have children, but when awakening comes where has it gone? And who made it? The one who makes also comes from Zero. If the maker is not true, can what he makes be true? It all comes from Zero. From Zero many things happen, but nothing is true, whatever it may be.

You see many people here. What is the base of it? Ignorance is the base even though you see by eyes. The appearance of things is never true. In a dream a plane comes here. You board the plane and you go to America. When you awake, is it true? Knowledge brings many things, but Knowledge comes from Ignorance. Knowledge made the dream, but it came from Zero, from Ignorance. It starts from Zero and ends in Zero, so it can never be true.

The world is nothing but a black-hole. There is no light, nothing. Nothing exits and everything can be broken in a fraction of a second. But you have become very objective here by your eyes and take everything as true. Even in a dream you have become objective and you see yourself doing many things. When you awake do you say, "I have done it!"? Good and bad, and what is correct are simply the notions of the mind. Reality has nothing to do with these thoughts. Thoughts come upon it and thoughts go, but Reality, the base always remains.

The world is nothing but a complete dream, take it for granted. When you sleep, you forget everything. You forget your wife, your house, everything you forget. Unless you forget everything, sleep doesn't come. One thought can keep you awake. But when you are in complete sleep, the Zero state, a thought comes and then the dream appears. It comes from Zero and if you go to the root of everything, it all comes from Zero or space. Suppose you get angry and slap someone. After one second where has it gone? Gone with the wind. The wind comes from space and returns to space. A cyclone comes from space and where does it end? In space. Nobody can say where it has gone.

Thoughts come in the same way. Can you stop your thoughts? The mind is thought. The mind always wants to think. So how to find that Reality? One thought comes, then another thought comes, then you forget that thought and in between that, Reality is there. It never goes away.

Knowledge pervades everywhere. You were in the womb of the mother and that connection is made. The connection is simply Knowledge. Good thoughts come from this Knowledge, and bad thoughts come as well, the bitter and the sweet. If you have bad thoughts, do you become bad, or if you have good thoughts do you become good? No! If you feel that you are the body then these thoughts affect you.

Awakening should come here. The world is nothing but a long dream, nothing else. It depends on you now, how you take it. After understanding you can play your part and do your duty. So act well on your part and therein the honor lies. Whatever part you have taken act well, but understand it is a part and not myself.

Women say "we are women" and men say "we are men." What to do? The body is nothing but flesh and bones. It is your thoughts that say you are this or that. So you are made from thoughts and thoughts come from Zero. You don't exist. You feel, "I exist," but that existence itself is wrong. Understanding should come. Understand that everything comes from Zero. What is correct in Zero, tell me!

Suppose a man becomes a woman in a drama. He acts like a woman and becomes the heroine, but his innermost feeling is I am a man. Your innermost feeling required is "I am He" and nothing else. But you don't accept that, what to do? The eyes are always habituated to see wrong things, they never see the correct things. After the dream, what remains? It is the same way here. All that is created comes from Zero, so you must go beyond Zero. But where to go?

A realized person goes that path into space. Be there and understand it is space, then forget the space and you are He. How much time does it take? The mind does not want to accept it. There is no word for Reality either, nothing to be used, but we have to say Illusion or Zero, so we also say the word Reality. There is no word for That, and words cannot reach there, they come back from there.

So what starts from Zero cannot be correct. Whatever part you take, you do whatever you like, that is your choice, just understand it is not true. But you take it to be true and then act. That is the difference. That is the difference between one who is realized and one who is not. Bow down anywhere or to anything, He is there, He is everywhere. Except Him there is nothing. What you see and perceive is nothing.

You see a dream, the dream came on you. Who made that dream and who demolished it? When you awake, the palace you have dreamt of is gone, nothing remains. When one dies, what remains? The world is gone for him. Nothing remains. As long as you are in the dream, you feel it is true. When a bubble breaks in the ocean, the other bubbles cry, but the ocean laughs. When you become the ocean, then nothing to worry about. Understanding should come. It is not very easy and it is not difficult either. Philosophy is very easy.

All are He, what else is there? Be in it and out of it, that is the main point. Understand yourself, "Who am I?" Be like the screen, everything comes and goes on it, but the screen remains. The screen doesn't do anything. It doesn't take the touch of anything. It cries and it sings also, but it always remains untouched. Understanding should be there. Do everything and say that it is not true. So, what is not correct is always not correct. Be out of it always. Forget everything. If you are not there, who will enjoy? You can enjoy, but don't take it as true, and then enjoy. Be in the water, but don't get wet. You take the touch and feel sorry, and then all the troubles come.

The young boy of one year is there. His father has just died and he doesn't know it, so he still cries for milk and his mother has to get it. So, is ignorance better than knowledge, or not? What you know is nothing.

All the mythological books praise only you. They cannot give you the real thing. Even the Master also cannot tell. He takes you up to that point and then he says, "Now you enjoy yourself." There is no duality, there is only Oneness. To forget everything is the same as deep sleep, no? Same way, forget here, but don't sleep, and you become He. You don't want to forget here, that is the main point. Forget everything, and say that everything is okay, but the mind should say that it is not correct, or not true.

* * * * * * * * * *

November 23, 1999

Questioner: I know that an experience can never be true, but maybe some experiences can be helpful for a deeper understanding. Is that clear?

Maharaj: Understanding is experience. If you ask, "What is this?," (pointing to a glass) and when understanding comes you say it is a glass. So understanding comes with this experience. But finally, there is no experience in it, because nobody is there to experience it.

Questioner: Reality never experiences?

Maharaj: It never experiences, right. In the same way, one should understand that non-understanding is really misunderstanding. The whole world is non-understanding due to Ignorance. You say that everything is true. You say the body is true, but when you sleep it goes away. It doesn't remain. Do you remember yourself? When you sleep can you remember yourself? Can you say, "I'm Govindas"? You say it is true, and that is non-understanding or Ignorance

For the one who understands, he has not to understand, nor is he in Ignorance because he is always there. When everything is one, what is there to understand? All the ornaments are different but if you understand it is gold, then? If gold understands, then all the ornaments are not there. They exist due to your mind. This is a chain, this is a bangle, this is this, and that is that, but it is nothing but gold. Gold has nothing to understand.

People understand this way, "I must have an experience." What kind of experience do you want now? You are there without telling because the words cannot reach there. Understanding brings the triad: knower, knowingness and known. Understand in this way. In the beginning, it is okay for you to say, "I experience this, I experience that." It will do, but still it is not true. One must go a little farther ahead.

Questioner: I am thinking of experiences like mantra, or meditation, or the bhajans. That kind of experience.

Maharaj: That experience is okay now. You have to experience that. You have to because your mind has to be changed now. It was in darkness and it comes in the light. When it comes in the light understanding becomes more. Try to understand yourself. Understand yourself now! Everything is there, but I am not in any way touched by it. All the pictures are seen because the screen is there. No screen, no pictures, but when the screen is there it doesn't take any touch.

You always say, "Is it true, or is it not true?" The screen never worries for that, it never feels anything. So when the pictures go away, the screen doesn't cry. Does the screen cry? The pictures end on it and all the people go home. Showing something, it makes others fools. Illusion is like that. Reality is also like that because Illusion doesn't exist. Illusion can be seen, Reality cannot be seen. Why not? Because it is there and That which is, cannot be seen. You see something only because it is not true. Only that which is not can be seen. You say, "I see this, I see this."

All the names are different here, no? But there is no differences here, if you understand. If your mind works like that, then what remains to be understood? When everything is one, what to speak of, tell me! Somebody comes, but he has no name. So, then do you say hello to him, come in? When the name is there, that is what makes you say hello, come in. Do everything, but understand it is not true, that's the main point. As long as the body is connected with the Knowledge it is sure to take the Knowledge. Knowledge is sure to come but still say, what I understand is not true. Whom I don't understand is what is true, what to do?

The screen shows the picture, but still it is not the picture. Be the screen yourself, and then no question of experience remains for you. Actions appear in the Illusion, which is not, and you experience. Everybody has a different name, so then you get the experience. It is not, so you get the experience. But what is Oneness? Can you understand and experience that Oneness? You cannot see that, and you cannot understand that also.

So worldly people say that Saints are fools. "What is there is what we see," they say, but the Saints say, "It is not true, and what you cannot see is true." So, Saints are fools and worldly people are right in their own way, but the Saints are right in their own way. For that which is not, what is there to see, can you tell me? The only difference is that. Everybody is the same. Everyone has got two eyes and one nose, but the difference is there. Where? The shape, shape is the difference and the shape makes you all what? What is not true, you say is true. You say "This is this, this is this." So, one should try to go to oneself first. Find out "Who am I?" first, then everything goes off and nothing remains to experience.

The Saint sees everything, he is not blind. He has eyes and a nose. He can smell good and bad. He takes the smell, but he says, "Oh, nothing is good and nothing is bad." The wind comes with a bad smell and goes away. It can bring a good smell also. All this is due to Knowledge, and that Knowledge is always there. But one should try to forget the Knowledge. As you have got the Knowledge, you are still sleeping.

Why do you get the dream? Due to the Knowledge. What is not you see, what to do? A beggar becomes a king and a king becomes a beggar in the dream. Same way here also, you can be a beggar or a rich man, but a beggar is always free of troubles. Does he have any troubles? But a rich man, how many troubles has he got, tell me. So, somebody may ask me, "Shall I be poor?" No, don't be poor, have whatever you like but understand it's not true. Realized people understand this, so they are always free. They say everything, why not! They taste also, good taste, bad taste but it is a bodily affair, not my affair. Try to understand this way.

So who has no experience? I have to say that now here. The screen doesn't experience anything. It shows many pictures, but the screen, the Reality is untouched by anything. So the pictures change each moment, what is there? Change comes due to Zero. The world comes from Zero, take it for granted, and everything is sure to be Zero afterwards. So when you sleep there is no world. Understanding should come that everything is not true. That is the real understanding. Ignorant persons take it true and they cry for that. When a bubble in the ocean breaks, who laughs? The ocean laughs, but the other bubbles cry. Why do they cry? They think one like me has gone. They worry for that.

Reality has nothing to do with anything. It shows everything, otherwise you can't see anything. It is the base, it is the real basement (foundation). If one hundred and four floors are there, but no basement, then? The Reality is there, but it is not to be experienced by you. You means something else. You become something else or not? "I am So-and-so. I am this, or that." So, you can't experience the Reality. Experience is for the worldly affairs, or thinking, or mind. Up to the mind experience remains, but finally that experience is not true. The mind experiences many wrong things. It's a rascally chap. It is not. It doesn't exist, but still it says it does. What to do? Who can control that, tell me? I, myself, am everywhere. If one understands that, then it can be controlled, otherwise not. Bad or good always comes in the mind. So forget the mind, nothing else. Action remains with the mind only. With no-mind, no experiences. What experience can a mad person have? Nothing. He can make love with a dog, because he has no brain, no-mind. Everyone is like that, what to do?

Tukaram says, "Everyone is mad." All worldly people are mad because they run after the wrong things. A deer runs after a mirage, because it thinks water is there. If someone says, "There is no water there," it will say, "You are a foolish person, I can see it." Then it runs all day and when evening comes the mirage goes off and he says, "Oh, I was unlucky." But the water was never there. Everyone wants happiness. Who doesn't want happiness? But they can't get it. All run after happiness. They do many things for happiness. Somebody drinks alcohol, brandy or whisky to get happiness. Some Saints say to do this and not to do this to get the Reality or happiness. That is also wrong. They are not real Saints. Forget everything and you are He at this very moment. Doing is not required.

Experience everything, what harms you, but you are not an experience. You will never become an experience to anybody. The realized person experiences everything, but still never takes the touch. In this way one should be out of it. Be in the world, stay in the world, no harm. Why to throw out the world. This is marble, no? (Maharaj points to a marble counter.) Why to break it? Let it be there. It may be a good thing to see, but say it is not true. The mind should be of that type. You run after it. If someone tries to break it you say, "You are a foolish person, what are you doing?" Doing something is always wrong. Reality is so open, no need to say anything, and nothing is to be done. Don't do anything. Know yourself and you will know the world. Christ was not a foolish person. He understood, if you know yourself then everything is known. "Nothing to worry," I always say.

When the ladies prepare and cook rice, they don't pinch every grain. They pinch one and then say, "It is done, so now come and eat." So pinch yourself. "I don't exist as something," is what the pinch should be. If you don't exist the world doesn't exist either, take it for granted. Where is it? As the "I" is there then the "you" is also there. When the "I" is not there, then where are you? Pinch yourself, that ego, with "I don't exist." That is the main point in it. If you understand that way, then you are out of the clutch of Illusion. Illusion is so strong. If you want to sleep and a thought comes, it never allows you to sleep. A thought is Illusion, no? "One thought came and I could not sleep the whole night." If no thought, then you'll snore like anything! Who is good and who is bad? You can't say. It is all due to the mind. As you say you exist here, that existence should be taken off. "I don't exist," should be your understanding. If you don't exist, then nothing remains.

Why is the world there? For a dead man where is the world? He may be a king or a beggar, whatever he may be. In this way, try to understand Reality. There are no experiences for Reality, experiences are just your thoughts. You can only experience what is not. Everyone wants experiences, what to do? "I was in this state once before," an aspirant will say. When you sleep you are in that state close to the Reality, but you can't know it then. What to do? When you sleep you forget everything, no? So when you forget everything, what kind of experience can you have? A woman on the pilgrimage talked about being dead for five minutes and everything was nothing. "A profound experience," she thought. Some disciples of Masters talk like this. So I tell them, "Can you get that experience here or not? You were dead, no? That was a very nice experience, but can you feel that experience now?" I want to ask her that! The mind craves experiences but they are never true. What comes and goes can never be true. When you don't exist what kind of experience can you have? Though I exist, but still I don't exist. In this way the understanding should come.

Reality is very confusing. It is difficult to understand. It is everywhere, but still you can't see it, because the eyes show the wrong things. It shows what is not. The mind also shows the wrong things, only what is not true. The eyes must see, you are not a blind person, but still, say it is not true. That is the right way to understand and my Master, Siddharameshwar Maharaj gave that understanding. It is difficult to say, "I am in the water, but no water is there." For the one who says it is not true, there is no water, the water doesn't remain. Being in the water and out of the water is the same. These are the highest points, but people can't understand.

Yesterday somebody was also telling, "I got this experience, and that experience," what to do? Mine and mind are not true. When you are not true, mind is wrong, and me and mine are also both wrong. When you say it's mine, ego remains. When you say it's yours, mind remains. You remain, so mind remains. Why do Saints say that nothing is there? Why? Because nothing is mine. What is not yours, you still say it's mine. You say, "mine, mine, and mine." Saints are not blind men, they see the world, but still they say nothing is true. He feels this marble and says it's hard, but no need to break it. He acts as a sensible man. So where to be no-mind? If you give Reality to it, then mind comes. If you say it's not true, mind doesn't come. It depends on you now. So me and mine are both wrong. There is no me and mine in Reality.

Does the screen ever say this is a good picture, or bad picture? It doesn't take the touch of anything, but it shows everything. In the same way, Reality shows everything and it depends on you now how to take it. How to accept it. There is a way to accept and the Master shows that way. So he is great, and once you get that greatness yourself, do you feel for him or not? Worship him only, nothing else. Whom to worship then? Nobody remains to worship. Still there can be fighting between the disciple and Master.

In the Gita, at the last point, Arjuna and Krishna fight. One should fight with the Master also. The Master doesn't mind. Then you can understand yourself. It clears your doubts. The ego must be understood. It takes a strong conviction to leave the ego. Then you can leave the "I" and you can forget everything. Otherwise the ego comes again. You say to the Master that "You have made me the Reality. I am the Reality now, and you can do anything you like. I am prepared to stand against you." It is your Knowledge, but I am prepared to stand. It is a hard way, a courageous way but it may be a necessary step, a required step. But if you say, "I have become He now, I understand everything, then the "I" remains. The "I" should be resisted or forgotten and then you are everywhere. If you say it is mine, it is limited, and if you say yours, it is unlimited. Be unlimited and keep your doors open and let everybody come in. Forget everything.

So, experience is of the mind. The mind wants something to know. Tell the mind that what you know is not true and when you go ahead like that, you can understand yourself without any experience because you are always open. Anybody can come in, no harm. If a thief comes, let him come in. If a rich person comes, let him come in. Let them both come because you don't take the touch. You may be a wealthy or a poor person, but nobody is wealthy and nobody is poor. If the ego comes that ego should be understood. Unless you understand that ego you are lost.

So I always say that it is a stumbling block, Knowledge comes and that is a stumbling block. "I know everything, why should I worry, why should I do this?" Do everything, but say "I don't do it." Drink the wine, but the kick should not come to you. Drink the wine and if the kick comes, then something else has happened. If you can count your change after drinking, take it for granted you didn't get the kick. A realized person doesn't get the kick, the world is there, but he has no kick of it.

If understanding comes, then experience doesn't come. Everyone wants that experience, but forget that experience. When you are always He, what to experience? His name is Bob, is he to say anything about it? Is he going to repeat, "I am Bob" every time. What is there to say? But when something comes in the mind and he says he's Bob, that is ego. Forget that, you are always there, no need to remember Bob. Bob never forgets Bob. How can Bob forget Bob? He's He. But Bob is not true, and that is his understanding, and that is the real understanding. Be there, but say "I don't exist." Short and sweet.

Go ahead, have the wine, but no kick should come. Everyone has the kick of what? Of Ignorance. You say everything is true, what to do? "What can I do now? My mind is in duality. What to do, should I do this or that?" Be strong enough to throw off that kick. The kick should not come to you. "Nothing is true." (In this example,) the wine is what is true, the kick is what is not true. See everything, but say nothing is true, then the kick doesn't come to you. Saints are paupers, and if a king should approach they don't have time to talk to him, they don't care for him. Why? No kick of "The King" comes in the mind.

In this way one should try to experience Him, without telling. "I've got this experience," you say. When experience comes you are lost. There is no experience for Him. He is so open. Eyes get the experience in the mind, but it is so small. A mosquito is there, how can he conquer the human body? Pinch him and he dies. The mosquito is the ego. Forget everything, forget the ego and say that "I am He," without telling, and that is the experience, nothing else. What is your name?

Questioner: Alexia

Maharaj: When you are young, you are Alexia, when you're older, you're still Alexia. That Alexia doesn't differ. Does it differ? You say "I was doing like this," when you were young, and now it's "I am older and I can't do this. I was climbing stairs in a second, now it takes me ten minutes." These are bodily affairs. Experience is the same. If you become old, the body becomes old you don't become old. Reality is Reality always, you are That. Where to forget, tell me and how to forget? Due to this Illusion wrong things come in the mind and you forget yourself. You are ever He. Do everything but say it is not true. Have that courage!

Somebody talked about witnessing. No, I don't agree with this concept. What is witnessing? Do you take it true or not? What is not, what to witness? What is there, witness That only. Everyone is He and that is real witnessing. Many Saints say to witness. What to witness? In a fraction of a second it becomes Zero. Why to witness this? I can break this marble just now and make it the smallest particles and it will go off. So what will be witnessed? What is the witness? Wrong things should not be witnessed. Reality is always there, forget the witnessing. Witnessing means the triad comes. You become something and then you experience something. It is the process of knowing or experiencing all these wrong things. Witnessing is not true. The witness has made the whole world. In that Knowledge everything which is not has become true.

Questioner: So when the teacher says witness this, in actuality it means the mind is still existing.

Maharaj: Yes, the mind exists otherwise who will witness?

Questioner: You are putting something together?

Maharaj: Yes, yes. Knowledge has become something, and that is witnessing. Forget that and what remains to witness? All people talk about witnessing and they may also speak about doing meditation. Okay. In the beginning meditation is required to make your mind subtle. When the mind becomes subtle, then? Questions do come in the mind, but then these points don't remain. "I have to witness, I have to witness." What to witness? What is not, you witness. If there is something in the mind you can't sleep. One thought keeps you awake. You were in bed eight hours, still you couldn't sleep. Witnessing is like that. If you forget the witnessing, then you don't remain, otherwise you are still there. The one who witnesses always remains.

When you cook pulses, in order to make it go faster and easier on the stomach you put in soda bicarbonate. Coming here is like that. Put the soda bicarbonate in everything and make it go faster and it won't pain the stomach. When you witness you take it as true. Forget that, throw it off! Soda bicarbonate is not required when you don't need to cook the pulses. Reality cannot be cooked in this way. It can only be cooked by understanding. When you cook something you say, "I've done it, I've done it." Do you take the pride in it or not? So cook everything and say, "I've done it." But still say it is not true. This way the mind becomes stronger. The mind should be strong.

People go to many Masters, but you must go to a Master who can take out the smallest particle. When you get a shave, the barber cuts like this, first down, but still the stubble is left. Then he shaves upward to take it all out. The stubble is trouble. Be trouble-free. There is no trouble for you when you say it is not true. If it is true, then troubles come. If it is not true, how can troubles come to you? So everyone runs after the wrong things. People say that they are lost, or unlucky. What is unlucky? Unlucky is when you run after the wrong things. If you understand that you are He, you are always lucky. If you run after the worldly things, the world brings you trouble. You are not to go after anything. When you sleep you are out of the troubles for a few hours, but when you awake you worry about what to do, what not to do, this and that. There is no limit to it. Forget all this and you are limitless. Then there is nothing to worry for. "I have no limit," say that. If you understand that, then every limit goes off and nothing remains. Everything becomes untrue. Stay in that way.

So experiencing is not required. He cannot be experienced. If you experience Him, then you do not know Him. Even knowing is not correct, because who will know whom! Experience is *of* something else. So no experience for Him. He is so open, what to experience? People run after experience and finally they die. That is the main point. When you are living, be in it and be out of it. How much time does it take? So I always say, "Be in the water but say that the water doesn't touch me." Have that much courage to say that. You may be wet, but still you say, "I am not wet." Understanding should be like that. So experiencing is not required, and what you experience is not true. The one who cannot be experienced is true, short and sweet.

Any other question now? Your question is over now? (There is a period of extended quiet in the room) Come on now, ask a question otherwise I will stop myself.

Questioner: What duty does a realized person have?

Maharaj: He has no duties, he is duty-less. What duty does he have, tell me? When you sleep, are there any duties in it? The one who realizes, he sleeps. The doer is not true, so no duty for him. Duties are for whom? Laborers! The Master or King has no duty.

Questioner: So it is our duty, Maharaj? Are we the laborers as disciples, and we have the duty?

Maharaj: As long as you are a disciple you have a duty to say, "I am He"! Then, no duty. How much time does it take? Be out of it, and you have not trespassed in my room. If you put one leg in this room, I can put a charge on you. If you are out, then no charge on you. The disciple has a charge, a trespassing charge. What to do. You are trespassing the Reality. Don't do that, say, "I am That." Then what remains? Nothing remains.

So, the disciple as long as he is a disciple, he thinks like one. What to do? It depends on you now. Suppose a king does some labor. Who will call him a king? Nobody. It depends on you now how to act once you have the understanding. Be a king or a laborer, but still say "No duty for me."

So, when someone sleeps he doesn't worry for anything, but if he then feels what about my belly? Why should he worry for that? Everybody carries his stomach with him wherever he goes. Forget that belly. If the belly still remains afterwards, then he has not understood. Forget everything and don't worry. The Master is there. Master means the one who has given this understanding, and it is the disciples only duty to understand. The Master is there and it is his duty to see that the belly gets or not. Why to worry? If you don't get you die, let the body die. You are not the belly. Make your belly empty and that is the real way to understand the Reality.

No duty, duty doesn't come for him. Duty comes where? From that which is not true. The duty comes from there. When you sleep what duty are you doing, tell me? You are going to Zero, and that is the duty. If you understand that Reality, then there is no duty for you. It doesn't remain. There is no duty for a realized person. If someone asks a question, he replies because ignorant persons are there. They are full of unhappiness, but they have the real happiness in them, and still they ask about what to do. What to do! So the Master is benevolent and gives. But what to say when everyone is He. He speaks, but what to say? He shows that all are He, so go. Run away, don't talk to me! I am speaking today, why not speak? Still it is no duty. The Master does nothing.

One should feel that "I am All, I've got everything." But people are such that they don't understand. The Master is a pauper, still he has got everything. That he understands! Be that way. Be the pauper and say, "I am the Master of the world." Why? Because all this is nothing. So to be the Master of nothing is very easy or not? For that which is not, what is there to be the Master of? You have become a slave of Zero. Don't be the slave of Zero, be its Master and then enjoy yourself. That is the Reality.

Questioner: Are all feelings of the mind?

Maharaj: No-mind, no feelings. In deep sleep are there any feelings?

Questioner: And what about the feelings one has for the Master, the gratitude?

Maharaj: That is also a feeling and if he wants that, it's okay, but if he doesn't want, that is okay too, but there is a difference between the two.

Questioner: Realized persons also have feelings, they experience feelings?

Maharaj: As long as the body is there, mind is there, so feelings must be there. The difference is that the Master uses his feelings in the right way, and the ignorant person does not. He doesn't say that which is not true, is true. The actions of a realized person make sense, those of an ignorant person make no sense at all.

Questioner: What about feelings of liking and disliking.

Maharaj: Why do you say it that way? There is no disliking. Everything is good for him.

Questioner: Everyone is the same?

Maharaj: Yes, all are.

Questioner: Are all the disciples of the Master the same?

Maharaj: The same yes. To feel otherwise, how can one be a Master? He gives the Knowledge to everyone, or not? The professor gives the same to everyone. The one who takes becomes a first class student. Some accept easier than others. But then the ego comes in for those that feel that they have more

Knowledge. Kill the ego. The real disciple keeps mum always. The Master gives the lecture to all. Some hear, some don't, it makes no difference to the Master. No feelings are there. When feelings come to the Master, he uses them in the right way and that is the main point.

****

November 24, 1999

Questioner: When does the disciple fight with the Master and why?

Maharaj: The Master says "You are He." Now by his grace, you have become He. The disciple acts like Him. "So, this is my world now. You can do anything you like against me, I don't mind." He says that way. So if you want to do anything, you can do anything against me, no harm, I am prepared for that. Follow me? That is the meaning in it. It is the hardest way. The disciple has been given the understanding that "You are He," so, "I am He," now why to worry for anything? Some things are not to be told in public, but I don't mind to say. Then what do you have to do? There are three different ways to approach the understanding.

The first is that "Everyone is He." The second is "I am He." The "I" is in a subtle form here, otherwise how can he fight with the Master? You have made me this. I am prepared to accept anything, so do whatever you like against me. That is the hardest way. The third way is the middle way, "The Master is He, I don't exist." So, the disciple worships the Master like anything (enthusiastically). When "You are He, everyone is He," then? "I don't exit." So there are three kinds of dedication here. "Everyone is He," is okay. Everybody is there, but there is still some distinction there. With the second way, "I am He. You (the Master) made me He. Now do anything you like to me. I am prepared to accept it." The third way, the middle way, is the best. "I don't exist, only He exists." Don't worry, let anything happen, say "I don't know anything." And when anyone bows down to you say, "They bow down to my Master, and not to me." This is a kind of dedication. The second dedication is hard, but it is strong. You have to take the Master as duality. Then do anything you like there, but that is also a little duality.

Of the three ways the middle is the best. The ego is sure to come one day, "I can do anything, I am everything," take it for granted. That is subtle ego. But you can fight with your Master, why not? Kabir was considered a half-saint, and his disciple Kamal a complete one. The Master doesn't mind anything. He says, "Everything is correct." What you do, I don't mind. Realized people find the shortest way. There are so many ways, no? Ego always remains, take it for granted, no matter who he may be. Whatever you do, it (ego) is always there. So always be on guard, on the alert. Otherwise the enemy will come inside the walls and take a life. Take a life means, you forget yourself. One should not forget oneself. The Master is there. You have got the respect for him in the mind, and keep that respect always. In the middle way, "He is everywhere, I don't exist." Then the question of doing anything, or what to do doesn't remain.

Differences always come in the mind. "I like this and I don't like this." The mind is a very shrewd thing. To overcome the mind is not easy, but once you merge that mind, or put your feet on it, it will never resist you. You can say, "I know I can do anything," but what is the meaning in it? When you are He, what is the necessity to do anything? Saints often make the mistake of wanting and they fall down. When the mind goes somewhere, are you under the influence of the mind or not? The mind always wants something. Don't be under the influence of the mind. Cut your mind. Thoughts come but nothing is required to do. Understanding should come in this way. "He does everything, I don't exist." As long as you exist there is some ego, a subtle ego that remains.

If there is lice in the hair of a woman, another woman is required to kill the lice. But with your ego, you have to find it out for yourself. Say, "I don't exist." When you don't exist why should thoughts exist? The ego is such a nonsense thing. Be out of its clutches. It is not at all there, yet still it is there. So when you say, "I can do anything," does "*anything*" mean that something remains for you or not? When you are He, what remains for you? Does anything remain for you? Everything is Zero, nothing is there.

When you understand that everything is Zero, that nothing is true, and still you find something in your mind, what is the use of it? A thought comes and that is the mind. It is just like a mosquito, it bites you and takes your blood, take it for granted. When nothing is true and everything is Zero, what do you want to do? Doing something, you are still in something. I want to say that. When you say Zero and you still want to do something, it means? It is Zero, what to do now!

By the grace of the Master you have understood everything is Zero. It is completely Zero, so what to do and what not to do? Never think of doing anything, and that is called Nishkarma, which means that there is no action for him. He does everything but still there is no action for him. It takes a strong heart and mind. Have that much courage to be that. People say "Doing this and that, I am going to be He." NO! Forget everything, it is Zero. That which is not, how can it touch you? When it touches you, that means you give value to it. Then you become the smallest creature. "I like this, I like that." What is there to like? It is just like bait that catches the fish.

When you want something, is it there or not? Whatever it may be. Doing anything, it is not true. He doesn't do anything. What's in his mind is, "I don't want to do anything, because there is nothing to do." In Zero, what to do, tell me! All have gone, so to whom to speak? No need to speak to myself. Don't be involved in the smallest aspect of anything. It is nothing but Zero. Try to understand. People become hasty, they want to do. "I have realized, I can do anything." Does anything remain for you to do? What can you do? If something remains for you, you become the smallest creature, a jiva. (A jiva is the individual being or creature.) You are not Shiva also. (Shiva is considered to be "Pure Consciousness" or God.) At the moment you are He, and at the moment you are a jiva too.

You do things for what? Only for this body. Understanding should come. A pinch of salt in six liters of milk will spoil the milk and make it sour. A thought is like that. You are the Thoughtless Reality. There is nothing to worry for. Then should you die? No question of dying remains because he does everything without the mind. He doesn't put the mind in the actions. He does action, he has to as long as the body is there. Act, no harm, but understand it is not true.

There you can fight with the Master, because the Master doesn't remain Master now. Both have become one, so with whom to fight then? Krishna and Arjuna fought afterwards. You can say anything to a Master. It is your wish, no? So you can do anything you like, the Master doesn't mind. But that is the hardest way. It is not easy. The Master has given this understanding and can defeat you in one minute, why not? He has got that Power. When you understand this way, you are out of the clutch of Illusion. Illusion doesn't exist. Illusion is an illusion.

His name is Ramesh. Where is Ramesh? Find out Ramesh. When you don't exist and you think you exist as something, or have achieved something, who has achieved? These are points of understanding. Understand in such a nice way that you are never touched by anything. Otherwise the mosquito (the ego) is sure to bite, whomever he may be. He may be the mosquito of a Saint, but still he can bite. Don't be a Saint or anything, that is the mind's work. To do something is the mind's work.

Why do people put on saffron clothes and malas? To show something. Why to show, and to whom to show? Anybody there to show? You come into duality by showing. "I am So-and-so. Oh, you didn't ask my permission, why have you come in?" Nobody is there at all, except you. Whoever comes is He. If you understand that, why should appointments be made? Forget the appointments, when you make duality, appointments always remain. In the West you phone and make appointments. So both parties know the appointed time. In the Indian language and culture there is no word for appointments, there is no time for the person. You can come as a guest at any moment. He comes as a God and you act like a God with him. Nowadays, instead of coming as God, the guest has become a demon. Nobody likes uninvited guests now, but have the courage to accept anyone at any moment. Then what is the difference between the Saint and the ordinary person? Why are appointments required?

Some woman came to see me. She had just come from the Sai Baba ashram. She tried for eight days to get an appointment with him and could not get one. What to do? Saints are of that type. You, yourself are a Saint. You are a Saint when you are in search of a Saint. Reality is always open at any time. In temples now they put gold ornaments on the Gods and then they close the doors. When you lock the doors, you've made a jail out of it, no? He becomes a God, so ornaments come to him.

So don't accept anything and say, "Nothing is wanted by me." If anybody asks you tell them, "I don't want." Without asking someone gives, no? You have to accept it. But still say, "Why? It is not required at all." I always act like that I tell you. People bring so many things. Medicine they also bring. "Oh, it is very good medicine," they say. What to do? One should understand that, "I need nothing, I don't want anything." Then you are He, otherwise this Zero point will bite you like anything. A vulture bites after the body is dead. Don't be a guest of the vultures. Say, "I am He, everybody is myself." In this way one should live and remain like that.

In sleep you don't worry for anything. In the waking state you worry, "What will happen, what will happen?" People are sure to give many, many things even if you don't want. If you want, you can't get anything. If you ask for something it becomes begging. Why should you beg? Without begging, if someone gives you water, say it's milk. Understand that way. I didn't ask for milk, but still he gives water. Understand that there is nothing I want. This body wants, it is a rascally thing. You have taken a body, no? When you understand this then, you become the "Master of the Masters."

He doesn't worry for anything. Be like an animal that waits for things to come into its mouth. Everything is sure to come, beyond your wildest expectations, take it for granted. But this body and mind doesn't allow you to throw it all off. It is a stone around your neck. Throw off the stone and diamonds will be at your feet. Why to worry. Still, there is no value for the diamonds. If you throw diamonds at a dog he will have no interest in it. He will only want a bone. But you run after everything, what to do? People run their whole life after what? Money. There are many priests like that, they say many good things, but still their God is money. A dog doesn't touch money, so are you worse than a dog, or not? Don't touch money. Say "I don't want." In India it is said, when someone wears saffron clothes and if someone puts money in his hand, it should have a burning sensation. He should feel, "I don't want." The mind then becomes so strong. You become He. Do anything you like, the Master doesn't mind, but never forget what the Master has told you.

During Diwali, Indian New Year, just before my Master died, my Master said, "I give the Power to you now, but make the right use of it. I have given every Power to you now, don't worry, you are He." Use it in such a way that you can never lose it. The mind is such a nonsense thing, what it will or will not do you cannot say. So try to forget the mind, "I have no thoughts," say that. I am the "Stateless Reality." Let the states come and go. Do the states remain? No, they come and go. The doctor gives the medicine and the fever goes off. But the fever of the mind never leaves you. It is just like the malaria fever, it comes again and again. So say, "I don't exist" first, and then say, "I don't want anything, because it is nothing." What to get when there is nothing? When you want something from nothing that means you are entangled in that, engrossed in that.

Sometimes you see ants in the sugar. They go after it and they die in it. They eat so much that they die. Be a content ant, and say no sugar for me. Forget the sugar, forget the mind, forget everything and you are always He. Right now everyone is He, but your mind doesn't accept this. Your mind should accept it. So, my Master said that the Power that I have given you, that Power means you are He. Understand that Power and act accordingly. Don't use it for the rotten things. The Power makes you That, it is so strong.

Ayurvedic doctors give you something like herbs, and they give it to you in a small pill and charge you one or two thousand rupees. You can take it like that, or you have to take it with these strong sweets. The pills are in a condensed form so you can digest it, otherwise you would have to eat one and a half kilos. In the same way, the Master gives such a strong dose, and you should digest it. Otherwise, it comes out of the body and gives you pimples. Try to understand yourself. Why not! You are He now. The Master gives to you lavishly without any thinking also. "You are He, go!" Your mind doesn't accept it, what to do? The mind should accept it. If the mind accepts it, there is no fight with the Master, I tell you. When you are completely full, then...? When one takes two or three shots of whiskey what happens? He is ready to slap somebody and take some slaps. You can take the brandy, but don't have the kick of it. Kick is the worst. The world is nothing, but the kick of the nothing is so strong. It never leaves you. Everybody says, "I want," nobody says, "I don't want." Nothing is required for you.

Try to understand yourself and you can fight with the Master. Otherwise what? The Master doesn't worry. Why should he worry? He says, "Myself is He, why to worry?" If you have one crore (one hundred-thousand) of rupees with you, should the Master worry? Have that much courage to fight with the Master. So, Lord Krishna, and Arjuna his disciple, were fighting. They were fighting for the understanding. But that is the hardest way. "You are He, I don't exist," that is the easiest way. Understand that everybody is He. Why to worry and for what to worry? If you want something from someone, then you worry. If I don't want anything from anyone, then...? He may say good morning, that is okay, but He doesn't care about saying good morning also. Why? He doesn't want a good morning from anybody.

Titles make all people happy. "Oh, I've got this title. I've got this degree." Forget that degree! Those degrees are upon you. If you are not there, who will get the degree? Tell me! That is the fighting of the Master and the disciple, still they are both one. Don't worry for anything. As long as you think, "Oh, I should get something from him," then you are a beggar. The Master doesn't like the beggars. The Master likes those that are He, nothing else. Have that contented understanding. Be content. For that which is not, what is there to have again and again? Forget yourself and the world is for you. Understand that an overdose is not required. Overdose is always wrong. Nothing is true and nothing is going to happen. So, never ask your Master for anything. "I want this, I want this," you say. When you want something the ego is always there. You want something which is not. For that which is not, what is there to have? When you want what is not, then you are in Ignorance again. So be strong enough to accept what the Master says. Fight with him no harm, fight with your father, no harm. Be strong and do anything you like, but be careful that the ego doesn't come in.

The ego is a watchman and if the watchman is killed, then nothing remains to be killed, and nothing to fear. Have that much courage! Let anything happen to this body. Let it happen and don't worry about it. And if someone comes to kill you, take a revolver and shoot him. But go to the gallows with a laughing mind. Take your punishment for wrong things, why should you worry. No watchman is required. It is just to keep this body. So many people want bodyguards. Why is a bodyguard required? To guard the body, no? But if the bodyguard is killed what will happen? Have the courage to kill yourself, nothing else. When you kill the watchman, you kill the ego. It is just to save this body that is ego. Kill your ego and do anything and everything. Why? Because you are doing nothing! Then the question arises, and people wrongly understand that they can do anything, no? So, don't have any wish. A wish is just a poison. In our language, Marathi, a wish means poison. When you have a wish it is a poison. Why to run after poison? All people run after poison, why? One is sure to die one day, and still he doesn't get what he wants. Is there any end to all this asking?

There is a politician who wants to be Prime Minister and is offering one crore of rupees to each minister if they vote for him. Does he have 364 crore? The mind knows no end! Have the power to kill your son. Arjuna was asked to kill his son by Lord Krishna. You can't sit on the throne unless you kill your ego, that is the meaning in it. In worldly life would anyone like to kill his son to be on the throne? No! But here the Master says kill the son, or ego. The ego is the only thing that troubles you. "I'm something, I'm something, I'm something." Understand that you are nothing. Something is nothing, something doesn't exist.

When you sleep what remains, huh? Tell me. Someone says, breathing is there, let the breathing be there, you don't care for that. Unless breathing is there, you can't sleep. It is a necessary will, what to do? Then you can get dreams, many dreams there. Knowledge is there, so many dreams come to you. Don't be after the dreams, say that "I am He." So, one has to fight with the Master to understand him clearly. The Master doesn't mind. My Master was there, and people were arguing about who was the greatest god, Shiva, Ganapati, etc. So how can you decide who is the greatest? Everyone has their opinion, so who is right? So, my Master suggested that they bring their favorite God down here and let them fight. Whoever wins the fight is He, the real winner! People have so many wrong notions in the mind. In the mind so many questions are there.

Questioner: I want to be clear when you are using the word mind. What you say is that as long as the body is there, actions and thoughts will come. The problem is that they are taken as true. So the thoughts and actions are not the problem, it is the taking them as true that is the problem.

Maharaj: When you say it is not true, then do actions become Zero or not? Let's say there is a bomb in the road and it has not exploded. They bring the bomb squad to take out its power, to de-fuse it. The explosive power is the mind. Understand the mind, what it wants. This explosiveness has no limit to it. By understanding you have to do that, that power has to be reduced. Then the mind becomes your slave. It is prepared to do whatever you want. But the mind has come upon your head now.

In Indian mythology, Ganapati has got very big body and he sits on what, a rat. When the rat sits upon your head, he does everything, and Ganapati doesn't eat, the rat eats everything. Ganapati of course is an idol. What the Master does with understanding is he puts that rat under you so you can sit on it. So the rat will be in pieces, because he is very small and Ganapati is very big. So your thought, or mind, has come upon you, and it destroys you. Destroys means, it eats everything, and still it's not happy. Rats are never happy. They go to Ganapati and sit on his head. The Master makes that rat sit under you. The mind is nothing. It thinks many, many things, what to do? Can the mind have it all? Tell me. Everybody wants to be a king. Who doesn't want that? Everybody wants to get something. A king means that you want something. And when it is nothing, then what to get? When there is no-mind, there is nothing to want and nothing to get. Don't give the value to anything. You give the value and then you loose your own value.

A diamond doesn't say, "I'm a diamond." If a diamond says it's a diamond, it's not a diamond. It will shine anywhere, whether in a dust bin or next to white gold. Understand yourself first, and then your mind becomes what, a small mouse. Forget him, let him do anything, let him eat, but still have the control over him. So Ramdas says in his book to make a thief your storekeeper. If the thief tries to take something, he won't forget the owner is around watching him. The thief won't let anyone take anything, but sometimes he wants to take himself. It is a habit, no? Everybody has the habit. Some people like to feed everyone, and afterwards without anyone noticing, they take for themselves silently. In the same way, if a thief tries to take something, be on guard. A thief has got four eyes. We all have only two eyes. He sees from behind also. The mind has many eyes, it wants everything and wants you to dance on it's one little finger. Tell the mind you that know what it's up to, like a thief. Forget the mind. The mind is only your thought, knowledge. Knowledge is Zero, it comes from Zero. That which comes from Zero, how can it be true?

The mind cannot exploit you, but you can exploit it You don't even have to control it. You only have to understand that it is not true. Controlling means something should be there to control. For that which is Zero, what is there to control? That Zero has come upon you and you yourself have become Zero. Be the "Master of Zero" and then you can fight with the Master. No harm. As long as you are Zero, how can you fight with him? The Master is beyond Zero. Understand yourself. Understand that Power. The Master gives you that Power. Have the courage to use that Power. Don't be entrapped by many other things. Many other things come to entrap you. Say that everything is nothing. And when it is nothing, why to worry yourself. You are He always. Be That and remain That. So, anymore questions? You can ask me.

The mind is such a thing; it has no existence. What to do? It dances on your existence. It has mesmerized you. Don't let it do that. You have that power to say it is nothing. But still the mind dances upon you. It makes you forget yourself. You run after everything. And when it comes to the senses everyone is mesmerized. Don't take the advice of the senses. Some Saints don't speak. Is there any real meaning in not speaking? It is wrong not to speak. If someone asks, you have to speak. How can an ignorant person understand the inner meaning of the teaching unless the Master speaks?

In the past, Saint Ramdas and his disciple Shivaji were there. Shivaji was in danger, and he sent a messenger to Ramdas to let him know. Ramdas gave the messenger some nutmeg, and Shivaji, when he received the message, didn't understand the subtle meaning in it. It meant to run away from there by hiding in a fruit basket. It has to do with the Marathi word for nutmeg. Things must be made clear to the disciple, so you must speak to them, tell them. And tell them very boldly, "You are doing wrong things." But these Saints today want things from their disciples so how can they tell them that? So these teachers keep mum. And people view this as a teacher's greatness. There is no meaning in it. The mouth was given to speak. Speak of things of value. Speak of that which can take you to the Reality so you can understand. So you should not dance on the point of the mind. Be the Master of the mind and do anything you like, don't worry, because nothing remains to do. I want to say that. As long as something remains to do, you are in the clutch of Illusion. Forget that Illusion and be He. That is what I want to say!

Questioner: It is difficult on the disciple's part to understand what the Master is doing.

Maharaj: As a final result, the professor fights with the professor. The professor makes you a professor, then you have to fight with him. Arjuna fought with Krishna after he understood. Ignorant persons also fight, but no need to fight. Just accept what the Master says. If you have questions, then you can ask a hundred times. No harm. A thought is always a thought and not true, that you must understand. The Master should be a real Master. The Master should not feel that the disciple is fighting with him. Now, he has the capacity to fight, and I like him. Capability must come in the mind, no? Why are two lawyers fighting in the court? The judge is there and one side says this and the other side says that. Fighting is required. But get the degree first.

Questioner: After realization can a Master have traditional experiences, like marriage, children, and sex.

Maharaj: That is his choice. Still something is in the mind in that case, no? The mind remains. The mind still wanders. It is nothing, what to do! When you are doing something, you are in the mind. You are entrapped in the mind. It is difficult to understand since the disciple is ignorant. So try to understand the Master. He doesn't do with the mind. That's the main point in it. So the question of witnessing doesn't come. The mind is the witness always, it witnesses everything. When you feel something in that which is nothing, do you go down or not? Then the disciple is in Ignorance, but feels full liberty in it, and thinks this is for me! The Master has done it, so can I. Be the Master and then talk!

People like to imitate the Master but they don't understand. Imitation is always limited, what to do? An imitation diamond can never be real. Don't imitate, otherwise you are under the influence of the mind. I always put force in understanding; understand, understand! Unless you understand you can't be He. To truly understand the Master, you must become He. The Master gives you both a red and green signal. Understand the ego, that is the red signal. That is the most difficult. Put an end to your ego. "I don't exist."

The Masters have found out the real way. Say you don't exist, otherwise the ego comes for you. You can fight with me, why not. You have got that ability to accept, but there are many difficulties in this way. The simplest way is to say "I don't exist." That is the best way, and then the ego can't come in. Unless the watchman is dead the enemy cannot come inside. Why are bodyguards required? At the moment this is a dead body. Because the connection is there, you say it is true. With force you can say it is not true, otherwise you cannot say it. But you do the same things over and. over again. When you are a correct accountant you do not worry if the auditors come. You check your own account, but you are too busy with others accounts.

When you eat lamb in India only one stroke, or cut, is required to kill the animal. No second force. With two strokes nobody will eat it. It is a Muslim custom. One should know how to cut, there is a correct way. Only one stroke is required. With one stroke be out of it. Kill yourself, your ego, with one stroke. You don't remain the killer then. Then you can go to the pilgrimage, otherwise you can't go. Understand. You have that power to understand.

* * * * * * * * * *

December 10, 1999

Questioner: Could you speak about the three types of Maya (Illusion)?

Maharaj: Everything is Illusion. How can there be three types? For understanding, you have to say that only. I told you in Andheri , but you don't hear, you don't remember. One is "Mahamaya." That is "Pure Knowledge" itself. Next is "Vidyamaya." That is when Knowledge moves a little, and it makes many things out of it. It is still subtle at that time. When you sleep you are in complete Ignorance and a little awakening comes, and that is called Vidyamaya. When you are in the womb of the mother and you take the birth that is Vidyamaya. It means to kick in to understanding. Unless you take the birth you cannot understand. The third type of Maya is when you get the dream, and that is called Avidyamaya. When you see the whole world, all objects, that is called Avidyamaya. You see the whole world, Knowledge and Ignorance have both come up, that is Avidyamaya. You see this, it is marble, this is Avidyamaya. Avidyamaya means it is nothing but a Zero. It is when a thought comes in a dream. Sometimes when you are in deep sleep, a thought comes but you go back to sleep again, so you don't see the dream, that is called Vidyamaya. It is when Knowledge comes, but you don't give birth to it. So, it is called the woman who is the highest, a barren woman. She doesn't give birth, so she is called a barren woman. The barren woman is Vidyamaya, what to do? If she gives birth to something, she is called Avidyamaya, which is due to combination of both Ignorance and Knowledge. Without Knowledge you can't understand anything. When you ask, "What is this?," is it with Knowledge that you ask or not? Without Knowledge nobody can ask anything.

Vidyamaya is Knowledge. You get the Knowledge when you take the birth. And Avidyamaya means that you have become something; Prakash from Japan for example. That is Avidyamaya. You must be practical when you discuss these things. Otherwise people say these words, but don't understand the meaning. "My name is Prakash from Japan," you say. How can a man from Japan get the name Prakash? It is the same for everybody. That which is not at all, which doesn't exist, but still you say that I am here. What do you mean? That is the main point and that is ego. Due to Ignorance the ego comes. But that ego is the Reality also. It is so strong that ego.

When you get a dream, you become something else in it. A beggar becomes a king, and when he awakes he says, "How can I be a king?" I sleep on a torn mattress. He comes to know at the moment, and that is Knowledge. That which you see, the whole world that you see, that is called Avidyamaya. It is that which doesn't exist. Vidya means that which exists and Avidya means that which doesn't exist. But you say this is marble, a pot, whatever; or your name. Man is very keen on giving his name always. If I ask someone their name and I don't ask you, you will say, "Oh, Maharaj didn't ask me." You should not feel that way. Instead you should feel that I am everybody. Follow me? One who comes here should understand that much at least. That he didn't ask me is better, otherwise you would have become Avidyamaya again. So, when you don't look the thief takes out something. Understand clearly between what is called Mahamaya, Vidyamaya and Avidyamaya.

When you become this Mahamaya, nothing is there. So you are God, you have created the world. You are the creator of the world, take it for granted. Unless you take birth, who will create the world? Mother and father, friends and everything happens then. You are always in what is happening. You never think of yourself. The one who thinks of himself is out of the clutch of Illusion. Find out who you are first. Nobody wants to know himself. So he, my Master, has written the "Master Key to Realization." You can use that key for all; you can use it for any car. No master key, then you can't take all the cars, only your car. Then he is called a thief with a master key. He tells you to do anything you like, don't worry, but know that it is not true. He gives you the reins for the horse. He sees that you won't fall. You can sit on the horse, but if you don't know how, riding the horse will make you fall. These are also the reins of the Master. The Master says that you are He, now go! You should know how to pull in the reins, and one should also know how to loosen the reins. The car is in your hands, and the brakes are always there to stop it. Understand everything, don't worry. You are He. Use some brakes on it, then you can go astray, no harm. If the horse goes the wrong way, then you pull the reins.

The same thing happened to me once when I went with Maharaj to Kashmir. We went with horses to visit a town. We were galloping and following a disciple who was a mischief monger. He took us aside to the forest, just a few of us, but he led us astray. The rest of the disciples went the right way and made it to the destination on time. We were told by a tall stranger that we were not going in the right direction, so we took the reins and retraced our steps and arrived two hours late. Maharaj was sitting there when we arrived, but he didn't ask us anything about what had happened or anything. He knew everything. One should know when to pull the brake. Here there is no need to apply the brake, the horse will take you correctly to the destination. The mind of man has such a nature that it sees everything and wants to touch it.

If you take a putter and try to putt a golf ball in with one stroke, it sometimes goes out. One who is very clever can put it in correctly. The Master gives you the reins in your hands and says, "Go!" Have the courage to know where to stop. Many people have fallen or gone astray. Don't worry, understand your Power. Then, do you come back the right way, or not? You remain there always. Many people go the wrong way after understanding. Understanding is required, and brings you to Mahamaya, the "Original Illusion," the beginning. It starts from somewhere, no? Then it becomes a river and then to the ocean where it becomes salty. It's the same thing for yourself. You have forgotten yourself and go ahead more and more, and you go to the ocean. Ocean means that the whole world is an ocean for you, and you become salty. How can you get more? "I must get more!" All these things come in the mind. Then, anger comes, wishes come, many things come. There is no end to it. You all are running ahead on and on. Knowledge should be ended. Put an end to the Knowledge.

Knowledge is so big. There is no end to it. If you understand that Knowledge has an end you become He, otherwise not. Knowledge is limitless, so put a limit to that limitlessness, and you are He. Knowledge doesn't do anything, it just goes ahead and ahead. How far? You can't say. The Master says that Knowledge is not true, and that is called the end. Knowledge should end. Knowledge is limitless, there is no end to the Knowledge. So go to the end of that limitlessness and you are He. Nothing remains. No Knowledge or Ignorance remains there. It is very easy. So I say, "Sit, you are He." It is very easy. What experience do you want? You don't give an end to the Knowledge. Understand that there is an end to it. If you understand the end to the Knowledge, then you are He. That understanding means that I give you the limit now.

Forget the Knowledge and you are He always. You do not have to experience or do anything. What experience do you want? Forget everything. You may have many factories, dollars, or anything, but when you sleep, do you forget or not? But it is a temporary forgetting, you don't forget forever. Say it is not true, then an end comes to that Knowledge and that ends Maya. So there are three types of Illusion. Originally it is in Knowledge. Knowledge is so strong, it expands ahead and ahead. There is no limit to it. When you understand Mahamaya it means a limit to the Knowledge. You can understand, otherwise nobody can understand. One who doesn't experience how can he understand? How do you understand the ocean? You have to go to the depths of the ocean then you can fathom the ocean. When you go to the depths of the ocean, the ocean doesn't remain. Finished! Completed!

So, what do Saints do? They give, but they are asleep in awakening. Awakening should be there. The Master puts an end to that limitlessness, but you are afraid. You want to do something else, to show something. "Oh, I am He." People put on saffron clothes, malas, and what-not. No need. How can you say that you are He? People don't know. Once someone came here and asked to see Maharaj. I waited a minute and said, "Whom you see is He." He thought something else about me, no? How can he know? He cannot know. If he knows then he will never ask, who are you. No need to ask anybody who are you. All the people ask, who are you and you willingly say "I am Doctor So-and-so," or "I'm Mrs. So-and-so," or "I'm Master So-and-so." You take pride in it, and that pride is nothing but Illusion. Forget that Illusion, and be as simple as He.

Everybody sees Him, but nobody sees Him. They say that he is Bob, but nobody says that he is He. Only the Master says that he is He. Everything has come upon Him. So many things have come upon You. When many things have come, put an end to it. That which is limitless understand that limitless. If you understand limitlessness, you are out of it. What are all people doing? So, in 1926, my Master wrote the world is galloping towards hell. Hell means destruction. Everybody should go to Zero. This world is nothing but Zero, but you don't accept that it is Zero, what to do? You want something to be there. No toilets are there but the Saints are there, so don't worry. You are not happy because you go ahead more and more in different states, and it is limitless. And the one who understands that the limitless is Zero, then, he says, "It is Zero, nothing is there." He goes to his Self. Then you can understand Maya, Illusion. That which is not, you say everything about it. Illusion means that, no? You say, it has manifested. It, Illusion, manifests by mind. I use simple words always. Who manifested? You don't know that.

Ramdas has written a small chapter (in **Dasbodh**). "Unless you know the king you can be arrested at any moment." Unless you know the king you are not happy, because a beggar or laborer can arrest you at any moment. Then you become laborer yourself. "I must do something otherwise what will happen?" Nothing is going to happen if you don't do anything. What is going to happen when you sleep? Nobody awakens you. When a king is awakened he is told all these things that happened in the city. Knowledge worries always. If you want to be worry-free put a Zero on everything. It starts from Zero and ends in Zero, what to do? Everything comes from the space and goes back to the space. If you move in the space there is no end to it. So, come back to the Self. The eyes are running up to the moon, the stars and the sun, no? You do that in a fraction of a second, the Self is so powerful. He comes back and you see the moon, and the whole world.

You are so powerful but you have forgotten yourself and you have become a beggar. "Give me something, give me something." What can people give you? They give you nothing. You want happiness and satisfaction, no? Can anybody give it to you? Nobody can give to you. Know yourself first. Find out yourself. Don't go in the space also. Don't go to the Himalayas. (A visitor had come to see Maharaj and indicated that after seeing Maharaj he was going to the Himalayas.) Why go to the Himalayas? Why go anywhere? Where you are, you are He. So Ramdas says in his book **Dasbodh**, "Where you are, whichever place you are, you are He." Parabrahman is He, and He is everywhere.

Some Saint told this man to go to the Himalayas and sit in a cave for four years. Afterwards he went to Balsekar, another teacher, and Balsekar told that man that he had wasted four years of his life. But Balsekar doesn't also say that you are He at the moment. That is where we differ. Or, some Saints say that you can get it after many births. Who knows the births? Can you know your birth? You will never die, if you don't get the birth. Why do you die? Because you get the birth, otherwise not.

Saint Tukaram was asked how a fish can sleep in water. It is running water so how can they sleep? He said, "Be a fish and know." Why should you be a fish and know that? Don't ask me. The wrong things you are asking. So, Maya is nothing but Illusion. That which is not has become so strong for you. So, Saints make you Zero. When you meet a Saint he makes you a Saint. But if you meet a "so-called" Saint, he will give you many names. He has become Govindas, (Looking at a disciple in the room who was given an Indian name by another Master), what to do? He doesn't know Govind, or das, or both. Are you a servant of Govindas? Why to give names? Just for pleasure. Why do mothers and fathers give names? Just for their pleasure only. They have committed a mistake, and now they have to put a name on it. If they don't put a name they are lost.

Don't commit a mistake. Reality never commits a mistake. It shows everything, but it is out of the touch of it all. What you see and perceive, and what you feel, the Reality doesn't accept it. The screen shows everything but doesn't accept crying or fighting, or singing, or even if God is there. God may be there, but he is gone in a fraction of a second. Three hours limit, then the end comes to it. Once I went to see a movie years ago, a movie about Saint Tukaram. All the people were there and they bowed to the image on the screen. I laughed at them. It was not Saint Tukaram; he is dead and gone. Somebody represented him. Why do you bow down to him?

You yourself put an end to the limitless, and the one who puts an end to the limitless is He. There is no limit to it, and people feel that. But "I have become limitless" is also wrong. There is no limitless. Put an end to it. Knowledge is limitless, put an end to it, and then you become He. The question doesn't arise of your limit now. You are out of the limits. Be out of the limits. Wrong meanings are made of it. It is not their fault. They don't understand the Reality. What is the Reality? Find that out and you lose yourself, and He is there. One who goes to find Him out loses himself, and then He is there. Then you don't remain anything. As long as you remain something, you remain in the limitless. So, Knowledge is limitless, and put an end to that Knowledge.

They have a ritual here in Bombay of putting a huge image of Ganapati in the ocean and it dissolves. People immerse an image of God in the ocean to finish the celebration. What people will do when understanding is not there is really amazing. When you do something without understanding, there is no telling what the mind will do. It is wrong or not? That is Avidyamaya. Objectivity has come, and you see objects as true. Illusion is always Illusion. Three kinds or not, it is Zero. Understand that way. Any other questions now?

Questioner: The Master gives the understanding that all is He, and that all is not true. Yet with understanding there is a subtle remnant of ego. The Master has a subtle power to remove that subtle ego. Can you speak about that?

Maharaj: One has to understand his ego. The Master can help only, but you have to find out your own ego. Where you have committed a mistake, you have to find that out. Otherwise, how can you take it out? There is a thorn in your leg. To take out that thorn another thorn is used. Then both thorns should be thrown off. If you don't throw out that second thorn that you used to take out the first, it will pinch you. So, Knowledge is that. He gives you Knowledge and then Ignorance is taken out by that thorn of Knowledge. But then he says to throw off that Knowledge also. Knowledge is ego. If you use that thorn of Knowledge, it is okay, but if you put that second thorn in your pocket it will pinch you again.

Knowledge always pinches you. "Do something, do something, do something." Understand and throw it off. But if you don't understand, you can't throw it off. The Master can help you, but how can he take out your ego, tell me? You should understand your ego. Many kinds of egos are there; anything may happen to you. Take out that ego. "I am a Saint. I know everything." All of that is ego. You feel that Knowledge is true, that is the difficulty. Put an end to the Knowledge. Knowledge is very vast, it is limitless. You have to put an end to that Knowledge. The Master shows you how to put an end to Knowledge. He gives you the tools, but in the end you have to solve it for yourself. His advice can help you, but *you* have to take it out. You should know that place where it pinches you. The doctor gives the medicine, but if you don't take the medicine, then how can that disease go off?

Understand that Knowledge is not true. Take out that Knowledge. A thorn is a thorn even if it is a golden thorn. Ignorance is taken out by Knowledge, the golden thorn, but the Master says "Be careful now." Unless you throw off that Knowledge, you cannot know yourself. The subtlest ego always remains. So he is always on the watch and when the ego comes in the mind, he says, "Aagh, why?" Suppose a Master gets one thought that he should have ice cream. He wonders at the moment why has he got this thought. But he comes to know that one of his disciples is there, and his disciple is ready to give him ice cream. He didn't get the thought. It was the disciple's wish. The Master fulfills others wishes. He has no wish. It was not originally his thought. How can a wish come to him now? His wish is for his Master only, nothing else. He does something only for the Master, otherwise, he doesn't do for himself.

Someone says that this is a very nice chair. (Someone had bought Maharaj a new chair.) I say, "Yes, yes, a very nice chair," what harms me? It is a comfortable chair. It is his wish. I had no idea that I should have a new chair. I never think of it. Then, do I have to accept it or not? "It is very good," you have to say. But the Master finds out the root of it, from where this thought came. So if any ego comes in the mind, he finds out that ego. He dissolves that ego. The ego has no value. The ego is all Illusion, and all wishes come from Illusion, that which is not. When does the wish come when you want something? From where? From Illusion. You always want that which is not. Find out your ego and throw it off, if it has come at all. The bugs come from your own perspiration. Do you kill them or not? In the same way, ego comes from you. Thoughts may come, why not! It is not a dead body. It is not a dead mind. He is no-mind agree, but still, it is not a dead one. Reality is no-mind.

Thoughts come to me, they must come. This thought is for this, this thought is for that. When I see you, thoughts must come to me. He gives way to the mind, but he checks on the mind. So the Master helps you but it is your choice whether to throw it off or not. As long as you know how to pull the reins, then you are okay. All are coming here, okay. Tell them, "I don't know anybody," have the understanding that all are He. I don't need to know that he is Bob, or he is Govindas. No need to know. He understands, so he doesn't need anything. Because he knows that everybody is He. His base is there (realization), and on that base he goes ahead.

So the ego can be taken out with the help of the Master. He helps you, but it is your choice whether to throw it off or not. Unless you throw it off, he cannot do anything. It is your choice because you are He. A king has no law. He makes laws, but they don't affect him. If a king makes a law, such as a curfew that nobody can come out after 8pm, and that all those caught will be arrested. If the king comes out, then? The police salute him. Why? They are his orders. "These are my orders," say that. So these are my orders, it's my choice now. Take out that ego. The Master makes you He, but you are always He, so why to worry? You worry for anything and everything, but understand "You are He," and then you won't do anything, follow me? That understanding should come, then you won't do anything. As long as the mind works, you'll do something, something, and something. Forget that. His Knowledge is such that he can help you. He must help.

If you go in the market place of the Mohammedans they have an expression that means; "He is one of us." If you happen to be a Hindu, then "He is not one of us." The price they offer you is different, that is the meaning. He (the Master) has nothing to worry, because everybody is He. He will take out your ego at once or not? He helps you because you are He. Many egos may come, just say that "I don't care for you." As long as the mind and body is there, the egos are sure to come. Throw them off, just like a thief. If a bad man comes, you'll give him a slap. He can give you two slaps back, but still you can overpower him. So, one should be That. Doing nothing is He.

When you sleep what do you do? When you want to do something, the ego enters. Say, "Go, I want to sleep." The Master shows you how to sleep. Be awakened, but be in sleep. Say, "It is not true." That is the only thing you can do. You take it to be true, and then you run after it. The deer sees the mirage and runs after it. If you tell the deer that there is no water there, he will say that you are a foolish person. He says, "I see water, I see happiness." The realized persons, they keep mum. What to tell? Let them run. Run and run. One day you will stop or not? How many hours can you run? The mind is of that type, it runs away. In a horse race, the horse stops at the winning point. Then he is victorious.

The Master makes you victorious. Be the winner and put an end to the running. Otherwise you can't be a winner. When a horse runs after the winning point, there should be someone to stop him. At that winning point you stop, the running stops, and you are He. Let everything happen as it comes. Let everyone enter, eat, drink, don't worry. If you put food in the mouth, you chew it. Master has given you the understanding now chew it. Unless you chew it nobody can help you. He has given that understanding, and that understanding helps you to chew again and again.

Why to run after all this nonsense? Just like a mirage all run after that. One day you will stop, the sun goes off and the mirage goes off, and the deer says that he has been unlucky not to get the water. But the water was never there. You want happiness from others, but nobody can give you that. Unless you forget yourself, you won't be happy. You don't remain you, then you are happy. The "you" should be broken. Break the "you." When you put a brake on the car it must stop. Put a brake on the mind and you are He. Then it becomes no-mind.

Master is helping you to take out your ego, don't worry because you are He. That is the main point in it. The Master is not the body. He is HE. You take him as the body. Then, what to do? Master says that "I am He, you are He, everybody is He," but you take the Master as the body. "I must see him," you say. When you understand "I am He," then you forget everything, otherwise not. He and you become one. Oneness can bring everything. That ends the matter. Both should go off. (Master and disciple.) When Oneness comes in the mind, you become He, and the Master helps you always.

* * * * * * * * * *

December 22, 1999

Questioner: How to pull the poisonous tooth out of the snake of the mind? So when the snake bites, you throw it off. Could you talk again how to throw the snake off, and how to keep the damn snake from biting?

Maharaj: The mind is just like a snake. It always bites. If you don't give importance to that, then nothing comes. Understand that "This is not true." The mind should understand that, so when the snake bites you know, "I've taken out its poisonous tooth." The mind has got this poisonous tooth when it takes everything as true. The mind always takes it true. The mind does many things, let it do, but still say that it does nothing. You feel many things, no? "I've done this, I've done this, I've done that." All of this is nothing but Zero. When you understand, that how can the snake bite you?

The mind is a snake, I agree, but it can't bite you when you understand that nothing is true. That should be the base of understanding. Then, Reality opens up automatically when the base of understanding comes. If clouds come, you can't see the base then, so how can Reality come? Same way here, thoughts may come. A realized person must get thoughts. How else can he teach you? Many thoughts are coming, but he knows that they are of no value. Suppose you have so many dollars in your pocket, but if nobody exchanges that money here in Bombay, what is the use of that money. It's of no use. It becomes Zero for you.

Suppose you want a goat and you will give forty dollars for it, but the seller wants forty-three. Then there is no exchange. If you don't give the value, then what? If nobody here exchanges your dollars, then you'll be stranded here, no? You can't help it. You will have to beg from somebody to give you some rupees. The value is given by the mind only. If the mind doesn't give the value, then what remains? Every moment you give value to the mind. "My thought is this, my thought is this." Tell your mind that "I know everything about you. You always come from Zero." But anything that is there in the mind, the mind accepts as something true, what to do?

In Sedona, Arizona, a disciple drew a Zero next to me on a board and made a photo. Correct! Nobody gives the understanding that all is Zero. Everybody gives value to Zero. Those that have only gone up to Knowledge, they give value to Zero. Reality is always there if you understand that nothing is true. The base should be confirmed. The mind should confirm that the base is Zero. Do anything, nothing to worry for, I tell you. What will you do when it's all Zero? When everything is Zero, what to do? Somebody asks, "What should I do Maharaj, what should I do?" I always say, "What you want to do, do it," but "I don't do anything" should be your understanding. In Zero there are so many things. How am I to know all this nonsense? I put a big Zero on it, so nothing to worry about. "Can I do this, can I do this, Maharaj?" "Yes, yes, do it, if your mind says to do it." I have to say that, nothing else. What to say when it is nothing!

The mind is the greatest factor. If the mind becomes no-mind, then Reality opens automatically where it is. Why to open it also? Who is going to open it? In the beginning you have to say these things, and to do some practice. Finally you are told to let all of these thoughts and everything be there, no harm. Still, what is there? Reality is always there wherever you are. Once open, then . . . ? People say, "It tastes very nice, very nice." When you taste it yourself, then you understand yourself. Taste for yourself. One has to taste. Put a Zero on you now. "I don't exist," and that can bring you to the Reality, nothing else. Things don't do anything to you. This water pot doesn't trouble me, on the contrary it gives water, cold water. But you worry for this, and don't worry from where it has come. It is from your mind that the pot has come. When the mind goes off, then . . . ? If no-mind?

So, Saints have no-mind. They can do anything, I tell you. People appreciate them, what to do. "Oh, he is a realized person, he can do anything. You cannot know him." But if you are realized, then you can know him nicely. You can say that, don't worry. A realized person says he is a Zero, that he doesn't exist. So, why to worry about himself? His mind is quite different. An ignorant person feels he has been put on the earth now, and then winning and losing comes to him. You are never losing the game. You are always a winner, but you take it to be true, so winning and losing comes to you. So, when you win there is a joy there. This means that when you do something and you get it you feel joy, but if you lose, you cry, what to do? Winning and losing always comes in the mind.

The one who goes beyond winning and losing, he is called Vijay. He is kept at an Indian temple. His name is Vijay, and he never loses. One day you are a Prime Minister, and the next not. He, the one who understands doesn't remain himself, that is the difference. You remain as long as the winning point comes to you. "Ah, I've won it," or "I've lost it." Here, there is no winning and no losing. You are never a loser, why? Because it is nothing. It is a big Zero, so what to lose and what not to lose? If you lose a thousand Zeros, what harms you? And if you get one Zero, you say, "Oh, I'm very happy, I've got one Zero." The realized person laughs at it all.

So a realized person laughs when people say, "God has given me this, God has given me that." Where is God? He, the realized person knows "It's only my thought." God is my thought. If I, the Reality, would not have been there, how would God have come into existence? God has no existence. "All of this is a theater of the world," you say. "The Creator has created it." But he is a foolish person to create the world, I tell you. Many people say, "Why has God created such a dirty world." I say, "Go and ask him." You have created it. You left the womb of the mother and created it. When you take the birth, you create everything, no? "I'm Michelle," you say. And then a Master gives you another name (The disciple Maharaj is referring to was given an Indian spiritual name by another Master) to make you what? More ignorant. In India, a woman gets two names. When she marries, another name comes from her father-in-law's side. So, she has to say both names. Now more duality comes, no? So, why is a Master required to make more duality? Put a Zero there, on everything. "You are not Michelle," I would say that. Live on Michelle and die on Michelle, no other name is required.

When you play chess and move the king, what is it? Nothing but wood. A piece of wood. You give the value. The mind gives the value. The mind is so dirty. It always bites you, take it for granted. That is its habit, it must bite, otherwise how can you call it a snake if it doesn't bite? People throw stones at the snake, so they get scared and run away. This is nothing but throwing stones on what? The Reality. Reality doesn't go anywhere, it is always there. That is yourself, so why should you worry for anything? When everything is nothing but Zeros, what will happen then? Will the world go to the dogs? People often say that. Where is it that it will go to the dogs? The world is not true, it is only a thought in your mind.

Let the tooth of the snake be taken out. Take out the tooth of the mind and let the mind bite you, no harm. Then you can play with the mind. It is just a toy for you. For a realized person it is a toy. He does many things with it, no? Is it not a miracle? I am a man who has become so ignorant. I am nothing, I am the poorest man, but that understanding given by my Master has made me the Reality. Is it not a miracle? Reality is the miracle.

You always cry in your mind. You may be a multi-millionaire, but still you don't feel you have much because someone else has got more. What happiness have you got? No happiness. Because you are always in the habit that what you have got in your hand, you are not happy with. With Indian people they give ladoos. (An Indian sweet.) Suppose you are sitting next to someone and he is also given a ladoo. You say, "Oh, he got a bigger one, and I have been given a smaller one." The mind is of that type. A realized person puts a Zero on it, whether it's big Zero, or a small Zero, what harms him?

So, let the mind come again and again, and fight with the mind always. The mind comes, but know that what it creates doesn't exist. When it doesn't exist why do you fear? The father says to the son, "The devil has come. Go to sleep!" The father knows that nobody has come, but the boy doesn't. The boy fears and hurries to sleep. Fear makes you small. Even the smallest ant also fears. They run here and there not to die, but then they eat too much sugar and they die anyway. Reality doesn't make you die. It keeps you always alive and fresh. There is no change in it. Is there any change in it? No change in Him. The body always changes, mind changes, Ignorance and Knowledge also change, but Reality doesn't change. The screen never changes. So many pictures come and go, why should the screen worry. So, if afterwards you remember a dream, what harms you? You know it wasn't true. You were a king in the dream, but if you act like a king here, people will beat you. And when you say that everything is a dream, what remains for you?

But this mind is so stupid, it always wants something, something, and something else. So, win over your mind. Have the winning point over the mind. The mind is full of thoughts, nothing else. It comes from Knowledge and Knowledge is ego. Everything comes in there. Suppose you buy a cow. The horns are sure to come, the milk is sure to come, everything is sure to come. Everyone has got the sun, so the heat is there. And, the ground is there for everyone.

In the paper, it is told that the moon will become brighter tomorrow. It is all foolishness. Who knows if it is brighter or not, tell me? Scientists say these things. By saying it, has the moon become brighter? It is as it is. It comes nearer so they say brighter, nothing else. Who has time to measure these things? You always eat, no? "I've eaten very nicely," you say. You never measure the shit afterwards. Do you ever measure it? People always measure the shit, what to do! They don't understand the Reality. It is very open, it is very simple. You are That, so what harms you when you are That? Who doesn't allow you to be That? Your mind, nothing else. The mind has become so small when what you believe, a thought, you take it to be true. Also, what the mind doesn't bring, you don't accept it. When you become no-mind, Reality opens up for you. If you understand the Reality, then what remains for you?

When you have no work, you sleep, no? People don't want to sleep. They want to do something more and more. So, it is said that idle hands make mischief. You always bring mischief. The mind makes mischief. The mind of a realized person does not make mischief. What is there to do? Everything is a Zero. Why to make it a big or small Zero? It has no value. If you understand this way, Knowledge becomes what? Your slave. Bring the right thing in your mind always. You can bring in worldly affairs, no harm, but it is still Zero. Do you agree?

If you are a prostitute you always want to attract the person, a human body. She laughs to get your attention. If you say to her that I know what you do. I know you and what you are. Then? She will make a face like this. (Maharaj makes an ugly face.) She will never laugh. By laughing you want to attract somebody. You are laughing at everything, no? So you are accepting everything as true. He never laughs. He sees everything, but so what, nothing is there. It is just like a dream. Let the dreams come and go, who cares for them? Do you care when you are in sleep? Dreams come, let them come. You know awakening is always there, but that awakening is also nothing but a long dream. If you understand it is just a dream, if you understand that way then the world has no value for you. You give it value, what to do?

All doctors are foolish, I tell you. Someone told me to get a cardiogram. What can it tell you? I know my cardiogram is not going to change anything. Why change anything? I never take the wrong things in the mind. You take the wrong things in the mind, so it becomes bigger or smaller and many things happen. Blood must run, no? The cardiogram is okay then. Why should you worry? There are so many veins in the body, but people unnecessarily worry. I went for the cardiogram, but I never told anyone if it was a good one, or bad one. Why say anything? It is a bodily affair. That which is not, you worry about. Never worry for what is not. Always be out of it. Suppose something happens, let it happen. Let's say a realized person doesn't take the medicine and he dies. What harms him? What harms a realized person? Whether his body is there or not, he's unconcerned. It's gone. But for the ignorant person, as long as the body is there, worries are there. You want to do something, and doing brings worrying. You always want worries. You read the books and papers for what? For making more worries. "Oh, this has happened!" You want to know everything. Why? Nothing has happened, and nothing is going to happen.

In a dream many things happen, do you worry for that when you are awake? When awakening comes, if you understand that whatever happens is not true, then let it bite. He understands the bite, "Oh, very good. Bite me, I am happy, but don't bite a poor chap because they will cry." They always cry. So it is called mastery. Try to get the mastery. Master of what? Master of Knowledge. Here the mastery comes when? When you say that everything is Zero. That is the way to be happy. Be happy, always. The mind is such a small thing. You worry for that mind and lose your happiness.

Millions of thoughts have come from the mind. So what is mind? Nothing, it doesn't exist in you. Why does space have to worry when the wind comes and goes? It doesn't worry. You make a file of the thoughts that come in your mind and you say, "I've done this, I've done that." Doing is the mind's work, the mind does, and remembers everything. Everybody has got a mind and according to his mind, "It is like this, I've got it better," or "I've got it worse," no? He thinks he will get it better, but how can what is nothing ever be better?

People don't understand. They go here and there, here and there. You are doing the same thing the birds are doing. For what? For eating. You run after it, so there is no difference between you and the birds. Where I sleep, I'm okay. I never worry. Whatever comes is okay. You want this thing and that thing, your mind never stops. The mind bites you and you always take the touch. Let the mind bite, but be out of it. You can become bite-proof when you say that it is not true. There was a man who took opium everyday but one day he couldn't get the kick from it. So one day he got bit by a snake and he got a kick. He became so poisonous after continued snake bites that one day a snake bit him and the snake died!

Be the Reality. Be the Reality in such a way that anything that comes, it becomes the Reality. Be so strong over it. Why should you worry? You worry for this small mosquito. (Maharaj claps his hands as if to kill a mosquito.) In India when someone claps his hands they do it to be important. Don't be important, be the Reality. Let everything come and go for you, why should you be touched by it? It is nothing. When you say it is Zero it cannot touch you. Have a strong mind. If a snake bit that man and the snake died, how vicious he must have become. Be so vicious yourself that anything that comes to you becomes the Reality. Because there is nothing except the Reality. He is everywhere so never worry for anything.

What is this body, it is nothing. People cry for the body, what to do? "It is going, it is going." Let it go, why should you worry. If your head is there, so many troubles will be there. No head, then no problems. If it is broken then what will happen? Nothing. Reality is always there, okay! It never fears anything, so it is fearless. Never worry for anything. "This will happen, that will happen." The mind always thinks in the future. Now the year 2000 is nearing, it is seven days away. People worry something will happen. Nothing will happen, take it for granted. Let the computers go to hell. What harm is there. They made a mistake, no? You made a mistake and took the birth, and you are always unhappy. They made a mistake with Y2K, no? If it is not the Reality, it is always wrong. There is no fulfillment and completeness in Zero, or the world. The world can never be complete because there is always some lack in it. The mind is your world, it always wants to do something and then something else. But there is always a mistake in that something. You are never satisfied.

Rama is a God, but still he has committed mistakes. And that monkey Hanuman, that monkey is sure to commit mistakes. Monkey means mind. If the mind doesn't make a mistake, there is no charm. The mind should make a mistake, otherwise no charm comes in it. If you eat bread and butter for breakfast, you still want some chutney to make it taste better. Something is missing always. The world is not complete, something is always missing. Reality is always complete, nothing missing, but you never worry for it. And if you become That, what can a mosquito do to you? It can kill the body, you can get malaria, but whatever happens let it happen, and say that "It is my choice now." You be the Creator yourself and understand that "I have created the world, and all that I've done is correct.? Have that much courage now! Due to the body you say "I am this," and then you all cry.

The writer writes the story. He doesn't care how it turns out, and in his mind the heroine must die at some point. The reader says there is no charm in the story if the heroin dies, but the writer says he can't go ahead unless she dies. The pen must go ahead, writing should go ahead. You write everything by mind and then it gets stored in the mind. Always you are writing and remembering. You never write of the Reality, what to do? All goes to Zero when you understand the Reality. What is there, the world is just like a mosquito. The world is so small a thing, but your mind has made it so big that you are overwhelmed by it.

This Y2K mistake, who created it? People created the mistake. In a dream anything can happen. If three Zeros come in a dream, what happens? Nothing happens. It's a dream, and a dream is always a dream. It cannot be correct. You have to confirm that in your mind. Once your mind has confirmed that nothing is true, you will never need to go to anybody. No need to go to anybody. What is required? Somebody wants something, so he goes, otherwise nobody cares for anybody. If you go in the street who cares for you? Nobody has got the time for you. People don't understand themselves. They just want to make an outward show. You dress well just to show your value. The mind wants that. The mind always wants an outer show. Forget your mind.

Be the ruler of the mind. What is there? Anything can come out from this mind. What will come? If the mind goes in the right direction and not towards worldly things, the understanding of Reality comes from there. When the mind sleeps, it goes to Zero. Reality is very near, but you cannot know it in the Zero state. When you sleep you are happy, the mind is at rest. But when the mind is awakened you cry. See how much you pamper it. Don't pamper it. Tell the mind to go away. Say, "You are just my thoughts."

So, in the mind you have to be convinced that everything is Zero. Will anything go away, tell me? The house will remain the house, it doesn't go away. Say Zero, it's okay, and if you say that you are Mr. Paul, be Mr. Paul, but not in the mind. It depends upon your mind now, and your understanding. So, liberation and bondage is the mind's work. You are ever free, why to worry? Nothing is there. The mind always catches you. Take out your mind and then do everything. People say the world is true, and if you say that it is not, you become a mad chap. Be mad and give them a slap. "You are mad, I am not." Okay? What do the realized persons do? They slap your mind, nothing else. If you know yourself, then? But you don't want to know yourself. You fear you'll be lost. What is going to happen when you say the world is Zero? Your mind becomes the greatest of the greatest when you don't give the world value.

Questioner: What are the actions of someone who truly wants to know himself? How would you recognize one who truly wants to know himself? How does a disciple act who truly wants to know himself?

Maharaj: A disciple should put a Zero on everything, but on yourself first, otherwise you can't win, no? You want to, but you fear nobody will accept you. Put a Zero on yourself. Be mad!

Questioner: Does that mean you sit all day in contemplation? Practically, how do you do it?

Maharaj: What to contemplate? What to contemplate, which is not? You must have the understanding. There are four people in the house, and one is mad, so nobody cares for him. In the same way, be mad here. People won't care for you. You want to keep your prestige. I am "So-and-so. I am John, an American." Whatever it may be. People are mad. You may be a multi-millionaire, still I say you are in ignorance. The millionaire runs after money only. Even in a dream he also wants money. Everyone is after money. So it is a bondage. Money and women. These are the bondages, and then you become the smallest creature. You are always after that. What to do! So, what do you have to do? Understand that it is not true. That is the way. Be mad in the eyes of everyone. "Oh, he is a foolish person," they will say. If you give him gold, he doesn't want it, but everyone else runs after it.

There was a Saint who was sleeping on the road in the afternoon, and a king in a chariot came and stopped right in front of him. "Why are you lying here?" the king asked. "Come with me in the shade and you will be happy." What did the beggar say? "You are blocking the sun where I am lying so please be out of it, I don't want anything." The mind should be of that type. Unless a change of mind comes, you are its slave. Be the Master, have the mastery. Throw off your mind. You can do it but the "I" won't allow you. But you must do it. The mind always wants thoughts. Tell the mind, "No thoughts are required, come on!" Can you do that? Do it! Who is going to force you? But you love to follow after the mind. If someone sings, you say "Oh, very nice." Don't be happy with others, be happy with your mind. So if you want to be realized, you have to throw off the mind. The mind is the bondage, nothing else. And then let mind come back, no harm.

First, throw off the mind. Everything cannot be understood at once. When you understand the Reality your mind will automatically become no-mind. An ignorant person cannot do it, but with understanding you can do it. That which is not, is not at all. It is Zero, and Zero can be changed into any form, but still it is Zero. Understand this way, and be out of it. If you want to be a realized person, you must really want it and give your life to it. Otherwise it is of no use.

Someone asked yesterday why the people who came last year are still coming this year? "No need for more, or to come," I say. What is the use of it? They want something, but the Master says that he has nothing to give. Who will come then, tell me? Somebody wants something, so they come. But you can never expect or accept that something, that is the difficulty. I give out the Reality only. You are That whether you come or not, so I don't worry if people come or not. Saints say that you can ask anything you want. I can give to you, but you must have the power to accept. That understanding, accept it. You feel that, "Oh, I can't do it." What to do? It's better not to go to a Saint then. They are foolish persons. They take away everything, but give such a thing that has no end. Okay?

Questioner: You say that everything is not true, and this seems an activity of the mind. Can understanding become so strong that this activity is not required and the understanding stands on its own?

Maharaj: Understanding means you know something. If you say this is not you go to the Reality. Then the mind stops. The mind doesn't go there, mind has no power to enter there. The mind is a thought. Reality is thoughtless, the stateless state. If mind becomes like that, no harm. The mind is in states always. By understanding you have to throw off everything that is not true. You have to, but instead, everyone is throwing off the Reality. Nobody wants the Reality. The love of Illusion is so strong that nobody wants the Reality, what to do? The mind works there, I agree, but mind itself goes off and becomes no-mind. The mind doesn't remain and it is absorbed in the changeless. As long as change comes, it is the mind, and duality remains.

Suppose one woman gets married, does she forget herself, or not? No matter what her life was before, she still forgets. In the same way, the mind goes to the nirguna. Nirguna means no attributes. Then it becomes nirguna itself. It becomes Zero. That depends on how you take it. There is nothing to leave and nothing to take. There is only Zero, and you are the Self without self. Only one thing is sold by a realized person. If you want the Reality, take as much as you like, but if you want Zero, I've got nothing to give you. But you go after Zero, you run after Zero.

Tukaram understood. He was selling chillies and gave people as much as they wanted, but he didn't want money for them. He was thinking that if I do business and I earn money, tomorrow it will make me more business, and I will be caught up in it. He never took any money. What are you going to take? You are going to take Zero, no? Why you should worry? You can't erase the Reality. The one who takes the Reality becomes He, and is free of all this business. He, the realized person, says to accept what he says. Why should he have thousands of disciples? To look after him? Why? This body is a dirty thing, sure to go one day. If it goes today what harms him, if it remains, okay. He gives everything, but you are in the habit to attract bad things, the worldly things, and not the good things. What is attractive to you? It is the mind's attractions that you want, always. The mind gives the wrong things, what to do? It doesn't give the real attraction. Reality is always there, but who can accept the Reality? How should the Reality accept you? It is everywhere. Do everything but understand that it is nothing. "I do nothing" should be your understanding, but still you want the results. Be out of the results as much as possible. Say that I am the Reality, without "I." Be That, and that is the right way.

* * * * * * * * * *

December 27, 1999

Questioner: Since I met you, money has been very difficult for me. And I wonder if this is a lesson or a test? Can you speak about lessons or tests?

Maharaj: Worldly affairs are always such. They are never completed. Anyway, it is by your doing that wrong things always come in. First, the world itself is always incomplete. Even with the computer, all these people found out that a mistake was made with Y2K. What is the meaning in it? In this world nothing is complete. Whether you get money or don't get it, money is a very secondary question. Why is money required? Because you want to fulfill the desire of the mind. Always the mind has desires. The mind wants those desires fulfilled. One should understand. You met me and you don't get any money. You said it that way, yes? What is the meaning in it? So you are after money and not me. Say when you want something, "I am the enemy of money."

I am the enemy of money I tell you! Be the enemy of money. Say, "I don't want you." And if it comes to you in the thousands, let me know. Your mind should always be away from it. The mind always wants. You cannot get completion in this world. You can never be correct in every way. What is the world? It is just a dream of yours. You feel it is true, due to what? Ignorance. You take the birth and the dream has come to you. When you sleep, you get the dreams, no? Otherwise, you don't get the dreams. One man slept all night and another didn't. So the man who slept got many dreams and then asked the other one, "How many dreams did you get?" "I never slept," he said, "so how can I get any dreams."

You have forgotten yourself and you run after what? You are just like a deer running after a mirage. You think there is water there. The idea that money can give you happiness is clearly a wrong thing. How can money give you that satisfaction? Tell me! A desire is satisfied, okay. But do desires remain or not? Do they go away? Many desires come. So you have one lakh. (One lakh equals one-hundred thousand.) Then you want two lakhs. And if you get two lakhs, you want twenty, and so on. For the whole life what do you do? You run after money. You never run after yourself. "Know thy Self, then you can know the world." That is what the bible says. What is there in this world?

Everyone in the world is a foolish person, I tell you. By my Master's grace I understood that nothing is true. Then, you will never run after anything. If money doesn't come to you? What then, tell me. I'll tell you now. With the mind you should be away from it. What is difficult? One can earn money in any way. A thief can earn money in any way. Huh? You want to keep your ego. You are hungry and you say, "I am poor, I don't have anything." The ego makes you that. You don't want to show others "I am unhappy" but every moment you are unhappy, what to do? It is just like a screen in a theater. You see the pictures on the screen, no? All the pictures come and go, but you keep any link to any of it? When you sleep, do you forget everything or not? Do you keep any link? You want to forget yourself so then you can go to sleep.

Your name is Marta. There is nothing in the name Marta and in sleep you want to forget it. A drunkard drinks one bottle, three bottles and then he says, "Oh, I want to sleep now." Why? He wants to forget. One has to forget that which is not true. Otherwise insomnia comes. It is a disease, and you go to the doctor for sleep. "I have got insomnia. What can I do? I can't sleep." Sleep is necessary but it is still not true. If the whole night dreams come, then can you sleep? It becomes a disturbed sleep. You say, "Aagh, I had a disturbed sleep." The whole day when you are awake you are thinking of the world, nothing else. All thoughts come one after another, just like a picture show, but you keep the link with it. What you want, you keep it. If somebody says, "Oh, you are very beautiful." You keep it in your mind. Always the ego breaks you. Remember that. She may not be beautiful, but the mind keeps hold of it. If someone says, that you are an ass or a donkey, you want to forget it. But you can't forget that also. Why? Because you want to pay him back with his own words and say, "I am not a donkey you are!"

You must understand your own mind. The mind is the only factor. So it is told by Lord Krishna, "The mind is the only factor that makes bondage or liberation." But you are ever free. You are subtler than what? Space. You can understand and fathom space, but you cannot understand and fathom yourself. Can you understand yourself? Huh? The Power works all day in the body. At anytime you can understand. The eyes see, but when you are tired the eyes don't see. A monument statue is made, no? They make nice eyes in the statue. Does it see? It cannot see. Can it smell? No, nothing. It is a monument only. Then who smells? You smell. There you can find out. Who? Who is there? Sleep may be a disturbed sleep, but still, you go to your own Self there, but you don't know it. What to do? Forgetting all this, you go there only. You are ever near the Reality. Or, "You are the Reality," short and sweet.

The problem is that you don't want to know that Reality. If you know the Reality, then? "The world will break," you think. The world won't remain. The world won't go away, so don't fear. Everything is there and the world isn't going anywhere. But why have the Saints left all this? The world, or mind, brings troubles always. Saints want to be out of trouble. They will never accept what is not true. You always accept what is not true. The eyes cannot see. It is the Power that is in you that makes you see. And if that Power is disconnected, then? Your body will be thrown away no matter how beautiful it may be or not be. Nobody cares for anybody. Find out that way and understand yourself. When you awake, the world is there. Where is the world when you sleep? Where is the world?

This question is not good and not bad also. Why? Why are you asking that question? Because you want money. Say that I don't want. Then you may ask, "What can I do?" Do nothing. Forget everybody. Does a small child have money? Still all people love him. You feel that money makes others love me. So it is told that even prostitutes can make money. What is there in it? Prostitutes make money. They make lots of money. One should understand this way. Be out of Zero. The real cause is Zero. Zero is the real cause of the world. So it is told, "It is an idle hand that makes mischief." If you want something, so you do something and you run after it. Don't worry about it.

Nobody wants to go to school but when you go, then? Everyone cries to go to the school. Why? And when you take the birth, also you cry. What to do! "What has happened now? Where am I, and what is going to happen?" Why do people cry? Now, you enjoy birthdays, you say, "It's my birthday." You are never born, and you will never die. Understand this way then the question of death doesn't come to you. The body takes birth, and the body dies. Let it die! You say, "Oh, I have such a nice body, I can do anything." Do anything, no harm, but don't be after it. You are always after the worldly things, nothing else. The mind always works and wants to work. So, no money coming in, huh? Be a beggar in the street. No harm. Beg for your lunch, once a day just to keep the body alive. It is not easy to do that, you feel, but once you become habituated then? One becomes shameless, no? And you are always happy.

The mother slaps the boy and he cries. But again he goes back to the mother. Why? Because she gives something to him. He knows he will get something, and this is the way the world is. The world is what? Nothing but an Illusion, take it for granted. That which is not, you say is true. You keep the voice in it, no? (Looking at the tape recorders.) Can you keep the man in it? "I heard Maharaj," he says. But what is the use of that Maharaj? He is not there, only his words. Don't worry for anything. You worry always. If you never worry? Then what will you feel? You will feel happy.

Worries make man feel older and older. But the Power in you never becomes old. You are so Powerful. But this is all nonsense. (Pointing to the body) It is nothing but a shitmill, I am sorry to say. But you want to be the owner of the shitmill. What happens? You take the best of food, no? The next day what happens? But you like this body.

(Maharaj tells the story of the fish ladies.) They sell fish all day, and one day they were tired and needed a place to sleep on their way home. They see a gardener and ask him if he can put them up for the night. He says, "Most willingly you can stay." He cleans the house and puts fresh flowers around to give a nice smell. But they were habituated to have the fish smell when they slept. They got mad and started to abuse the gardener and accused him of not wanting them to sleep there. But they were so tired, so they all put their heads down to sleep, but they kept their fish cloth with them so they would be able to sleep. Follow me?

You are all habituated to this body and its habits. What to do? The world is such. It makes you cry and cry and never makes you happy. If you want to be happy forget the world and forget the body! Say it is not true. When you forget the world where is the body? It is part and parcel of that. But you want a good toilet. So people like to put some perfume in the water also, but still the dirt comes. They can't help it. Can anybody help it?

When you take an airplane they give you a hot towel to stay fresh. How to be fresh? You are in captivity and you are always tired! They try to make you comfortable. They give you lunch, or show a movie to appease you since you are sitting all the time. The destination comes, and then you are happy. Life is a destination that you have to go through. You have taken the birth and you want to be happy. The mind always wants happiness. You are happy to see the picture show. One picture, two pictures, then the mind gets tired of seeing. What is the use of it? If you talk to someone for two or three hours, you get tired of the person. You are ready to say goodbye.

The mind works always, but it never gets satisfaction because you want the body. Always you want the body. Body is what? Full of disease and troubles. Everyone has his pains here or there. There are forty people in this room. Everyone has his bodily troubles. Everyone says that Saints talk nonsense. They say that nothing is true, but you feel that it is true. People run away from the Saints. They don't like the Saints, I tell you. But the one who understands the Saints, then? He becomes happy. He says, "I don't want to go home. I want to sit here." Then the Master says, "Go home!" (everyone laughs)

At school when the bell rings all the children run from the school. Why? They think that they are in bondage. But what of the one who doesn't feel in bondage? Be happy. With what? With yourself. When you sleep you forget everything, but you still remain. And you are always happy. So when the world is going on, let the world be there. What harms you? Does anybody trouble me? Nothing troubles me, I tell you. Say, "No person can trouble me." Forget that someone is a man, woman, or child. Say that they are all myself. When you understand yourself, you are never tired of yourself. You may be in hell or in heaven, but you never forget yourself. So the Saints have said, "Know thyself, find out the Reality." What is the Reality in this? If the Reality is found then whatever one does, there is the Reality. Then nothing to worry about.

You worry for money. What is the meaning of money? Stay home wherever you live. Don't come here I tell you, or accept what I say! What is the use of coming here? Troubles may be there, everyone has got troubles. You have taken life for troubles. Taking birth is a problem, and many problems come the whole life. And death is also a problem, for everybody. It is not easy to die and it is not easy to live also.

So, how to find out the way? Say it is not true! It is incomplete. It can never be complete. Be so strong about this. Then you can say, "God is also not true." People ask, "Why has he unnecessarily made this world?" Why has God created this world? "Go and ask him now," I say. What is the use in asking me? I was happy before all of this nonsense was created. "When I was poor I was happy, now I have got money and so many troubles have come," you say. Everything comes as troubles. The mind is of that type. It always wants something. Keep your mind away from that which is not true, then you are happy wherever you may be. A diamond is sure to shine even if it is in the dust bin, or in gold, or white gold. It is sure to shine, but you have forgotten your own shine. What to do?

A diamond is just carbon. It is just a stone, but under pressure it becomes a diamond, and then the shining comes. But the cutting needs to be there, otherwise it is just a stone. People like to wear diamonds. They say, "I look very fine and nice." It is all right. But what is the end of all this? You will die yourself. But if Reality is found? Reality is so brilliant because the shining never goes off. If you understand that shining, then you are He. Then what remains for you? Always be He and stay. The world is nothing no matter what it may appear to be.

It is Zero in the moment. Break it (the world) and it becomes Zero. Everything starts from Zero and ends in Zero. What to do! Then there are no questions. You were a drop when you were in the womb of the mother and one day you become a drop again. You are put in the grave and it all vanishes. Why do you love this (body)? Don't love it! Love yourself, that never dies. He never dies, never goes anywhere and doesn't do anything. But he who understands does everything but knows that he does nothing, so he is out of it.

Let the world be there, what harms you? You are never happy with the world. Why? You want something else. The mind always wants something else. What you have got you are never satisfied with, whatever it may be.

An Indian woman has won Miss World now. Is she happy after becoming Miss World? Ask her? "I have got the title now!" Title is not good. The title makes unnecessary trouble. She wants to look more and more beautiful. How can she be more now, tell me? What is there is there. People cannot understand. Can anyone eat money? You have got lakhs of rupees or dollars. Can you eat that? You have to purchase something to eat. Give up your dollars. The body wants some fruit, fish or vegetables, whatever it may be. Nothing to worry. People eat non-vegetarian foods and some people say that, "They are dirty." Of what is this body made? It is made of flesh, bones and blood. Why should anyone say bad to them? Nobody is bad and nobody is good also. The body requires food and drink, that is all.

When it is cold you may take a brandy to add heat to the body, nothing else. Have you become bad by taking brandy? Someone who hasn't taken brandy, has he become good? This is all the nonsense of the mind. The mind makes so much difference. Many Saints say, "Oh, you have to eat vegetables, then you can come to me." What to do? You eat ladyfingers (okra), no? You have to cut them, no? They have life even though you can't see it. Then air and germs come in. Can you stop those germs from coming in? You can clean and clean, still it is there. So it is told in our mythology, "That if you want to live, you must eat life." One should eat the life. Do you breathe in and out, or not? Without breathing one cannot stay alive. Breathing means you want some wind and it has so many germs in it. You eat them all.

In some cultures they eat man's flesh. They say it is tasty. I don't know. They cut the flesh and blood comes out. When you have a cut, you lick your wound. (Maharaj pretends to lick a wound) Lick that blood so it will go off. Understanding must come. What is the world? It is your thought. You made the world. You took the birth and that is your thought, and then some name is given to you. Her name is Susan but I call her Marta. What is in the name? Some fat woman like her was in America. Her name was Marta. So I call her Marta. I forget many names. What to do? Due to old age I forget. I can't remember many people. Okay. I say okay, how can I remember? Many people come here and go away.

Everybody goes to church. Does Christ see anybody? He doesn't see anybody. (Maharaj laughs) Be He! Myself is everybody. Go! Why do you go and pray at Church? "He" doesn't speak. "He" doesn't talk. "He" doesn't hear, and "He" doesn't see. You go to see an idol. Be the idol yourself. See everything and say nothing is true. Have that much courage. Whatever happens let anything happen, what harms you? If I say this is not a marble mantle, can it harm me? I say it is stone. Oh lovingly you say, "It is marble," and people take pride in it. Is it nothing but stone, or not?

I always give the example of the man who was counting his money. Everyday he would count his twenty thousand rupees. Counting and counting, and when he finished counting, he put it back in the earth where he had hidden it. One day, another man saw him counting and thought, "What is he doing there, he is only counting." The next day he took the money out and replaced it with stones. The next day the man went to take out his money and saw only stones. He began crying. "Ah, ah, all gone." The other man said, "Why are you crying, you are only counting, no? Count the stones instead, it is as good as your money." But the mind cannot accept it.

"The mind is such a rascally chap. It is a mischief monger," I always say that. The mind makes so much trouble for you and you have to suffer for that. You take the pride of mind and say "My mind has said." Take your mind and make it no-mind. Say, "I am not the body, I am the Reality." Let people say anything. They will say "You're mad. You have become mad." Why should you worry for what they say? Do you know yourself or not? If you have twenty thousand rupees with you and you wear torn clothes, do you feel that you are poor? No! You like to make a show. Even not to show is also a show. You think, "If people think that I have money, they will take it from me." There are so many thieves in the world.

When you go to a marriage ceremony you try to look good for the people to see you. You try to look special. But no one looks at you, they look at the bride and groom. Nobody cares for you, but still you go with all that pomp. You want some acceptance there and that is ego. Take out your ego, forget your ego, forget yourself. Ego means everything that is unnecessary. The mind is a very different kind. It always wants something, and something, and something more. But what it wants is not true. The mind never asks for the Reality. Does the mind ever ask for that?

Nobody wants to go to the Saint because they talk of something else, and you are always thinking of what is not true. Two drunkards are happy together because the other thinks, "He is just like me." But if one says, "Sorry, I can't come," Then what? In life, birds of a feather always flock together. People make friends. Why? For the purpose to make the mind deeper and more satisfied. But the mind is never satisfied. Today's friend is tomorrow's enemy. That depends on you. What the mind will do and not do, only God knows!

If a rich person makes a nice party, he sits in the hall and says to himself, "If I become poor tomorrow what will happen to me?" He begins to cry and people cannot understand why he is not happy. He wants to keep the ego of it. The mind knows the world is going to go off. Nothing can be done to stop it. Why do people cry when someone dies? No one wants to die oneself, so they cry. Die yourself when you are living. Understand this: "I am not the body, I am not the mind, I am not Ignorance nor Knowledge. I am beyond Knowledge." Knowledge is just a thought, Why to be so strong defending Knowledge? What kind of Knowledge do you have? Knowledge is the wrong thing that you have got, whatever it may be. Does Knowledge go away or not? Do you forget or not? Tell me! When you sleep you forget everything.

So Knowledge is not true. Is it true? You are so happy you say, "I have so many degrees," and "I am So-and-so." Are you a degree? You are nothing like that. The ego wants that. The ego wants happiness. Forget everything, then you will be happy. Don't say, "Will I get money or not." Don't get money, I tell you. You are always rich. As you are there, the whole world is there. Otherwise where is the world? Be in that fashion. Be that way.

If you have torn clothes, there is nothing to worry about, because you know "I am not this." Never worry for anything. Then, when worries go off you become no-mind. You don't become a foolish person with no-mind. Your mind always troubles you. No-mind takes you out of your troubles. Never worry for anything, whatever state you are in. It is only the body's or mind's affair. You are stateless. All of these states come and go. You are always He. Never accept anything less. Okay? So is your question over now?

Questioner: Is understanding still Knowledge? Is it a knowledge of nothing?

Maharaj: Yes, nothing. That is the understanding. Understanding is that. It is nothing, but you take it to be something true, due to that understanding. If you go beyond understanding, then you are ever there, because understanding brings ignorance. It comes from ignorance. Go beyond that. Go beyond space. Space is Zero, so go beyond space. If you understand that you are beyond space, who can touch you, tell me? Then what Knowledge can come to you? Knowledge comes when? When you take the touch of it, when you say, "I exist."

Questioner: When the mind goes off, you are He then but the mind is sure to return at some point.

Maharaj: Let it come.

Questioner: So the understanding is also there, but it is understood to be nothing?

Maharaj: Yes. Then you know that nothing is true and that He acts in everything. He does everything, but the mind understands it is not true. The base should be of that type. See the whole picture and still say that it is not true. It is just the thought of one person. But you lovingly see the whole picture and again take it as true. When you understand that everything is nothing you become a Saint, otherwise you stay as an ignorant person.

Ignorance has no bliss. Knowledge *and* Ignorance are both wrong. So, understand and do everything, but you are not to worry for it. I give you an example. Five or six friends were sitting together. Then secretly one man twinkled his eye to the host. Then the man who twinkled his eye began to scold the host. The other people got upset. "Why isn't the host answering back and he is taking all those bad words," they thought. The host just sat back and laughed. He understood that it was just a joke.

Take the world as a joke, your joke. Then make that joke dance on your little finger. The ego wants everything and makes you feel that everything is true. Take it as a joke and say it is not true. Be out of it, otherwise you will have to stay in the world, no? As long as the body is there the connection of Knowledge is there. Body is there and you have to think and work, but still you can be out of it. The realized person thinks everything, but says what? "Everything starts from Zero."

Two men are fighting and a third man comes in and asks, "Why are you fighting?" One says, "He owes me twelve rupees." The other says, "No, what I owe you is seven and five." All are fighting like this. You always want it in a different way. So, make it all dance on your little finger. Make that Knowledge dance on it. (Maharaj holds up his little finger in the air.) Knowledge is nothing.

Understand that "Ignorance has come on me, and that is all that Knowledge is." Then you can be happy anywhere. If you dance then you can't be happy. So, don't dance, make the Knowledge dance.

When a tabla (drum) player plays, do you dance or not? But does he dance? He makes you dance. Drum your own drum, but don't dance with it, and that is the way to be out of it. If you dance all night then what happens? You can't drum the next day. So make others dance. The fellow who does that understands that everyone is a foolish person. Nobody is wise, and I am also not wise. Say that, otherwise the ego comes, no? Ego is such. I am also like a foolish person, but I know something most don't know. That is the difference, nothing else. You are subtler than space and nothing can stop you. Can anybody stop you? Nobody can stop you. Be subtler than space. The wind comes, can you stop the wind? Anybody? No, nobody, whomever he may be. But the wind goes where? Back in the space again. It goes to Zero. So be out of Zero and dance with it. Make everything dance. You drum, but don't dance. Okay?

Questioner: Did you know Dattatreya? He lived in your lifetime?

Maharaj: No! He lived more than five thousand years ago, before Christ. Dattatreya is my child. That I understand. The attributes come, and that is the child. What to know? A man with three heads, can he be there? It is a punishment on him to sleep that way. To be a God is a punishment. To one who is punished, how can he be a king? All gods are nothing, they are only thoughts. Who knows if Dattatreya was there or not? He is just written about in books. He went to twenty four Masters. The attributes cannot be happy. How can they be happy, tell me? From where are they born? You say, "I die," or "that man dies." The attributes come and go in the body. They are not true. How can they be true? Guests all come and go. If you see them as God, then you are lost in heaven. The world has come up when you took the birth. It is not there at all. One leaves the body, then the world is finished. Nobody and nothing is true.

* * * * * * * * * *

December, 30, 1999

Questioner: Maharaj, I had a guru in Holland for ten years. Sometimes he said to me, "You are a little bit strange." One day I asked him, "What do you mean by that?" He said, "Because you don't stand for what you are." I didn't ask further then and in a few months he died. Yesterday I heard you say, "Have the courage to be He." Could you explain to me what you meant by that?

Maharaj: You are He. You think you are the body, a woman. All this nonsense has come in your mind due to your birth. You cannot stand on you. He (her Master) wants to say that. He should have explained to you how to stand. One should understand "Who am I?" first. You are not the body, not the name, and Ignorance and Knowledge are also not you. One should understand that way.

That is the duty of the Master to make you understand. How can you stand? How can one stand? When you understand that you are He, then what remains? You stand forever, you never lie down. Standing forever means understanding, and that understanding needs to be practical. In the beginning one understands theoretically, and then practically. Practical means you are He, that is practical, nothing else. How to be He? So he told you that you do not stand.

First, stand on the Knowledge. "I am the Knowledge, I know everything. The world is in my thought only." The whole world is your thought. People cannot accept that. Due to Knowledge the world has come up. How does the dream come up? You are sleeping, and you are in Ignorance. A thought comes, and it becomes a dream. You become a queen in the dream. You say, "How can I be a queen?" It is the same way here when understanding comes. The Master says, "You are He." Understanding comes when you leave the dream. Unless you leave the dream, you can't understand what "I am," and "what I was before."

It's the same way here (in the waking state) also. Everything comes from where? From Zero, and it ends in Zero. Nothing is true. You feel that it is true here due to the eyes and the mind. The mind always accepts something as true. In a dream also you feel it is correct. In a dream you can have a child in one second, and here it takes nine months. There you do not have to wait. Nothing is to be done there because your Power is so strong at that time.

The world is made by that Knowledge. And that Knowledge is yourself, one should understand that. Then you become the Creator of the world, otherwise you can't be the Creator. As you have become something, so you say, "Why has this happened? Why did my son die so early?" It is due to your thought. When he was created it was due to your thought.

I give an example: In a story the writer makes the heroine die early. That is the author's right. The director says, "That is bad if the heroine dies, then what remains?" The writer says, "If the heroine does not die, my pen cannot write more."

In the same way, as you have taken this body, you say "It has happened like this." No, it was your own thought when you created the world. In a play also, one may become a beggar or a king. Who makes all this? The writer, and you take a part in it. So, a king wants to play the part of a beggar. He takes the ego of it and he says, "I've done very nicely as a beggar even though I am a king." Same way here, as you have taken the body, you forget you are the Creator. But you are the Creator, Knowledge is the Creator, nothing else. Does a madman have any world? He does anything he likes. He has no world. His world is only his thoughts.

Why do people do things together and have social functions? Because they are all of the same mind. It makes these worldly affairs true because all are so engrossed in it. But it is nothing but a dream. When you sleep where does everything go? Tell me! You forget your body, you forget your mind, you forget everything. You even forget the place where you are sleeping. I often forget where I am when I awaken from sleep. "What is this, where am I?" Forgetting is there. Forget everything. Forget the whole world. See it, enjoy it, but say it is not true.

Have that much courage to say that it is not true. Do everything, there's nothing to worry about. Due to the connection of that Knowledge in your body it is sure to work. Eyes must see, ears must hear, and tongue must taste. Still, say it is not true, have that much audacity. You eat something sweet, does it remain? The sweetness goes off. When you feel some disturbance in the mind, you cry, and then it goes away. Does it remain? You are always changing, wherever you may be, but you never forget yourself. I always say, "If you are in heaven or hell you never forget yourself." You forget everything, but you misrepresent yourself that you are a body and mind. In this way you have to stand. He always stands. He never speaks. What to do. If He sleeps, the world will go to the dogs, because all this is just his shadow. The world is just a shadow of Reality.

Who made all of this? The question always arises and everyone thinks that the Creator has made it. Who has seen that Creator? Tell me! How was the world created? My Master said, "What bloody fool has seen that?" Was anyone there? Were you there when the world was created? People say so many things but without any experience. But the experience of the Self is always there. A thought comes and something is created. A dream comes. Can you know what your dream is? After awakening, who demolished that dream? So, nothing has happened.

You saw the palace, and you are a queen. Everything is there, and you did many things. Does even a piece of it remain? As soon as you awake everything goes off. Then who created it? That Knowledge has created the world. You say it is true. Why do you say true? Because you are all of the same mind or quality. Birds of a feather flock together. All say the world is true, or has been created. The one who understands says, "I don't know who is God." He is so strong about it. Who is God? You slept and something happened, no? Who created it? Because you have forgotten the Reality, Reality is forgotten and you cannot go there. The whole world comes up as a result.

Questioner: That which is permanent and unchangeable, how come on That, this appearance has come, and is constantly changing? It is a contradiction that the one who is permanent and unchanging produces that which is changeable and transitional, or the world and the Reality.

Maharaj: It doesn't produce. He doesn't produce. If He would have produced it, then nobody could have made it untrue. He is forgotten and Knowledge comes, and Knowledge brings everything. You are in complete sleep, doing nothing and a thought comes. From where has it come? From your Zero state. Who created it? If He would have created it, somebody would have demolished it also. Understand this way. It is just a shadow. I have to use the word shadow. If you go after the shadow, can you get the person? A shadow changes every moment. Shadows become longer or shorter depending on the light. Is the person shorter or longer?

He doesn't create, I want to say that. People think He has created. No! In a dream you are doing nothing, but still you are dancing. You talk and drink and are doing everything in the dream. If you eat in the dream is your belly full? No. You feel hunger when you awake. So what you have done is not true. You take the taste of everything, bad or good. Some people like bitter gourd. Somebody else tastes it and says the opposite. Why? It is the mind at work and it works everywhere.

I was told not to take sugar to prevent diabetes. Still, I take sugar more and more. I take all these tests and the results are nil. What to do! I have a cough so they want me to take an electrocardiogram. And the last one was better than the first two. How to find out? Better not to know anything. Knowing is the worst. A boy was enjoying himself and then he got a letter saying his father had died, so he began to cry. Knowledge brings all troubles. No Knowledge, then? If one doesn't know that an Indian plane was hijacked, what does one feel about it? Will one feel anything? When you know you say, "Oh, what will happen, what will happen!"

So knowing is not a blessing. Knowing brings troubles. You took the birth and knew, so now every trouble has come to you. Every problem has come for you. Ask your mind, "What problem has not come?" To love someone is also a problem, and not to love is also a problem. What can you do? Knowledge is there, no? Knowledge is so troublesome. Reality has no Knowledge, so He never made the world. Knowledge has erupted over it. You were sleeping doing nothing, still, it erupted over you. With a bad dream you are unhappy, and with a good dream you are happy. Both go off when you are awake.

If you awaken here, then it is nothing but a long dream. It repeats, so we call it a long dream. Why do realized persons call it a long dream? What was yesterday, is today. It is nothing, it never happened, but memory creates the link. Everything seems separate so you take it as true. You feel it is true due to remembering. You keep it in the mind. That is Ignorance. A man was crying yesterday, but is laughing today. What is the meaning in it? Why does it happen? I ask you now! Both are wrong, no? Nobody was crying, and nobody was laughing. So, you can change at any moment yourself. The world is so changeable at every moment. A good breeze comes and you say, "It is very nice," and if the heat comes you say, "Put on the fan, or the A.C." What to do? If you are sick, then you don't want the fan or air conditioning. Let me be hot, I don't mind.

Questioner: Is there any difference between realization, and a higher, or highest realization?

Maharaj: As you know, you go ahead more. That is higher realization. If you go to the 7th floor of a building that is still higher realization. (Everyone laughs.) But when you feel that everything is not true, that is the highest. The mind is always in suspense, "Is it true or not true?" The Master says, "It is not true." "How can I believe him? I see and do everything. I eat, and I go to the toilet also." In a dream you are doing many things there, but still you forget it all when you get up. Nothing remains. So, when one dies and leaves the body, what remains? Nothing remains. The world goes to the dogs.

Questioner: The human being is a combination of form and formless. Form is the body and formless is the Knowledge or Consciousness. So, the body and mind are not true, and that is realized experientially by those that are sensitive. The problem for me is how to cross Knowledge and yet "Be." Is it possible?

Maharaj: Understand that Knowledge itself is not true. Everything happens in the Knowledge. It must happen. One person gets a fever, and one does not. Say it is not true in the mind, and that is the difference, nothing else. The body gets the fever, "I" don't get the fever. Your degree cannot be measured.

Questioner: How does the crossing happen between the formlessness and that which nothing can be spoken of?

Maharaj: Only by understanding. That "I am formless," or "I am with form" are due to the beliefs of the mind. You are not formless or with form. No thought remains, so it is called thoughtless thought, or stateless state, nothing is there. Otherwise something would happen there. You never feel anything. When you sleep what do you feel, tell me? Sleep means everything is gone.

Form and formlessness doesn't remain. Because you see the form as real you have to say formless. It is not formless also.

You have to use words like "Reality" for example. It is not even Reality. What is it? It is not Reality, and one has to accept that Reality. There are no words there. On one side everything is true. You are in complete sleep and thought comes. You see the whole dream or not. Are you in form or formless, tell me?

Questioner: Formless is inactive at that time and Consciousness is active.

Maharaj: Consciousness may be there, I don't say no. Consciousness comes when? When you take the touch of it. In sleep you scratch yourself but you don't know. You murmur something, but if someone asks you what you were saying, you say, "I didn't say anything." Due to the habit of the body or mind you feel that you are doing something. Everything happens here but it doesn't happen. Everything happens in Ignorance.

Questioner: Can we conclude Maharaj, that the passage from Knowledge to Reality is automatic? It happens on its own.

Maharaj: Say that, it will do. But it is not true. That is the final understanding. Does the realized person not see the world? He sees everything. The question remains to be solved always. The world is a question. Yourself is a question.

(Maharaj then asks the original questioner her name.) Marijke. Where is Marijke, where is Marijke? "I am Marijke," you say. It doesn't stand. You feel it is true, but still it is not true. This marble counter will break your head, but it can't break you. It will break my head but it can't break me, because I am He, short and sweet. When you are He how can you break yourself?

Reality is so wonderful I tell you. One cannot imagine. And you are That. So how can you kill yourself? The marble is He too, but still it doesn't exist, it can't stand on its own. Can you put any blame on it? Electricity kills so many people. Can you put any blame on it? Electricity says, "I never know that anyone is dead." It also gives the light but it doesn't know what light is. The sun doesn't know that it gives the light to the world. If it does, it is not the sun. It's the same way here also. Find out yourself. You are not found anywhere, but still you are there, without telling.

Questioner: So all objects, sentient and insentient are He?

Maharaj: Say that, but say it is not true. In a dream you see many things. When you awake what has happened? You want to put something in Reality. Reality doesn't say anything. The mind wants something there because it wants to prove that everything is true. As long as the dream is there, it is not true. When it happened it was not true, and when it was demolished it was not true. Gone! Nothing has happened and nothing is going to happen. Everything is in the counting only. The year 1999 is going in two days, and 2000 is coming, and Christ has not come yet. He never says he is coming. You say it! Reality never says anything, but everything happens on Him. It doesn't take the touch of anything.

Questioner: So Reality is not aware of itself?

Maharaj: If it says, "I am the Reality," it's not the Reality. What to say?

Questioner: But the whole universe is aware.

Maharaj: I agree, because it is in Knowledge, but Knowledge is not true. The first day of the year 2000 all will sleep and then they will get up again. One day gone, and another has come. Everything happens like this. The mind is so creative. It wants to create. It is not easy to go across the mind. Cross it by saying it is not true. If you have that power and courage, let anything happen, just say, "It is not true. I am not anything. I will never be anything."

So, what you see and perceive is all just like the bubbles in the ocean. Close your eyes and where is the world? (Maharaj uses the example of "blind man's bluff" where one person is blindfolded and then he has to search for the other players in the game.) So, everyone is in search of Reality, but Reality is never blindfolded by anybody. It is so open.

Questioner: We use this Knowledge to understand, and yet we are also asked to give it up at the same time. How do we reconcile this? We are using the same instrument to discriminate, and then we must give it up at the same time.

Maharaj: Keep the same instrument, but understand it is not true. What it makes is not true. What results is not true. One has to sleep, then the dream can come. If I sleep the whole night and you don't, I may get many dreams. But if I ask you then, "How many dreams have you had," you will answer, "I never slept so how can I get any dreams?" The instrument is the same. To use it or not to use it, that depends on you now. Knowledge is an instrument, nothing else. How to use that Knowledge?

Questioner: How to go beyond it?

Maharaj: Yes, then Knowledge doesn't remain. It is never there. You see the whole world, but still it is not there. That is what you must understand.

Due to Knowledge you see. A dead man cannot see the world. Can he see the world? He may have crores of money in the bank but it is still null and void, because Knowledge has been disconnected. The whole world is just a show of that connection. Knowledge comes and the whole world is seen. Then everyone sees and everybody fights for money, nothing else. For what reason? Knowledge brings everything, but still it is not true. This you must understand. How can Knowledge prove itself? Knowledge cannot be proved true.

You cannot prove it because Knowledge goes off in a fraction of a second. You were just speaking, and then you die. Gone to hell, what to do? What happens? Tax your mind, always. You pay taxes to the government. Don't pay taxes to the government, tax your mind. What is true? The mind is the real chartered accountant. Be the chartered accountant. Ask your mind, "What do you want?" Ask your mind, "What don't you want?" There is a way to find out. What is mind? What don't you want? Ask it. It wants everything. The mind is like that. If you say, "What don't you want," the mind says, "I'm sorry, I can't say anything." What can it say, tell me? What don't you want!

Questioner: The mind doesn't want pain, Maharaj, it wants a lot of pleasure.

Maharaj: Pleasure, I agree. In a dream so much pleasure comes, but when you leave the dream, then? All gone. The mind wants more and more. From where to bring more and more? All the toys are kept in the house, but the boy says, "I want something else." What to do? Boys are of that type. "I don't want these, they are old toys. I want new toys," the boy says. From where to bring new toys? So, it just repeats, always. So the world is round, it repeats, what to do? Where to bring the new things? Nothing is new and nothing is old. It is your mind that makes it old and new.

"The mind is such a mischief-monger!" I always say that. It wants to make some mischief to fulfill its thoughts, nothing else. You do anything. You will do everything for that mind. You think that "I am the mind." The one who works with the mind is a man, and the one who woos the mind is a woman. He works with the mind and she also works with the mind, but the concept of man and women is just a covering on you. It is called "Prakruti" in our language.

Man means Knowledge. Knowledge gets the body, and enjoys with the body. Why not! But the realized person says, "This is still not true," because they have the understanding. The mind wants so much, there is no limit to it. People want to go to the moon, no? Now they have gone there, and gone to the bathroom there as well. And still God has made no reply. What is the use of all this! Because it is nothing. So why worry for all this Mars, and moon, and all this nothing.

Questioner: So to be in this Knowledge and enjoy all these worldly pleasures is okay, and there is no harm in it as long as you are aware that it is just Prakruti, the nature of Knowledge, and that one is not attached to it.

Maharaj: That is okay, one can enjoy, why not? But what enjoyment can you get? Tell me! You want it all again and again. (Someone says, "He forgot to mention pain, he only mentioned pleasure.") That is the main point. Pleasure and pain go together and pain comes again and again. I like to be single then my pockets can jingle. I married and I lost everything.

Questioner: Maharaj, will this understanding that you are giving, if we think about it constantly, and churn it again and again, will this convincing of the mind bring about no-mind?

(Note: Maharaj often uses the term "no-mind," however it is not the same concept of no-mind that is commonly seen in popular "spiritual" books of our time. The latter can be considered a state. Maharaj means where Knowledge and Ignorance both go off, the "Stateless State." There the "I" doesn't remain, only He remains. It is the Final Understanding. Still, the one with no-mind speaks and does everything, but the sense of doership is absent. "I speak, but I don't speak," is his understanding.)

Maharaj: Convince yourself today or tomorrow. It is sure to come. You have to churn it. Unless you churn and digest it, you cannot produce the milk. You are He, at the moment you are He but wrong things have come in the mind. The mind wants something always. The mind never says, "I want the Reality." Yourself is He. The mind wants everything that is not real, which is untrue.

Questioner: Does the mind have to die?

Maharaj: Let the mind live, but keep a watch on it. A jailer keeps a watch, be the jailer. Where is the jail? Don't make it a jail. But the mind says, "I am in jail." Be anywhere and say it is a palace, what harms you? This small room is a palace for me. Doing nothing here, I do everything. How much time does it take to clean this room. A minute. Understanding should come, nothing else.

Questioner: So Maharaj, with the arising of mind comes the imprisonment. And with the disappearance of mind comes liberation.

Maharaj: The mind brings everything, but it is always liberated. He was never a captive. You are always in your palace. In a jail, if you sleep, you are in a palace or not? Who is going to object? The jailer can't object. But the mind doesn't allow. There is no bondage and no liberation. All this is nonsense. You are never in bondage so who can liberate you? You want to remain in bondage, so

Maharaj has to come and liberate you. But he says, "You are always liberated, so fly now!" "How can I fly, how can I leave this room?" you say. Your mind says, "I can't do this. I can't do that." Understand the mind, the mind is Knowledge, nothing else. Understand the Knowledge. Then mind doesn't remain. The mind itself goes off. "I have no place to stay here," it says. If you put the mosquito net up the mosquitoes can't stay. Outside they can stay, but not inside.

Questioner: So Maharaj, the whole activity of realization appears to be a very selfish act.

Maharaj: It is not selfishness. You are not there. When you say, "I am this" you are selfish. Selfishness doesn't remain because all are He. The mind brings these questions, what to do. "I am poor, I can't do anything," or "I am rich and can do everything." A pauper says, "I can't do anything because I have no money." Parabrahman (Reality) is a pauper. Everything is seen on him, but he doesn't take the touch of anything. Be He and enjoy the world which is a nasty place, and which is not true. Be in it, and be out of it.

A realized person does everything but he knows how to be out of it. The world is nothing, it is a Zero. What to enjoy, tell me! Understand that. It is not easy, and it is not difficult. Be out of the room. Put a foot out and you are not a trespasser. No charge can be put on you. That is the beauty of the Reality. Then one can enjoy.

The Master gives that understanding. Then you are always liberated and never bound by anything. What to say about anything? (Looking at Marijke) The question came from you, about how you cannot stand for two hours. Tell your Master, "I stand forever." You can't tell him now, because you are ever there. Unless you are there, how can the world come up? Be original, that is the best. Otherwise, everything is an imitation. Don't make any imitation. Everything is imitation, not true. Be He and stay as Him. Okay? Any question?

Questioner: Why does He allow or permit Ignorance to come up?

Maharaj: The mind always wants theories. The mind runs after many things. You say, "I've been to many Saints, I have understood." It is all theories. The mind doesn't want the practical things because its death is there. Nobody wants poison, everyone wants the sweets. The death of the mind is there, so the mind doesn't want to accept it. The mind can make you a God or the smallest creature. The mind is not the enemy, but one should know *how* to use the mind.

So the mind doesn't want the practical. That is the main point. The mind boasts, "I've done this and that." But what have you done that is practical? Sorry. Make your mind a friend, and it will do the right thing. If you understand the Reality, who can conquer you? You are never to be conquered by anyone. The mind is nothing but your thought. One can change the thoughts, why not?

Suppose a man is a drunkard and wants to stop. He goes to a doctor and the doctor says, "If you take another drink you will die." "I will do it," he says. Boys play with toys. Now you are a man, and if someone gives you boy toys, you will be insulted. It is a change of mind, or not? The mind can be changed.

* * * * * * * * * *

January 7, 2000

Questioner: Can you get the Reality in a fraction of a second, even if the mind is not totally clear? Or must you go through the process step by step?

Maharaj: If mind is not clear then how can you get it? The mind should be clear always. The mind should understand: "This is not true." You take it true and that is the only drawback. There is nothing, but Reality is always there. When the clouds come, the sun cannot be seen. If the mind is not clear, then how can you get it? The mind must know that everything is Zero. Nothing is true. The mind itself is not true. Follow me? Then, mind becomes no-mind. Then you can understand. How can you understand without that? Suppose you have a fever and you eat ice cream. Your fever will become more. You cannot help it.

So, if the mind is not clear then what you ask is impossible. Things should be very clear, otherwise all would be That in a fraction of a second. The mind comes again and again. Thoughts come, so the mind should be clear. The mind should say, "Nothing is true, I don't exist." Then what is true? When one dies what remains, tell me? Does anything remain? Nothing remains. He doesn't remember himself. He doesn't know, "I am That." If he knows, "I am That," he will never die. The mind should be no-mind.

It is very easy, in a fraction of a second, yes, but the mind should be clear. Clear means that what you see and perceive with the mind, and what you see by the eyes is not true. Take it for granted. You see the whole dream. You are in Paris, or you are a king, or you become a queen there. Everything is there. In life you wait for a child for nine months, but in the dream if you want a child you get the child right away. No trouble, your Power is so strong there.

When you have faith, then you can do anything, why not? The mind automatically becomes clear. When the Master says, "It is not true," the disciple says, "I agree with you." But then you run after the world again. Many people say they have understood when they are here, but when they go home they become something and forget themselves. What to do? Reality, if forgotten, brings you back in Illusion. Many people who say that they understood went up to Knowledge only. It is a stumbling block, because Knowledge is not true. Still, the Masters give the Knowledge first, and then afterwards say that it is not true. How can it be true?

When Knowledge comes, the triad comes. The knower, knowingness and known; the three come. As long as the mind is there, mind, ego, and Knowledge are all one. You have to say these things in different ways, nothing else. A woman is there. Someone says, "She is my mother," and one says, "She is my sister," and another says, "She is my wife." Is she three? No, she is only one. It all depends upon your mind. The mind is such a crooked thing.

One can be realized in a fraction of a second, why not? You must have the faith in the Master. What he says is correct. He says, "You are not the body," so you are not the body. If someone says, "You have a nice finger," have you become that? Someone else says, "It is bad finger," and your mind is affected. When it affects you, how can you be He? The mind should be open. The mind should become no-mind. So, Socrates said, "I know I know nothing." He knew everything, but still he says he knows nothing.

You can take a picture of me and see a body there, but still I am not the body. One should understand. That is the beauty of it. When you are not, why to worry? When your child is there, and someone else's child is dead, do you worry?

One day at 1:30 a.m. we were playing cards with Siddharameshwar Maharaj and a dead body was taken away. So he asked all of us what we thought. No one said anything and then he said, "When you feel that your dearest dies and you don't feel anything more, take it for granted you have understood the Reality."

Reality never dies, whoever he may be. The nearest and dearest is the body, A child and husband are secondary questions. When you are dying, you cry for that body only. Don't cry for that. Say boldly, as I say sometimes, "If you want to kill someone, no harm. But when you go to the gallows, say that the body is going to the gallows, I am not!" The body has done wrong, so it must go. I don't go. I will never die. He doesn't do harm to anybody. The mind is there, and He works with the mind. Still being no-mind, He works with the mind and that is the beauty of the Reality.

If you understand the Reality then mind becomes no-mind automatically. One who understands is not a mad person. On the contrary he is a very understanding person. All his actions are done with aim. What he does, he does with aim. He is not aimless. You do many, many things without aim. There is no aim for you. You go and worship in the church, and you worship Mary. What is the meaning in it? It's Christ's church. If somebody worships my mother will they get the Reality? My mother never went to school. What is the meaning in it? Understanding should be there. So, one can be He in a fraction second, but your mind must have that Power inside. So if your dearest dies and you feel like nothing has happened, take it for granted that you have understood.

My Master understood everything, so he gave us that understanding. If your neighbor's son dies, you say, "Oh, the poor chap died," but you don't feel anything. In India, and with the foreigners also, if your neighbor dies, nobody knows. Do they know? They don't care. I'm living, no? Why should I worry? Gone is gone. Understand this way and you can be the right person to accept anything.

All people talk but they don't understand. They don't want to understand. If your mind is not correct, how can you be That? You do all the wrong things if you accept without understanding. Some people have understood, so why should they come back in the world again? They want more disciples. What is the meaning in it? Everybody is He, no? Then who is your disciple?

So many people have come back from the understanding. They want money. They want everything. When you don't want, everyone becomes your servant. The one who wants, even if he begs, nobody gives. Nobody gives him a chance. All are beggars. If you beg from the mind, the mind doesn't allow you to go to the Reality. If the mind says, "Ah, go away, nothing is true," then the mind accepts in a fraction of a second. I speak so many times, but nobody wants to go ahead an inch. What to do? Move ahead slowly. One can get it slowly, why not?

If you are only sitting here, can you get the place? How can you? If you want to go to Bhagewadi you have to go by car. When everything is nothing, then why to worry? Go ahead more and more. The Master makes you understand that nothing is true, and that you are He. It is very easy. In a fraction of a second you can get it. Forget everything. But you can't forget yourself first, so how can you forget everything. Can you forget yourself? You say you are the body, mind, and name, but finally, that name has no value. Your name is lame. Your name is not true. Forget your name. Forget yourself. When someone calls your name, you say, "Yes, yes."

Everyone wants to make their own name important. You never forget your name, but when you die you forget everything. When one sleeps one forgets also, but when you awaken you don't forget. When Oneness comes in the mind, the Master says, "You are the Reality, Go!"

(Maharaj proceeds to tell the story of Sukamuni and the king.) The king was ruling the country, but still he had the understanding that nothing can touch me. Sukamuni came to the king, who was realized, to ask for understanding, and the king told him to abandon everything. So, Sukamuni went home and came back without his loincloth. But but the king again told him to abandon everything. Suka then went back home and understood finally what the king meant. He meant, "Forget that you are a great renunciate, that had done this and that, and forget that Suka." Suka is the name given to the body, and I am not the body, and also not the mind. He never went back to see the king. He had understood. Forget everything. If you understand that way, how much time does it take? No need to say anything. But nobody wants to move ahead an inch, what to do?

You can go in the world and enjoy, no harm but understand it is not true. It is a poison, no doubt. But I can drink that poison, and I know that it cannot hurt me. The mind should not be affected by the world. The poison can't harm you. The body dies, you are not going to die. And the body doesn't even die, it becomes part of Parabrahman itself. Everything is He. Besides He, there is nothing.

(Maharaj then tells the story of Meera, the greatest lover of Lord Krishna.) The king had her drink poison so she would die. "Let her go to hell, I don't care." (She was his wife, and he was jealous of her feelings for Krishna.) She took the poison willingly and after two hours nothing happened. How can poison affect you? You are not this, the body, you are He. Poison affects whom? The body. Poison cannot affect the one who is not the body. No need to take poison, just understand that nothing can affect you. With wrong understanding then everything becomes troublesome nonsense.

Her husband had also seen Lord Krishna, so he asked her, "What do you see in that picture?" She said, "What I see in him, you cannot see. What can I do? I see him as the Reality, as Parabrahman, you see him as a picture." That is the difference. Be the Reality. That picture is also the Reality. He is everywhere. Automatically you become He then. Nobody makes you He. You can get the address. The Master gives it to you, but he cannot come there with you. You have to go there and enter yourself. Up to that point both are one. Except Him there is nobody. Knock on the door and become the owner of the house.

In Germany one man told me that he had seen the house eighteen years ago, but he never entered. I told him, "That's your fault." The door is always open and then you become the "King of Kings." Have that much courage. What will happen if you knock on the door? Are demons going to come? You can eat many demons. Demons are your thoughts. Both Gods and demons are in your thoughts. You breathe them in and out. So you are He, or not? Nothing can affect you, but when you say "I am this" you are lost. When you are He, you are in heaven. The Master gives the correct understanding, nobody else can. So try to understand him.

So, in a fraction of a second is also wrong. At the moment you are He. You are He at this very moment but you have forgotten yourself. You forget your name. If you are on the road and you don't know your name, people will run away from you. They will think you are mad if you say, "Where is Paul?" Paul has forgotten himself, what to do? If after understanding he asks, "Where is Paul?," then he has become the Master of himself. He knows that he is He. Paul is only a name given to this body. How much time does it take? Time and tide is not, it doesn't wait for the man. There is no time and tide in the Reality. Understanding should come.

Questioner: Sometimes you say that some Saints don't go beyond Zero and that some go beyond. So who is it that is trying to go beyond or not?

Maharaj: Yourself, your mind. He feels emptiness there (at Zero), but then he doesn't forget himself, and then feels emptiness. He comes back then, the mind comes back. The mind remains up to there. The mind can be absorbed in a fraction of a second also. Many people ask why the Master has not told them this. Nobody wants to give out the understanding of how to go beyond Zero.

Questioner: Many people and disciples of your Master were taught by him, but not all the disciples had realized. Not everybody has reached the Reality.

Maharaj: Why not? Because they don't want to go. If you have a destination and you get off before the destination, how can you get it? Can't get it. Why should you worry about this? Think of yourself! Don't think of others. There is nobody there except you. You worry for others. Why? To take yourself as something, and think, "I know, I know more. I get the first number and they get the second." That's the main point in it.

Forget everything. Don't say that anybody is there. When you compare, you enter a circle" "That person has understood, that person hasn't." Why should you worry? Understand yourself. You are hungry, no? Eat and be satisfied. Then you won't say anybody is hungry. If you think somebody is hungry, you will say, "I'm satisfied, why are you hungry?" You will say that way. Understanding should come. Difficult, I agree, because the mind works on this side always, the wrong side. It has its tendencies.

When you sleep, you go to the Reality but you don't know it. If someone says your name, you answer at once. You can't help it. You are habituated that way. "Habit is second nature," it is told. Don't do that, forget everything. And if you are not He, tell me, because I am responsible. Say that nobody exists. So, if nobody exists, where do you exist? When that understanding comes to you, you are He, and that is forgetting. Forget like this and you are He in the moment, not in a fraction of a second later. But you don't accept that, you don't forget this and that, what to do? Forget everything, forget the mind!

Nothing to worry about, but you want to be what? She always wants to be Mary. (There is a disciple in the room named Mary) Her name is Mary, so she wants to be Mary. So, can the mind be Mary? She is Mary, but she doesn't understand that she is also not Mary. What to do? Be Mary (Play on words, merry) always. Say that everybody is myself. Why do you want to know if anyone has understood or not? Everybody is He, no? Still you doubt what I have told you up to now.

My Master was there and some people were coming and some were not coming back. So the disciples were discussing this, and our Master asked, why we were discussing this. Coming or not coming, still, everyone is He. When you get the degree, do you go to the college again? No! In the same way, always think that everyone is He. Don't ask that question. Discrimination power rests with the mind. How can you know what someone else knows? If they understand, it is their choice. Also, who am I to say, because I don't exist. When

I don't exist, who is going to say? As long as the body is connected with the Power it speaks.

So, never to worry. And never say that after me, "he" should be appointed (a successor). Nobody gets appointed here. Nobody is to be appointed. The one who has the Power is sure to speak. He will make things so clear, and just sit like this with his own pillow and speak. People will be sure to hear. And that is what? The Masters's degree. That pillow is the Master's pillow. Take it yourself, but why put somebody else on a pillow? No need. He is a king, nobody appoints him. He doesn't appoint anybody. When everyone is He, why to appoint? Whom to say that you are first class, you are second class? No need to say. That understanding should come. Any other questions?

Questioner: Can subtle forms of energy or intelligence like angels or gods achieve the Final Reality, or do they have to have a physical birth to reach it?

Maharaj: After the death, what gross body is going to come? Can you say? Achieve here at the moment. You are He, no? So, what to achieve after the next birth? If you don't achieve here, how can you achieve in the next birth, tell me? You do everything here and then go away. Your body, mind, Ignorance, and Knowledge. Everything goes away. You go away, and where you go nobody knows. Has anyone written letters from there? Forefathers, grandfathers? Nobody writes a letter after they are gone!

Unless you forget, you can't get the death. So forget this Knowledge also, what to do? I don't agree with those who talk about the next birth. Why not this birth only? The tongue is there, put the sugar on it. It must be sweet, no? At the moment you can be He, why is the next birth required? You love the birth and the world. That world you love doesn't remain. If you become a mosquito, then what will be your world? The blood of a human body. These are all nonsense things. Why tomorrow, why not at the present time? You are He, but when you forget that, you take a body, and only God knows what will happen. I don't understand. I don't believe in this, what next birth is going to come?

Questioner: (Someone explains to Maharaj the original question about angels and gods needing a physical form to realize)

Maharaj: Where are angels? Have you seen them? I have never seen anything. You eat them, you swallow the gods and angels.

Original Questioner: Maharaj, you have said in a book that angels and gods were Knowledge, or in Knowledge.

Maharaj: It is in Knowledge. You say, "He is God," no? I say, "He is not God." What can God do to me? Some may say, "He is not a realized Master."

Okay, so he doesn't say anything. You don't understand the real meaning of what is written in the books of Knowledge.

I have never seen angels, where are they? Where have they all gone now? I have never seen Shiva., and Shiva is never seen. You make a lingam, and call it Shiva. These are all thoughts, so forget the thoughts. Angels and gods are thoughts, your thoughts. Angels and devils are there in your thoughts in the darkness, and in the morning when the light comes on, you understand that only your pillow was there, nothing else. Everything goes off when understanding comes. It is written in the books of Knowledge, okay, but what is the meaning in it? I only speak from the highest point. The mind makes all these beliefs.

Questioner: So from your point of view there are no angels and gods.

Maharaj: Gods and angels are in the world only, and the world is not true. It is Zero. All the gods and angels will be Zero one day, but you will never be Zero, take it for granted. So when you swallow, you breathe in gods and angels, what to do! They take birth from the wind. Both gods and devils come only from the wind. They are no entities at all. When you breathe, you can be a god also, why not? Or a devil, it depends on you. Forget everything. Gods and devils are your thoughts.

When they are only your thoughts, what value do they have? Tell them they are not true. Tell them to go. What can they do? If you have a servant and tell him to take his money and go, what can he do? They are all your servants. Gods and angels are your servants. Have that much Power, and nothing can affect you. Still, they affect you, because you feel that gods and angels are there. You like the angels. (The questioner says "Yes.") Where are the angels? If someone has an interest in a she-ass, a female donkey, and then even if an angel comes, he won't notice. His mind is on the she-ass. What can an angel do?

I knew a man named Mr. Shah, I never liked him. He had no distinct features on his face, but his wife was very fond of him. If the mind goes for a she-ass then? What are angels? Angels are nothing. The mind is the greatest factor. It is very difficult to explain to you. What to do?

Forget everything. When you sleep, do you forget everything or not? Do any thoughts remain? Angels and she-asses all come from thought. They are in your mind only. And when you sleep you forget yourself, and also even that you are a doctor. If you remain a doctor (The questioner is a doctor), you can't sleep, take it for granted. Forget everything at the moment. Why? Then you are free. The mind becomes no-mind. It takes a fraction of a second. You don't want to change the mind. Change your mind. Understand that way. There are no angels, gods or she-asses. Everybody is One.

Questioner: I had the idea that the Self works through the body-mind.

Maharaj: No, no, the Self doesn't do anything except show the picture. When you go to sleep and get a dream, do you have any idea what dream will come? It comes, like any thought comes. And whatever comes, you become that. You can become a drunkard there even though you don't touch a drop here. When you awake you say, "How can I be a drunkard, I never touch it." Still, you experience that. The mind gives such experiences. These experiences have no sense in them.

Questioner: So, no matter what I do or whatever experiences I have, it has no relationship with Reality. So everything is valueless.

Maharaj: Everything is Zero, and when you understand that everything is Zero, then you can understand the Reality. Understand that everything is nothing and you are He. You do not have to cross anything. Nothing to cross, just understand it is not true. Zero is nothing, so how can it be true? You take it true.

In America someone asked how to cross Zero. Understand it is Zero and you have crossed it. His name is Paul, and if you understand that his name is not Paul, you've crossed it. You know his name is Paul, but still he's not Paul. How much time is required to know it? Understanding should come, and if the Master is strong, he can put anything in your mind. When the boy doesn't want to eat the mother can pinch his nose and his mouth will open and she can put something inside. The Master can do the same. But if you don't want to know, or you don't want to open your mouth? Accept it, that is the main point.

Questioner: I try to forget the mind, but sometimes I can't, and I get angry with myself. Should I fight with the mind at that point?

Maharaj: When you can't put a check on the mind you get angry with yourself. The mind is a thought. Anger is a thought. But still, the best way is not to think of it. When a thought or anything comes, tell your mind that it is not true. Why should you be angry anyway? The mind has got the habit to think something always. The mind itself is Zero, so let thoughts come and go, why should you worry?

Let's say this room is made open to all, and all can come in. Why should you worry? When you worry, you don't make it open. The mind should be open. You can control the mind, why not? If sadness comes, you never think of pleasure. Do you ever think of pleasure? And when pleasure comes, you forget sadness: Both are there, and the mind always acts in a different way. One day you say "He is my friend, and the next day, "He is my enemy." The mind doesn't accept. Why should you be angry? Make the room open and anybody can come in and sleep. Why should I worry? What can I do? In the same way, make your mind so that nothing is bad and nothing is good. Then the mind becomes very easy to control.

When you sleep, do you control your mind or not? Does the mind go away when you sleep or not? There you want to forget, but here you don't want to forget. So, when you are awake you don't want to control your mind. You always want something more and more and more. The mind is running or galloping towards hell. It is always thinking of something more, and that is the same for everybody. If you like dancing you want to be better and better, or with anything else you like, the mind is never satisfied.

A man may have crores and millions of dollars, but still he wants more. Is it for eating? Can you eat dollars? The body wants to eat, but the mind doesn't want. The mind is of that type, it never eats. When you eat you are satisfied, but the mind is never satisfied. The mind is a broken thought. When food and water come, it goes off. So the mind is a broken thought. Understand this way.

Why should you be angry, anyway? Does a thought ask you if it can come? It never asks your permission. You accept it and you become angry, what is the use of it? Keep the door open, and anybody can come in. Rats can come, dogs can come, anybody can come, why not? The door is open.

When you sleep you forget everything; your body, your mind, everything. You don't want to remember. But suppose someone wakes you, you say at once, "I want to sleep," you want to forget. But once awakened, you want to know "Where are my things. What has happened,. What are you looking at?" You may get angry. What is the use of getting angry? You do the thoughts. You are the maker of your own thoughts

If you are eating lentils and there is a stone in it and your tooth breaks, whom to blame? You wanted to eat. You want to enjoy everything, but troubles come. Why do troubles come? They are nothing, they don't exist. Be always happy.

You can understand in a fraction of a second. So fast, faster than the mind. The mind works here. If the mind works to the other side, then at every point you become He. It takes no time for this. Whatever comes to the mind, the mind will say, "Not true!" You are always engrossed in the wrong things. If you take the right things in the mind, it takes you to the right point. I can say this so strongly. Why do I say it so strongly? This is the main point. Because I forget the things in my mind so easily that I can say to go against what is not, as soon as it appears.

* * * * * * * * * *

January 12, 2000

Questioner: This morning you asked me, "How do you feel?" And I said, "I am frustrated!" I came to you to find real happiness. That is what I want. And I am listening to your lecture which makes me frustrated because you negate what is important to me. So what should I do?

Maharaj: Yes, I asked you. You said, "I'm not feeling very well. I feel frustrated."

Questioner: What should I do? This is not the first frustration.

Maharaj: What is the first frustration? When you come here and want to know real happiness, which is yourself. But you're always involved in that which is not. When you come here, you should put a Zero on the world, that is the main point. Still play your part, no harm. You should know it's a play. You're playing a part. That doesn't mean that you are what your playing. You are not the doctor (the questioner is a psychiatrist), I tell you. You may say anything, "I've done this much, and I've done this. I know this much, I know this." This is all about Knowledge. Knowledge should be ended because your Self has no Knowledge and no Ignorance. When you dream, what do you do, tell me? You forget yourself completely and you do something else there. Do you take it true or not?

Questioner: Yes, I take it true.

Maharaj: You kill somebody in a dream. Short and sweet now. In a dream, you kill someone and you feel guilty. And then some knock comes on the door. You think "Aargh! The police have come to arrest me!" and you awake. Have you done anything? It's the same way here also. One should understand. Why does one have to go to a Master? For understanding, nothing else. Understanding of what? Your Self, which you have forgotten.

You take this "doctor," which you are not, as true. You never killed anyone in the dream, but did you experience that or not? Then somebody comes and knocks on your door and you think that the police have come to arrest you. "Aargh!" Then awakening comes. When awakening comes, does the feeling of killing remain? The feeling of killing goes off at once. "I've done nothing," you say. "I am a simple person. I don't even have a gun. I've not killed anybody. I have done nothing." But still did you experience it or not? It's the same way here, you experience many things. Go ahead, experience, but still say it is not true. Have that much courage. You don't want to say no to that which is not.

Have the courage. It is not, no? When you sleep does the doctor remain? Everything goes to Zero.

So, why are you afraid or frustrated? Huh? Nothing to be frustrated about here. Why to be frustrated? You have to know your Self, which you have forgotten. Due to Ignorance, you have forgotten it.

You people in the West often call a woman your friend. In India we say wife. That is the difference, nothing else. Friend and wife are both one, take it for granted. I take it for granted. When you say, "She is my friend," I think she is married to you. Anyway, not to worry about this. The social life is such. Here the social life doesn't allow you that freedom. In India and Pakistan people don't do anything unless you get married. In the West you have the divorce, also. Here this disciple, (Maharaj mentions an Indian disciple's name), says he can't divorce because he is bound to his wife. "How can I break it?" he says. It's a knot.

In India during the marriage ceremony, a knot is made between the woman's sari (dress) and the man's shawl and they both are combined there. (A disciple used the word joined.) Yes, that is the way. And that you cannot leave. You have to understand that. The husband says, "I will help you in every way," but nobody does anything. What to do? One wants that the woman should be relieved and helped, but nobody does it. It is just like in the court of law. You say, "I will tell the whole truth and nothing but the truth," and you say it with a Bible in your hand. But you say everything wrong, you can't help it. One should understand. One should know that this is a part I am playing.

Questioner: Yes, I understand most of your words, but still it is only an intellectual understanding.

Maharaj: It will come, no? The boy goes to school, and then he goes to college and gets a degree. When he gets the degree, he says, "I am a doctor, or a barrister," or whatever it may be. But that degree is not true. You have to find out your own degree! Find out "Who am I?"! My Master, Siddharameshwar Maharaj, always told that, "Know thyself and you know the world." The Christian Bible has told the same.

Shri Krishna has said, "Unless you know yourself, whatever you do is useless." Nothing is true. You may be married to many people, but still where are you? You don't know yourself, and you get married to others. So, he told me that he can make civil marriages (Talking about a western priest in the room who is a disciple). He can do it. He's not a married person but still he can perform the real marriages as a priest. But where are the real marriages for you? They are "so-called" marriages. Don't worry if you do that. Get them married! What harms anyone? One only has to say that she's your wife and he's your husband, and that ends the matter! Your mind is changed, nothing else.

There is no knot in America or France and Western countries because it is just a ceremony, but it's better not to dissolve the knot also. No need. You think you have to dissolve that which is not. You take it to be true. So, intellectually one can understand, but practically you cannot understand. Why? You have got some love for this whole world.

Questioner: I'm not sure exactly.

Maharaj: Not sure, but still you've got the love. Don't say that I'm not sure. You have! The day when you will feel that nothing is true, that is the Reality. Do you remain yourself or not? You without you now. You still take the doctor as yourself. You are from Germany, no? Forget everything. (Maharaj then tell the story of the argument over whether Bombay was to be with Gujarat or in Maharashtra. It was a political decision that was determined on January 26th, 1954.) Maharaj says: "Why should I think I am a Maharashtran, or a Gujarati. I never cared for that. I don't belong to anything. I'm not Gujarati, nor a Maharashtran, and not an Indian, and not an American." Don't be anything. When you are something, a fear remains there, because you have become something.

Questioner: I understand. I am not very much identified with my country or my profession. But still there are desires, for example, having fun, marriage, children and all these things.

Maharaj: Desires may be there. It's a bodily desire not yours. You don't know yourself. You take the body as yourself, the mind as yourself. You take the mind as yourself, and by mind you have become a doctor. Otherwise you are just like me.

Questioner: My mind?

Maharaj: The mind's work is not you. You have to go beyond the mind, and there it is just Knowledge. And when you go beyond that, you come to Zero. And if you say Zero is true, it is the ego, Illusion. You have to go beyond ego. Understanding should come, nothing else. When that understanding comes, then you don't remain yourself. You die yourself. You're not a living person. The body lives with Knowledge only. Everybody is living with Knowledge only, but understand that Knowledge has got an end. "I" have no end. Who are you to give Reality any end? There is no end you can show.

Knowledge has increased so much, and Ramdas in **Dasbodh** has showed that it is Zero. You have become something which you are not. What is required is to put a Zero on it. You have to! Very few can understand, agree! But still it is my duty to give out whatever it may be.

You are not the body, you are not the mind, you are not the doctor, you are not Ignorance, and not Knowledge also. In the beginning, the Master gives Knowledge, and in the end the Master says, "Put an end to the Knowledge, Knowledge is ego." Everyone thinks that "I know everything," or not? "I know what I know," he says. How can others know what you know? Nobody can know. Can anybody know what you want to know? It's impossible. But if you go to the bar, then I can think that you go there to drink, nothing else. You may drink or not drink, that is a different question.

Be in the world but don't be a worldly person. You want to be something, and then want to do something. Forget that, say that "I am not." When you sleep, do you forget you're a doctor or not? Do you forget your house or not? You forget everything, and that is called the Zero state. Living in this world, understand that it is not true, and be in it. That is the brave man's work. Have bravery. Follow me?

Questioner: Yes. Maharaj, two words you used, intellectual understanding and practical understanding. How do you transfer the first to the second?

Maharaj: When intellectually you understand..., say that there is poison written on a bottle with poison in it, no? You understand intellectually. (Everyone laughs) If you drink that, that is practical. (More laughter) Be practical in that way.

Questioner: If someone understands intellectually, then where is the basis for frustration?

Maharaj: It must be practical, but still you don't understand it is not true! That's my point. You take it true. And still you say..., what did you say? "I cannot understand you, Maharaj." What to do! When you say Zero, nothing is there. (Maharaj then tells a story regarding intelligence): When God wanted to give the intellect to all, it was declared, "Come at 4 p.m., I will give it then." Gujaraties were very shrewd people, so they decided not to sleep, and instead they came at 3 p.m. and just sat. (Maharaj was told this story by someone from Maharashtra) The Maharashtrans were sleeping and enjoying, so they didn't get to the place until 6 p.m. God had left by then, so they phoned God and asked him what they could do. God said, "I have delivered everything to everybody. Nothing remains with me. But when I was handing out intelligence something of it might have fallen on the floor, take what you can find."

And so I can dare say, that at the moment you understand theoretically, and that means you don't understand. It still has to be practical. Theoretical should become practical. Don't throw off anything. Why throw off this? (Maharaj points to the marble counter where his water pot is.) Without the marble top how could I put this pot there? It is useful there, so let the marble top be there to support the water pot, but say that it is not true. Understanding should be changed.

For a realized person, the wife is Brahman, and the sons are also Brahman, and the wooden table where you sit is also Brahman. Everything is He, then why to make a difference? You make differences. Why do you think of differences? When it starts from nothing, it can be made to Zero at any moment. If that understanding comes, then you are He, otherwise not, and that is practical. Theoretically everybody understands, but nobody goes beyond Zero. They don't know what is Zero. Somebody asked in Sedona, Arizona, "How to cross Zero?" How to cross it? It is nothing! Then, what to cross, tell me? You want to cross that which is nothing, no? When you say there is nothing in the house, is it Zero or not? You have crossed it, but you don't think that you have crossed it. And that is practical.

Why do you fear to say that Zero is Zero, tell me. I always openly say, "You are not here, whatever name is given." Where is your name? Can you show me your name? Whomever he may be. He may be God also, but he cannot show he is God, because God is only my thought. God is your thought, he has not created. Say "I have created the world." I have got that audacity or that power to say, "I've created." Knowledge created. "I am" is Knowledge.

But sometimes it doesn't happen according to your wish because you've taken another form. In a dream a king becomes a beggar. When you become the beggar you have so much time on your hands. Does anyone wait for a beggar? But when the king gets that dream very late in the morning, when he awakens he thinks, "All are waiting for me. But is this true, or am I a beggar?" He has to pinch himself.

You have to pinch yourself sometimes. "Am I this, or That?" You are so much engrossed in it. I always forget where I sleep. I forget. I don't remember where I am, I tell you.

Questioner: Excuse me Maharaj. As I understand it when I'm dreaming and when I wake up, I find the dream was false. Now I'm living, and when I die I'll find that this life was false. Maybe there will be one more life, and I'll find that was false also. Quantum physics tells me that this body is false because it's 99.9% empty space. My thoughts, if I observe for five minutes, I find they're not mine. And that leaves me like an orphan.

Maharaj: If you don't know it's not true, it remains. But when understanding comes, where do "you" remain?

Questioner: That "I" doesn't go off.

Maharaj: "I" is ego, no? Forget that ego. The Master makes your ego go to Zero. He has got that power. Knowledge is ego. Knowledge of first life, second life, third life, fourth life. Many lives you have got, but is that due to ego or not? You don't understand. "I have to take another birth." Who says that? You are birthless and deathless. Yourself is He. One should be He, anybody, whether he be rich or poor. Why is he called rich? Someone has ample money, so he's rich. Another has no money, so he's poor. Is he rich or poor? Can you define anything? You cannot define? You give the value to it. Money has been given value by your mind.

Does a dog care if you throw a hundred rupee note at him? The dog says, "You're a foolish person. I want bones to eat." And that bone has no blood. He chews the bone and gets the taste of blood and he thinks: "Oh, it is a very good bone." He thinks that the taste is from the bone, but actually it comes from his own gums and teeth. You take it true, what to do?

So it is told in the Morning Bhajan that when you chant the name of God, "Ram, Ram," it means "I am not this." Whatever name may be yours, it is the same. You are not this. His name is "Doctor." Your name may be anything, but still, that is not you. When you think like that, your mind doesn't put anything on you now. No birth and death for you.

Questioner: Maharaj, for 2 hours I have been travelling to come and see you. And suddenly I find that nothing exists. What is the relevance?

Maharaj: Nothing exists, but you exist. The hearer remains only because he is in Ignorance. To get rid of the Ignorance you come here. So, I am not going to pour more Ignorance in you. Ignorance has been poured in you even by spiritual teachers. Many Saints say, "Do this, and do that. What I say, do it!" I never say that. I say, "You are He. You are the Highest Power." It depends on you, how you take it now. If you put a Zero on all this, and say that nothing is true, then you can have that Power, otherwise not. Who gets the Power? The one who doesn't care for God, who doesn't care for Illusion, or doesn't care for anybody. Why? Because you don't exist. When you don't exist then why to care for others. Others are not there.

All are bubbles in the ocean, and when they break they become ocean. This example I often give. Then who laughs? The ocean laughs. The bubble has become the ocean now. All the other bubbles, they cry. Aaah! What to do? You never die, and you never take birth. But still you have the fear of birth and death, because you think you were born and have become something. Birth and death are nothing. It is not there at all. When you come here to the Master you are given something so strong that you cannot hold it. It is said that if you put the lioness's milk in an ordinary vessel it will break. It requires a golden vessel. If you put it in a golden vessel it remains, otherwise not. Why? Because the lioness has got the power to eat many people. She doesn't care. She's got such power, so how can her milk remain in an ordinary vessel?

When you become He, the Saints are like you. I was also like you when I went to my Master. I was an ordinary person. He changed me, what to do? So, now I have got the Power to change others. If they come here, I try to change them. If you say that "I've got nothing," what then? Nothing is not there. Nothing is always nothing. But what exists behind it, is it there or not! If I say, "Go in that room and find out if anybody's there." You say, "Nobody's there." But you were there. You forget that. You have forgotten yourself.

Ten people were travelling and they crossed a river. They say, "Let us count and see if everybody is here. One, two, three, four, five, six, seven, eight, nine. Oh no, there is no tenth person. The tenth person is lost." Everyone counted and still only nine were counted. All were crying, "One is gone, one is gone." Nobody cries really. It's all nonsense. Nobody cares for anybody, I tell you. It is a system to cry. One wise person was passing by and he asked them, "Why are you crying?" They replied, "Oh, we were ten and we've lost one crossing the river." He said, "Yes, yes, come on now, and count with me." He counted to nine and then the wise man gave a slap to the next man. "Oh, I've found the tenth!" he said. The others were still in doubt. How can it be? When they get the slap from the Master, then they can understand themselves, otherwise not. That slap means, put a Zero on everything, and then you will get that Power. What harm is there?

Questioner: Maharaj, I'm perfectly happy as I am living the way I am. Why should I go for something higher? I am perfectly happy the way I am.

Maharaj: Okay. Why have you come here then, huh?

Questioner: I don't know.

Maharaj: If you had not come here, it is okay.

Questioner: I was just reading this book. I find that everybody talks different language. Languages are so many.

Maharaj: Languages will be many.

Questioner: Osho talks one way, Ramana Maharshi another.

Maharaj: Should the meaning be one or not? One should know what Rama and Krishna told. Why have they told in that way? You don't know that, and you say, "I am happy." I am just asking you, "Are you happy?" Then why do you open your eyes? A happy man never opens his eyes. No need to open your eyes. You're not happy! You may be a rich person and say, "Oh, I am happy now. Everything is okay." Still something is lacking. The mind is of that type. It wants something more and more, more and more.

The Master puts an end to it. He cuts the mind. If one feels that "I'm okay," why you should go to anybody? If I don't want anything, why should I go to the bar, or to Parsi people who sell sweets? No need for me to go. Why should I? Any need? I want something, so I go. But you go to the wrong place. If I go to the bar and ask for sweets they will say, "We don't sell sweets here, we sell brandy and whiskey. If you want that, you can take it." You have to go to the right person to know yourself, but you don't know what you want. Ask your mind what you don't want.

Questioner: Misery, unhappiness; the mind doesn't want that. The mind always wants happiness.

Maharaj: Happiness, okay. But does it get it? So, it is misery when you've not got anything. One man was begging, asking someone for 5 rupees. He said, "Give me five rupees. No, then four rupees fifty paisa. No, then four rupees, three rupees, two rupees," then he said, "five paisa." The man said, "I don't have even 5 paisa (a fraction of a rupee)." Then the beggar said, "You don't have even 5 paisa? Then you are a beggar like me, so let us beg together." It is a nice business to beg.

But you say the wrong things. A business man may be earning twenty or thirty thousand a month, but if you ask him, "How is your business doing?" He will say, "Business is so-so." He will never say "I earn so much!" Why does he fear to say? Because he fears. He thinks that if he says that business is fine, "your eyes will be on my business, and I will lose it."

But realized persons have nothing to worry about. They don't lose their business. On the contrary, their business increases, whatever it may be. A realized person says that nothing is true. Have that much courage to say that that which is not, is not. Still, you want to prove that "that which is not" is true.

The mind always wants Zero, nothing else, whatever the thought may be. From where does it come? When you are sleeping, a dream comes. From where does it come? Who brought that, tell me? You don't know your dream also. In a dream you are in complete Ignorance doing nothing, but still you are killing somebody there, or maybe you have become a king. Maybe you are enjoying your dream, but your wife says, "Get up, why are you sleeping so long?" "Oh, I had a good sleep. Why did you awaken me?" And she says, "Go back to that dream." Now you can't get the same dream again because it was not true. What to do?

What is not true, you say is true. What is true, you say it is not true. That is your mind's work. The mind works in that way, what to do? It doesn't like to go to the Reality. It can become your friend or your greatest enemy. If you make him a friend, he'll take you to the Reality and die itself. Say, "I am no entity at all." That understanding should come. That is understanding, but your mind wants misery. Do you always think or not? "Should I do this or that?" The mind's work is thinking.

Suppose somebody is celebrating his 100th birthday and he begins to think, "What if I die tomorrow, what will happen?" He begins to cry and loses his good mood. All the people are enjoying his birthday, but he cries. Somebody asks him, "Why do you cry?" " Oh, nothing, nothing, nothing." He is so ashamed to say that he doesn't want to die. Is there any dead man who says, "I'm a dead person?" or anyone who is sleeping that says, "I'm sleeping?" He'll never say that. If he says he is sleeping, he's not sleeping.

In the same way, you are doing the same thing here. Forget everything. You try to cross Zero. Understand that everything is Zero, nothing else. Crossing Zero is the worst. It's very difficult. If you understand that it's a Zero, then you have crossed it, otherwise not. But you have the love for Zero, for what is not. You have got the love for it, what to do? Everybody has got the love for the eyes, no? If a cataract comes, you go to the doctor and pay thousands of rupees. "Take out my cataract!" When one dies what happens? You forget everything. No eyes and no nose; all gone to hell. Understand this way. Try to understand yourself, nothing else.

One should have the faith in the Master. Otherwise it won't work. Faith should be strong enough. What the Master says is okay. What he does is okay. Suppose you want to make a friendship with somebody. You say, "Oh, we'll go to the bar." Go to the bar! You don't have to drink, but give him that company. Do you give the company to him or not? He wants the company, nothing else. Everybody wants company. The whole world is your company but you have such a nature that you cannot make friendships with anybody. Whatever you like, you want to do that. Who will allow you to do whatever you like according to your mind? You have to give, in some way, here and there! If you put five rupees on the lottery then you can get thousands of rupees. Otherwise not. But if nobody puts in their five rupees on the lottery, how can anyone get the prize?

Here also, it is the same thing. It is nothing. Now put Zero on everything, and what you get is that you can understand yourself. It is not easy and it is not very hard. What my Master has given to me, you can get it on the spot without doing anything. Don't do anything. Bas! (Bas means "enough" in Marathi) Forget yourself. You say, "I exist." I say, "You don't exist." That is the difference. When you don't exist, who speaks? Who talks? Nobody! I never talk, I never speak. I'm a liar, short and sweet. The body is the liar, what to do?

When you go to the cinema the sign for the lavatory is shown saying that the lavatory is that way, but you say, "No, I want the lavatory over here." Who will give that to you? There is a difference there in the mind. The Master gives the address to you, and you want to get it just now. Go to that place and you'll get the place. But also that much time is not required if you understand yourself. But you want to keep that which has to be thrown out, that which you call yourself. You don't want to give that up.

Still, I say "Everything is Zero." Find out it is Zero and that is the work of the brave. Then, do you remain or not? One who says it's a Zero, does he remain or not? How much time does it take? The picture on the screen is either bad or good. Some say good, some say bad. Both have seen the picture, but according to the mind, one says "good" or "bad," or "It was a nice picture." It all depends upon the mind, and what your mind wants.

If somebody gives something to you, then you are happy. But if you don't want it, then it's misery. Find out what that happiness or misery is. Both are thoughts. Everybody is He, and everyone is the Reality, why to worry for anything? You worry because you don't understand yourself, and you don't understand Reality. If you understand, you are the Reality. Then, how much time does it take to make others real?

The black stone that you rub on the piece of gold gives the value of gold. It may be twenty-four, twenty-three, or eighteen carat. That which is useless, a black stone, gives the value to others. So, everything is useless, but if you give the value to Him, "Oh, He is myself," then what remains? You become yourself the black stone, and give value to others. Try to understand Reality. Don't say, "I'm lost, but when I come here..." I give such a Knowledge, but you may not like it. That is possible.

Not everyone can accept what I say. You may be in a bar but you want sweets, or you're fasting then how can you go to a bar? You may think you go to the wrong place according to you, but still that wrong place is not the wrong place. The Master says, "Everything is true, go!" and "Everything is Zero, not true." He says both ways are there. One should find out and understand the Master.

If I say that you are God will you believe me? You won't believe me but if the experience comes, then? "I am the father of God," you will say. And if then God comes to you you will say, "Why have you come? I don't want you." Because you want nothing. If you want something then God is required. Something is nothing and you want everything that is nothing. What can the Master do? So don't worry about it. Your Self is He, I tell you. Understanding should be changed, mind's understanding. Everyone is myself but the mind doesn't agree!

(Maharaj then tells a story from the Bhagavad Gita.) Yudhistir, who was speaking the truth, was asked by the father of Arjuna, "Who died on the battlefield?" Yudhistir said, "Someone died, but I don't know if an elephant died or a man died." You have to tell lies because nothing is true. The world is not true so he told lies there. You can't help it. You have to because nothing is there. There is nothing, but you say, "Oh, say something." I'll say anything to you, it's my choice. You want to put names on everybody. Fathers and mothers have given many names, and now Masters are also giving names. I don't because I don't like to give names. Why to pour more ignorance into someone by giving another name. Understand this way. You want to know, but still the mind doesn't want to know, that's the beauty of it.

Questioner: We want to know, but at the same time the mind doesn't want to know. Is it up to us, or is it up to the Master, or is it up to both Master and disciple?

Maharaj: Master has nothing to do. He's not the Master. Disciple remains and he wants something. Master doesn't want anything. So, it is the mischief of the disciples. Why the Master? I say, "You are He," but I am also yourself. I make these marriages. (Referring to the questioner who is a former catholic priest now performing marriages in the USA.) If water is put here in this pot, that is also a marriage. Both are combined there. The pot has got some water and then it is combined with more. So, what is the mischief of the Master? It's your mistake because you've forgotten yourself. One who doesn't know himself, he will ask somebody, "Who am I?" What does he have to tell you, tell me?

Questioner: But you say frequently that only the Master can take you beyond Zero. That's what I hear.

Maharaj: That's okay. If you want to go beyond Zero then I can take you. But you must say, "Zero." Keep your mind in that way. In Zero nothing is there. Master takes you ahead, why not? If you go to the market where Mohammedans are selling and ask the price of something, they say something that means he is our man, he is one of us. That means that if he's our man they give him a better price. Follow me or not?

Questioner: Yes, yes.

Maharaj: Where are you from?

Questioner: From Belgium, Maharaj.

Maharaj: If a Belgium man meets you he would say, "He's our man," And if he or your brother sells you something, you will get a better price. If you want to understand Zero, then the Master lifts you up, why not? What is there to lift, because you are He? But you don't want to be lifted.

Questioner: Why?

Maharaj: Why? That's your choice. It's your choice, no? To be lifted or not, that's your choice.

Questioner: If I don't exist Maharaj, how can I choose?

Maharaj: You've got many choices. You exist at the moment as something. Zero let's say. Zero also exists.

Questioner: There are many contradictions here. It is difficult to understand those contradictions. You say that we have a choice, then you say we don't have a choice.

Maharaj: That is correct, no? When you are in choice, there is choice. When you sleep what choice do you have? Maybe you are thirsty, or you want to eat, but you feel sleepy so you say, "Ah, let me sleep now." And even if somebody comes with the best of things that you really like, you still say, "Oh, no, let me sleep now." You want to forget everything. So, everyone has got choice and no choice, and you have become the smallest creature due to the choices and no choices.

Questioner: You say that we exist in the moment, and then you say we don't exist, we are not. You say both. How to comprehend this?

Maharaj: Yes, both I tell you. It is all wrong, but what I say is correct. Why? Because you don't exist. What is your name, tell me?

Questioner: Yogesh

Maharaj: Yogesh! Where is Yogesh, tell me?

Questioner: He's not here, I know. He doesn't exist.

Maharaj: He doesn't exist, but still you say, "Yogesh," what to do? Still you say, "I'm Yogesh." And sometimes people say, "I'm Mr. So-and-so., and I have degrees also." You want to make a big tail of yourself. The mind is of that type. Hanuman has a big tail. (Hanuman is the monkey God, servant of Rama, who symbolizes the mind.) He always wanted to have a bigger and bigger tail always.

If I ask everybody their name and I don't ask you, you will say, "Maharaj didn't ask me my name," and you will feel slighted. But you have no name. I understand, so I didn't ask you. That is my choice. Your choice, or wish is that Maharaj should ask me. All these things concern choice and no choice, and that is the mind's work. It is not your work. Choice is of the mind. You mix everything up, that is the difficulty

Questioner: Does time exist? Do we have a past, present and future? Does time really exist?

Maharaj: No, no time. It's all Zero. By the sun you count day and night. Ask the sun how many years have you passed. "I've never seen day or night," the sun says. You count everything on the sun, how can it be true? When the base is wrong how can it be true? Base is Zero, everything is Zero. So I'll put it in a shorter way. This can break my head. (Pointing to a marble counter top) If I break it into little pieces, then ? It will dissolve in space. One should understand that. It all depends upon your mind, your choices. If I take this (points to his head) and hit it on the counter top, blood is sure to come. But if I break it into little pieces, then how can it touch me? And anyway it touches the body and not me also! That is the other point. In one day you cannot understand everything. Come many times here and you can understand something I tell you. I'm sorry but you must have full faith, then understanding comes, The Master says yes, "You don't exist." Say, "I don't exist." Don't die, but again I tell you that you don't exist but still don't die. And that is the beauty of my telling, which you cannot understand. That is the difficulty

Questioner: Maharaj, is negating neti-neti, the same as remembering the Self.

Maharaj: Neti-neti, means "Aham Brahmasmi," I am Brahman and that is also wrong. How can you be Brahman? Where nothing remains, Brahman also goes off. Nothing touches me and nothing remains. Everything goes to Zero when you sleep. You forget yourself and your mind and only the breathing remains. Do you question anything? You scratch yourself but you are not conscious of it. You don't understand anything at that point. Knowledge is in a subtle form. But to understand what this Knowledge is, your mind must be there.

If a boy goes to his dying father and he says, "Papa I've come, I've come" The father can't speak, he can't respond. What is the use of it? Why should you worry? "Ah, my father has gone!" But you have no father, what to do? There is a saying that when you are living no one cares for you, but once you die then everyone cares for you. "Oh, she was my mother, now she has gone." Now that she has gone you've got that love.

You've got the body. You say, "It's my body, I am this." When one dies what remains of it? It becomes Zero. It has no value at all. This computer is such that it does everything, but it cannot re-connect. The body is a computer, but nobody knows when the connection or disconnection comes. And when you say it is in God's hands, it means Chaitanya, the Power. So, when the Power is there everything comes up. No Power, then it won't come up. Understand! If understanding is there, then it's okay, everything is okay. Otherwise it is Zero, which means you take it true.

When I say everything is Zero you still take it as true. And that is the madness of the ignorant person. You cannot say what he will take as true and what not. "I'm the best robber," he says, what to do? "I'm the best robber." He takes pride in it. How can you tell him? You should tell him, "You're the best robber, but don't rob me." Say that much. Have that much caliber to tell him.

"Don't rob me! Rob everyone else, I don't mind. I'm not going to tell anyone you are a robber. Why should I? I say "You are He."

One man was killed by another man and a third man witnessed it. Someone asked the witness, "What did you see?" He said, "I don't know anything." For he knew he was the killer, the one killed and the one who witnessed. All were himself, so what to say? Whose name should be given?

You don't understand, "Who am I?" first. Find out yourself; "Who am I?" "Know thyself and you will know the world." You cannot know the world unless you know yourself. Everything depends on your mind. If mind becomes no-mind and you go and ask someone on the road "Who am I?" or "What is my name?," or "What is my address?," they will take you to Pune (Pune is a city outside of Mumbai) and put you in an asylum. When you don't know your name, what will they do, tell me?

You forget everything. But a realized person doesn't forget anything. They know everything, and still they say it's not true. That is the beauty of it. Understanding is the beauty, nothing else. Once you understand, everything is okay. If you don't understand, then everything is Zero. Because you don't know you give some value to Zero. You say that it's marble, what to tell? You say, "I'm something, I'm Yogesh." What to tell to Yogesh? You're doing all yogas, what to tell him! You are the Lord of the yoga, is there anything to tell you? (The name Yogesh means "Lord of Yoga.") Let your yoga be there. Don't tell me your yoga because I am quite contrary to that! I don't agree with that! You are so open, why should yoga be made to know himself? Eye sees, no? Who sees that you're there? Who smells here? Nose smells. Who speaks here? Understanding should come, that is the meaning of it. So, know thyself, understand yourself.

Questioner: I have read Nisargadatta Maharaj and he says that even meditation is not necessary. It's a very slow process.

Maharaj: But has he given any other process? He has not given, no? Then what will you do? He wrote everything, but something remains to tell. I don't want to comment on anybody. I'm the last person to say anything. He was my co-disciple. He's here. (Pointing to his picture hanging on the wall.) He was a disciple of my Master, but he didn't show, what is the use of it?

When I was there in San Diego, one woman phoned me. She had been with Nisargadatta and was doing meditation for over 20 years. She said, "After the year 2000 I am going to leave meditation." If everyday you eat rice and dhal, do you get tired of it or not? Eat some cake! "Give me something," you'll say. She was also tired. I told her my Master had told me to forget meditation. Just be in yourself. He, Nisargadatta, didn't tell that, what to do? He would have shown that way. Meditation is not required, agree! If you go to the doctor and medicine is given you're okay. But how can you tell about him (Nisargadatta) now! He understood but he didn't tell. One of his close disciples told me that he never told us to leave meditation. But if he had said that you can leave meditation, and that meditation is not required, can you leave meditation or not? You have got that thinking power, no?

What the Master says you have to do it. One plus two is three. I say "One plus two is four.!" I can prove it, why not! The fourth means that I am there, the Reality. Who knows it? So one plus two is four. He, the Master would have told that, why not! I don't know why he didn't, it was his choice. I don't want to comment on anybody because I don't like to comment. He was my co-disciple and he was elder to me. But still, the mind can take you anywhere if you understand that, otherwise mind becomes dull. If you don't work the machinery it becomes rusted. Rust comes.

My Master told me to teach so that his Knowledge doesn't get lost. I started very late, in 1983. I never wanted to be a Master. What to do, tell me! If you're a Master people come, many may come. They don't know my English also. Still it happens. Why to be a Master also? It's really a job. So, don't be a Master. Meditation is not to be done forever, I tell you. If you're doing meditation, one day forget that meditation, also and go in the laya. Laya means absorb yourself in the Reality. Absorption is required.

When you are meditating, you are the meditator, the object of meditation is there, along with the process of meditation. You see something there, and a triad appears. Shankara says, "When the triad goes off, then Reality is there always." Nothing to say about it. If you are not here, then nobody's in the house. Wherever it may be, a palace or a room. Nothing to worry. Be out of it. You have to be out of it and then you can understand little by little. One cannot accept everything in a day. So, we meet tomorrow at 3.30 p.m.

* * * * * * * * * *

January 14, 2000

Questioner: Several days ago you spoke about experience and you used wine as an example. You said to drink the wine, but don't take the kick. You went on to say that the kick is not real, but the wine is real. This confused me. Up to that point I felt that both the wine and kick were not real, so I don't understand.

Maharaj: The wine is real up to that understanding, then the kick comes, otherwise not. If I drink water how can I get the kick? Wine is real, the kick is not. In the beginning Knowledge is real, and Ignorance is the kick. Due to Ignorance you say that all the things are true. Knowledge is real there at that point, but finally even the Knowledge is not true. What it shows, you have to say it is true. Still, that kick of the Knowledge is not true. But in the beginning, you say that gold is true, and the ornaments are not true. Finally, you say the the gold is not true, I agree, but when is it not true, then Reality comes in the mind. When you give the example, it is a thing that you can see, something to give you a way to understand . So the wine is real, but the kick is not real, agree?

Questioner: No, I still don't understand.

Maharaj: This is called a handkerchief. You say it is real, but it is nothing but thread. The thread is real, the kerchief is wrong. The handkerchief is in name only. Because you have taken the wine, you have gotten the kick; otherwise you can't get the kick. Knowledge is there so Ignorance comes, otherwise not. When you say, "I am John," John is not true. The connection of the Reality in the body is true at the moment. As long as the body is there, the connection must be there. If you pinch me here then you might say that a realized person should not feel it. He has a body, he must feel it.

I was in France the first time in 1996. I did not know French. The French nurse came to give me an injection. I told her thank you and the nurse said, "I pinch him here and he says thank you." Always the same thing, when you take one dream real, nothing is wrong. Same way here, name is wrong but Knowledge is true. If you go a little ahead then, Knowledge is also wrong. So it is said, "I cannot tell you Brahman also, I become shy to tell you Brahman." You give light to the Brahman. Reality gives light to the Brahman. Brahman means Knowledge and everything you see there. So you have to explain according to the comparison of the time.

She is fair and I am dark. If a black man comes, then he is darker. So, comparison comes. When comparison comes, one thing becomes wrong, so that one thing becomes a kick. The kick means thinking of that comparison.

Suppose one man takes some brandy and he says he can count your coins without a mistake. He has no kick then. The kick is there, but his mind is so strong he doesn't accept that kick. He can count very clearly at that time. He won't make a mistake. Here also, a realized person has got the Knowledge, they understand everything but they don't get the kick of that Knowledge.

A realized person acts in Knowledge always. Without Knowledge how can I speak to you? No Knowledge, then how can I speak? But I understand that Knowledge is wrong, and that what I say is wrong. But still, it is for *whom* I speak that is true. In America, someone asked me that if everything is Illusion, then who are you? I said that I was a "First Class Illusion." I have to say that way. What I speak is wrong, what I say is wrong, but for whom I speak is true. There is the difference. If everything is Illusion then I must be Illusion, no?

So, that Brahman, that Knowledge shows the whole world. It is not true, it shows the wrong things. And you give Brahman the light. You are Parabrahman and you give the light to Him (Brahman). The sun gives the light, but does the sun know that this is marble. He doesn't know. He has no kick of that. If no sun, then you can't see the whole world.

That "You are Brahman," means that Knowledge can see darkness and light. You cannot see the objects without light. Darkness and light are both in Knowledge. They are two sides of one coin. If I show you the heads, the tails is sure to come. And if I turn the coin? The opposite is true. The whole game is on that scale. It all depends on how you look. You have the power to understand.

Nothing is true, but you take everything as true. You take everybody and what the mind says to be most true. It all depends on your mind now. If someone takes a poison willingly they die. If someone tries to give you poison, you will slap him at the moment. "What do you mean, am I your enemy? Why are you giving me poison?" The action is the same for both, but the reaction is different. You see a woman, and a realized person sees Brahman. He sees both, he sees a woman there, but he says she is Brahman. It is quite different.

In an earlier time there was a writing slate, and if you wrote on it you could see the writing. But if you lifted the paper up, nothing was there. It's the same way here, you see everything here which is not. Take that paper up. That paper means Knowledge. Everything becomes Zero. You say that everything is true on the paper, and the realized person says it is not true. That is the difference between them. So, one is called realized and one is called unrealized. He sees the marble also, but if hits his head on it, it hurts. The body must get the hurt. If you say that I shouldn't get hurt, that is a wrong idea.

About eight years ago in Bombay a Saint was not able to walk on the fire, although he said he could. So he got burnt. He also said he could walk on water. He couldn't do that also, so he committed suicide. "I cannot do it now," so he jumped out of a window. The body must bum as long as the connection is there. It must bum.

If you understand that everything is one, then you can realize the Reality. Everything is Oneness. Scientists have discovered the "black hole," but they cannot experience it or go beyond it. The realized person can experience what the scientists cannot. No need for science. Thousands of years ago Indians have found this out. What you see and perceive is just Knowledge. Knowledge is one, and everything comes on this Knowledge, but that Knowledge is also ego. Your ego remains always, but that ego can be killed by only one word of the Master.

Knowledge is ego, take it for granted. "I have realized, and I know everything," is also ego. Socrates said that he knew nothing. Don't show that "I am something," because something is always nothing, what to do? That which is not, how can you say anything true about it? One is also not true. Oneness is not true, that is the main point in it. Oneness means I have become one now, I have become He. Where is the I? That is ego. Understand that way. So whiskey is right and kick is wrong.

Questioner: So the kick is in Knowledge.

Maharaj: Okay, that will do. Knowledge is of something else. Why has the kick come? You have taken the brandy or whiskey. If you take water can you get the kick? The kick is wrong, it is not true. You can say anything when you get the kick.

Around 1920, I was a young man at that time, and a man under the influence of the mind began to act like Krishna. Was he Krishna? It was the kick of Ignorance. He was an architect, a nice man, but when the mind goes off, what to do? Some ladies near him were shouting at what he was doing. He was a good person, but one can become bad or good in a fraction of a second. Reality doesn't become bad or good. Reality is always good, not to worry for it. Whatever comes on it, it takes up and accepts it, but you don't willingly leave it. You take the kick of it. You cannot leave it. Realized persons see the same things you do, but they understand it is not true, and it doesn't touch them.

All have the kick of Ignorance, no matter if he is a doctor, engineer, or whatever. It is just Knowledge. The Master is the doctor of what? Ignorance. He takes out your Ignorance. Does he take out your fever or not? He gives you Knowledge, understanding. And finally, he has got the power to make you understand that Knowledge is not true. Knowledge is due to Ignorance. Ignorance of Reality.

So, in the examples you have to say that brandy is true and the kick is wrong. Go ahead then. The Master takes you step by step. Say that everything is wrong, and finally, who I am, and who I see, and the witness, is also in Zero. If that understanding comes then you are He. What experience do you want then? At this very moment you are He. So, I say that everybody is He, don't worry. At the moment the handkerchief is true, but it becomes wrong if you understand it is only thread. In that way you have to give examples according to the comparisons.

So, the whole world is shown by that Brahman, that Knowledge. You give power to that Knowledge, otherwise you cannot understand. Knowledge cannot do anything. The body is required for the Knowledge. The eyes cannot see. They can only see when the Power is there, when Knowledge is there. "Why are you looking at my wife!" Foreigners don't worry about that. Somebody asked me what to do if somebody takes your wife. You take somebody else's wife and go. In India it is forbidden. In Italy, England, and America it works. They don't worry.

So what is Reality and what is the kick? Kick is the whole world of Ignorance. Due to Ignorance you see the whole world. You are in sleep, and you are doing nothing, but you sing there in the dream and you become the best songster there. When you awake, you say to yourself, how can I be that? All this is due to Illusion. Illusion makes all this nonsense. You are the Reality. The kick is taken to be true when you see the whole world. Ignorance is true when you see everything. How can it be wrong? "Realized persons are fools," people will say. They see everything and yet they say it is wrong. You see everything in a dream, do you take it true? When you awake, you yourself say nothing is there.

Yourself is the Reality, and what you see and perceive and experience by mind is nothing but Zero or Ignorance. Should you leave this whole world? No, no need. When it is wrong how can it trouble you? Let everything come, but understand it is not true. Your mind should not open it up. If your mind works on it, it will take it to be true. You take it to be true, otherwise you won't do anything. Understanding makes you He, and then that understanding itself goes off. Any other questions?

Questioner: Does it make a difference to you if you have a body or not?

Maharaj: My body is not true. It is not true, so no difference to me. You take it true, so you cry for it. If death comes, I don't care. Why should I care for death? It is a dead body at the moment. It is a living death. When the connection is there, it speaks, thinks and does everything. Connection and disconnection happen, so why should this bulb worry? Electricity doesn't worry.

This fan works by electricity. If electricity stops from its origin, the fan will stop, but the fan doesn't know that I've been stopped and that I can't give air. You feel it. The result is quite different if the electricity is on or not. You cannot make curd unless the milk is spoiled. You have to spoil the milk. Put some salt in it. This (body) is a spoiled container. If you understand the Reality, what is the use of the body? It is of no use, I tell you.

Questioner: So it can be a happiness to get rid of it?

Maharaj: To whom is the happiness? No happiness or trouble, no pleasure and no displeasure. As long as Knowledge is there, pleasure and displeasure remains. As long as the body is there, you have to say something. Good or bad, he has to say. Understand that it is not true. Everything is Zero, whatever it may be. The best of the things that you like, or the body likes, or the mind likes, is nothing but a Zero. That is your base.

The base needs to be very strong or the floors won't remain on top it. If someone gives you millions of dollars, and somebody takes it away from you, a realized person says, "I don't know." It has come, okay, it has gone, okay. It wasn't mine to begin with. For the realized person, everything is his, but still he doesn't feel it. If a dollar note has left your pocket, you search here and there, but he doesn't worry for that. "I don't care for that," he says. You should understand that you are not the body, otherwise you will cry every moment. All cry every moment. Everyone is crying, what to do? At the time of dying, all cry in mind, but at that moment you have no power to say that the body is not true.

The Power goes away, what to do? So if the body is dead or alive, both are equal to the Master. When the body is alive, everyone does wrong things. Everything is wrong, no? So, if someone says to me that I am an ass or a rascally chap, I say that I am a double one. That is the difference. I don't care. If bad words come to me, I say "Very good." Everything is wrong, no? That which is not, which is nothing, can you say anything about it?

So the realized person has the license to prove anything, because the truth is quite different. If ego remains he is lost. Let the ego go. "I am something, I know," this is all egoism, and all the "isms" are equal. "Ism" means ego. "I am there, I am something" is an "ism." "I" is a very strong form of "ism." Understand, and all the "isms" become Zero. He is beyond "isms." Everybody is the same, they work with the "isms," the ego. But try to discard them. It has come from you, that Knowledge, but still, discard it and say that "I am real." Bugs come from your own perspiration, and do you kill them or not? You don't allow them to drink your blood.

Your ego is your dearest son, throw of the ego. (Maharaj tells the story of Krishna and Arjuna and how Krishna, who was a shrewd person, a Master, told Arjuna he couldn't sit on the throne unless he killed his son.) Son in this case means your ego. He couldn't sit on the throne unless he killed his son. Understanding comes when you take out your ego, and then you are always He. No need to understand anything then. No need to read any books, automatically it comes in you. You are everywhere, in all things.

A man who was a realized person and his wife had a child thirteen years old of school age. The wife wanted the child to go to school. So the man took him to school. In the first class he was taught, "Om Namah Siddha." I am He, is the meaning of that phrase. The boy made 1500 verses on that. From where did it come? He had no learning, nor had he heard it before. So the husband asked his wife, "What to teach him now?" The Power is there, no? The Power can do anything.

So, for a realized person if his body is there or not, it is nothing for him. A cyclone comes and goes. Who worries for the cyclone? Only those affected by that, otherwise you just say a cyclone has come and gone. You worry for that because you take it true. The world is a cyclone, nothing else and you are a partner of the cyclone. You say, "I am this." The world then becomes a cyclone and everything becomes a problem for you. Birth is a problem and to die is also a problem. This happens and that happens, many problems appear. Everything has a defect in it because it is not true. When it is true, no defect remains there.

When you are He, why should you worry for death? The body is going to die, let it die. The mind should be changed. The Master doesn't do anything. Your mind gets changed. The Master mesmerizes you. He changes your mind, that is the mesmerizing. Otherwise, I would have to do something. The Master, he takes you up to the right point and from there you will never be mesmerized. You can mesmerize others now, you have that much Power. That Power is the best. Reality is at the base of everything. Why do you say that it is true? Due to

Reality. if no Reality, you cannot say true also. Reality is the base, everything is seen on it. No base, and you can't see anything.

You can put many colors on this wall. If you put black on it you can't put any other color. Black means Ignorance. Ignorance makes such a dirt that you cannot change the color. Take out that color. Master does nothing but still it is a hard job and he does it willingly, what to do? You say it's all mine. Come on, nothing and no one is yours. The Master proves that. Nobody is yours. Is anybody yours? No!

Your body has come from your mother's womb, but still she cannot do anything for you. If you have a disease, the Master can take on the disease, because he has that Power. Why does the mother have no Power? Because she is in Ignorance. The Master can take on any disease. The disciple says, "What to do, what to do?" Forget it! Tell him I've taken his disease. Go! He must be all right, I tell you. There is that Power in the mind of the disciple also, but that much love should be there. The Master can take anybody's disease, what is there?

The body is not yourself, so let any disease come. What harms you? Don't go for that experience, or try to help anyone, just say that I have the Power to accept anything. It is not necessary to do that, no need unless that opposite party has that much love for you. Then you can say don't worry. Have that much courage also. Courage is not a simple thing. The Master doesn't fear anything. Fear doesn't come to him. He is fearless. The body gets many fears, even a mosquito makes you fear. When a mosquito comes by, hmmmmm, you kill it at once. Why, because you don't want it.

Be Powerful, don't worry for anything. You worry for very small things. You cry for the smallest things. You break something and you cry. It has just become Zero and that is the only difference. Your heart should be so open that when the death comes, who cares for the dead body. It is a dead body at the moment.

When understanding comes you fear none. Nobody can make you fear. Everybody fears the thief. He doesn't do anything, but still people fear him. The Master doesn't mind anything; but your mind always says "I've done wrong." Be so open and heartless now. Don't worry for anything. No heart for you and no-mind for you. Be no-mind and no heart. If the heart is there the body runs, but if the heart stops then gone forever. Same way, if the mind becomes no-mind, then? The mind doesn't remain, but He remains always. Nobody wants to become no-mind, what to do? How can I be no-mind? People think I'm mad. But they're really mad, I tell you. Because I know that it is not true. You take it true, and due to that, you fear. Forget the fear.

You are subtler than the space. What can harm you? Everything is He, no? So nothing troubles Him. He doesn't fear anything, so He is fearless. The space which you perceive has some fear in it, but Reality that is there, which is subtler than space, has no fear in it. Space can be perceived and felt. Reality cannot, so forget the space and you are He, always. Everything comes upon you and goes away. Thoughts come and go away or not? Good thoughts go away or not? So what is bad and what is good? Bad thoughts come and you worry. What is going to happen? Nothing is going to happen. When it doesn't exist, what will happen? Thoughts are nothing, no? From your mind they have come. What can anything do to you? Bad and good thoughts come from your mind. Whether high tide or low tide, the ocean doesn't worry. It doesn't become bigger with high tide, or smaller in low tide.

So don't be small or big. This is all due to Ignorance. You have become this and due to that Ignorance you worry for everything. Never worry for anything. Say, "Everything is my thought." Then, nobody is bad and nobody is good. Then you are out of bad and good. How to be out of bad and good? Thoughts come, both bad and good, and you make a difference there, but both are one.

When understanding comes then nothing remains bad and nothing is good. You run after the good. You ask God for the good. That which is not, you don't understand. If you are not, then? Why to ask him for anything? Your ego should go off. The ego is the devil. Reality doesn't die. First, the Master says you become Brahman. The Master says that you are Brahman now, but that is also ego. Forget that ego, that Knowledge and say, "It is not true, and I don't exist." If you don't exist, what have you become? Nothing has become, because Reality is always there.

Nothing is done but you feel "I've done something." You see this room and you call an interior decorator. Does he make one inch more? Nothing! He says, "Put here, put there," and then you give money to him. No difference. The mind is of that type. It wants to make some difference. Forget that difference. Reality is one, no difference in it

Be the Reality and stay in it. You will be always be happy. Where would unhappiness come? When there is no duality, where does the unhappiness come from? Two's a company, Knowledge is okay, but three is a crowd. The whole world you have prepared is a crowd, and that is what makes unhappiness. Don't be unhappy. Have the Knowledge, but say it is nothing. Here there is no company, you are without company. He doesn't take any touch of it. So, be in the water but don't get wet.

Do everything, but say it is not true, that is the point. One must play one's part. You have taken a part and you have to play your part. The Master won't pay you, so you will be hungry. The belly wants. So do everything but understand that "I am He, at every moment. I do nothing." Your mind should not be heard from. Things may happen against your wish also, but the wish is not true. Then you can be out of it, otherwise not.

Questioner: When we listen to you it sounds very simple, but it comes again.

Maharaj: Put a whitewash on it. You should know whitewash. You put another color over it. It is not true. That is the real color. Do everything, but say it is not true.

Questioner: It helps to hear it again and again.

Maharaj: That is churning. Churn again and again. Cows churn the grass again and again and it becomes milk. This is all a game. Lose that game by understanding. Do everything, play the game, but say it is not true. When you say it is not true, you don't go after it. Everybody chases for happiness. Don't chase your mind. But if you chase my mind, you become no-mind. Be no-mind and you will be happy.

To be in the vicinity of the Master is not necessary. Listen to what he says and accept it. He makes you no-mind, don't worry. It depends upon you and how much you accept. Accept it in the right way and you will say bye, bye, to the Master. The Master has given by his grace, so whom to worship now?

I worship my Master only. And people wonder why I worship him. If one has no love for that, they don't worship, but Master's mind doesn't work that way. It is no-mind. But still he does that worship. It is not habit also. You do it for pleasure. What to do now after understanding? What to do? Everything is Zero, from every direction and all around, it is Zero.

As long as the body is there, Zero remains. He says that you are He, but you say that you are not He. That is the main point. The ego comes there, it is such a rascally chap. The Master doesn't want to prove anything. He doesn't want to be Master. If someone comes to him, he says this is my point. If you understand, understand. Otherwise go. The mind works both ways. It is your friend, and your enemy. What to prove, Zero is Zero always. So, we will see you tomorrow.

* * * * * * * * * *

January 20, 2000

Questioner: Siddharameshwar Maharaj said that whatever the intellect perceives it becomes. And you said that when you eat a pineapple, you become a pineapple. Does that imply that the experiencer becomes the experience?

Maharaj: How can you become a pineapple? When you eat a pineapple, how can you be a pineapple? It's impossible. You take the taste of the pineapple. If you eat fish, do you become a fish? No, you taste the fish. Same way when experiences come, to whom do they come? There is nobody except Him in the world, so who will taste whom? The question doesn't arise. Experience only comes up to Knowledge. Up to Knowledge you get the experience. Then you become the Knowledge, I agree. Beyond Knowledge there is Zero, nothing is there. And beyond Zero you have to go. You have to cross Zero. How can you be Zero then? And who will experience that? 'The question doesn't arise. If you understand yourself when you sleep, what do you experience? You experience nothing there, you are in Zero. But still you don't go beyond it. If you go beyond, then even in your sleep you are there.

In our Indian custom a boy asks his mother, "When you sleep where do you go?" The mother says, "You go to heaven." She doesn't know what heaven is, and the boy doesn't know. So, why do they say like that? You go to heaven, but nobody knows. Suppose you want to go to India on a plane, but you don't know where it is. So you might go past India. You have to get down but you don't know where. Without knowing how can you get down?

Same way here also, up to experience is okay. The experiencer becomes the experience. That is Knowledge, but you have to go beyond Knowledge. The Master takes you beyond Knowledge. And what is that? Yourself. Self without the self. There is no self there. You feel you become something, but there is nothing there. There is nothing except Him. He is everywhere and anywhere.

The gunas are there but He doesn't take the touch. If you eat a pineapple how can you be a pineapple? It's impossible. When you taste something, that is not yourself. When you experience yourself, still you are in ego. The question of experience doesn't come. So, you prove yourself by negation. In the scriptures it says, "Neti, Neti." What does that "Neti" mean? What you see by the eyes or the mind is not He. So He is also beyond that. So He is beyond "Neti, Neti." Neti means that you are not what you see. You say this is marble, (Pointing to a marble counter) but it is not marble. He is beyond marble. So when you say, "I am Knowledge," you are still in Knowledge because "I" remains there. Knowledge brings experience and what experience do you want? No experience remains because you don't remain yourself there.

Somebody asks, "Who is there?" You answer, "Nobody is there." But you are there or not? You forget yourself, always. You cannot forget Him, still you forget. Still, He is there, He doesn't go away. When you see the picture, the screen goes away (because your mind is on the picture), and you see the picture only. When you see the screen, then you don't see the picture. That is the difference. Difference is always there. And by experience how can you be He? You can become Knowledge. Up to Knowledge you can be, I agree. What he has told, that by the experience you get the experience. You become yourself the experience. What he has told is not wrong. But where there is no experience, it is not yourself also. There is no God also. It is all a whitewash.

If you put a whitewash on the colors, all the colors go off. Put a whitewash on everything. Whitewash means, it is nothing. What you see and perceive is not, it is not there. What you see and perceive and experience by mind is not true. He is beyond the mind. No question of mind comes there. The mind should be avoided.

So it is told by Krishna, "Your mind is the bondage." There is no liberation and no bondage on you. You are free from liberation and you are free from bondage. Suppose you say, "I am in bondage." Who is going to tell you that you are not in bondage? Due to the body you say you're in bondage. You believe in so many things. Understanding should come. The Master gives the understanding and he takes you beyond understanding. That is the teaching of a Master. Some Masters take you only up to Knowledge. They put you there and say, "Oh, you are that." You experience Knowledge but Knowledge is not true. Try to understand what Knowledge is.

(There are identical twins in the room) There are two brothers. If you see him you can forget his brother and if you see his brother, you can forget him. But still differences are there. They are twin brothers and after ten minutes the other was born. You forget one or the other, but still they are not lost. Paul is not Peter, and Peter is not Paul. He may forget it. If you forget the Reality whose fault? It's your fault. If you remember the Reality then? You are beyond Knowledge and Ignorance. Knowledge comes from Ignorance, take it for granted.

You people all like Knowledge, Knowledge, and more Knowledge. You want to know the Knowledge. What is Knowledge? Knowledge is Zero. If you understand that Knowledge is not true, then you can go beyond Zero. It starts from there. The whole world starts from where? Space. No space, then one cannot remain there. (Pointing to an object.) This can be broken and become space in a fraction of a second. Break it and it will run away in the air. It becomes space.

What you see and perceive is nothing but space only. That you should understand and experience! And if you experience that what happens? You go beyond experience. You can't be a pineapple by eating a pineapple. You taste the pineapple, no? You like the taste, I don't. It is my choice. That depends upon the person. What you experience is not bad or good. The liking of the person depends on his mind.

Everyone says, "God is great." I say he is not great. Do you agree with me? How can he be great? He created the whole world which is not true. How can the Creator be great, but still people say so. Understanding should come. The Creator is the worst. Your father and mother created you, and you came in the world and are experiencing the worst in it. Whose fault? Is it the Creators fault or not? You are a fault of the Creator.

So the Creator is not good, I say. They say he should be worshiped. If the Creator comes to me, I will put him in jail. He made a mistake. Saints are of that opinion, they understand that way. They say in the scriptures it is a Lila. Lila means play. It is God's play and you have to enjoy that play, the results of it. Whose fault is it, tell me? Understand this way.

You can't be a pineapple, agree? You taste the pineapple. If you become a pineapple, then what will you chew? Don't be a pineapple, have the taste of the pineapple. You can say, "Very good, very nice." Have the experience, but it is not true. What you experience is not true. You have to go beyond experience. And how to go beyond experience? The Master knows the way, how to go beyond experience. He teaches you, and he makes you understand how to go beyond Zero.

Understand, understand it is Zero! If you understand Zero, then you are beyond Zero or not? You don't understand. You take Zero as true. So to go beyond Zero means that Zero is not true. To go past Zero means to give an exam of Zero, then you have the mastery of Zero and then you get the degree. Say it's Zero and you get the degree. It is nothing, but still you give value to it.

A blind man gives value to light or not? He gives value to it because he cannot see it. Do you give value to the light? No need to give value to it. One should understand in that way. Is it true or not.? So, it is told to know thyself and you will know the world. People go in the world to see and find out how much Knowledge is there. But if you know yourself then, you don't take yourself as a body. You are not the body, you are this Knowledge. Knowledge knows everything. Why do you want to know? Because your ego is there. "I want to know." "I want to know," that is ego.

Unless you drop the ego you cannot be He. You can't experience Him, but He is there. After you leave the ego, if you forget the Reality, He is still there. No need to experience Him. Who will experience the Reality? You are He. Understand that way.

What do you have to do to know yourself? He is so subtle, subtler than the space. In space you experience something, but there is no space also. When there is no space, one is called the best person. Krishna said, "There are two kinds of people in the world: one is Knowledgeable, the other is not." Who is best? Finally, the one who is called the best is the one without Knowledge *and* without Ignorance. Where there is no Knowledge and Ignorance, you go beyond words. Words come from space. If you go beyond words then you go beyond space. No space, no words can come. Up to the space words come.

So it is said, "Words come back from there. They cannot approach me." When you go beyond space, what word can you say, and who will say? And who will experience? As long as the pineapple is there you will experience it. But there is nothing but Him in this whole world. What to experience? So don't be a pineapple or people will eat you. Say, "I taste the pineapple, I taste the Knowledge."

What is Knowledge? Knowledge is my thought only. Have that much courage to say. Then the Creator is your thought only. The Creator is not true, no? You say the Creator is true. I don't agree with that. Say yourself that you are the Creator, that will do. You create many good and bad things. Then you compare, and the mind comes. Who is rich, who is poor? The mind compares always. But if the mind goes to the Reality, it becomes Zero itself. All the religions are nothing but "isms," nothing else.

What is the real "ism"? I don't exist. When you don't exist, then what "ism" will you use? All "isms" go off. You get more Ignorance with Knowledge. "I like to know," you say. What to do? The one who doesn't want to know anything is the Reality, I tell you. Why to worry for anything. Does a baby worry? It doesn't care for anybody. If he wants to cry, he cries. If he wants to laugh, he laughs. So all this nonsense is the mind's work.

So, go beyond the mind's work and understand the Reality. The mind cannot know Him. In a fraction of a second you can become the greatest of the greatest, or in a fraction of a second you can become the smallest of the smallest. Be out of the clutches of your mind. The mind cannot experience Him. If you experience him, you experience something else. Until your mind gets absorbed in laya (dissolution), you will experience. After that, what and who will experience? When you collect your experiences you collect only Zeros. Reality is beyond Zero.

Krishna carried on doing many activities. He told wrong things also. He had four wives and said he was a celibate. What to do? Another Saint was there and though he ate so much food daily he said, "I never tasted anything. My tongue has not tasted." Understanding should be there. When eating, the body eats, I don't eat. You say, "I eat. I see." You cannot see anything. You say, "I speak," and that is ego. Try to know your ego.

Unless you know your ego you cannot know God. How to know Him? You are He, there is no difference between you and Him. Forget the body and mind and then what remains? Knowledge remains, and then Master takes out that Knowledge. That Knowledge becomes ego, and the ego erases the Reality. You can taste the pineapple but you cannot taste the Reality. You have to be the Reality, and then you are "Real."

People say that in this birth you cannot get it and after many births you will get it. I say that they are fools. To know oneself, how much time does it take? Know thyself, and you will know the world. I am not this body or mind. The mind is thoughts, they come and go, but you ever remain. Where do you go?

I always say, "If you are in hell or heaven, you never forget yourself." So that which cannot be forgotten is yourself. And it cannot be known also. If it is not forgotten, how can you know Him also? Without knowing you are He. Without experience. No experience is required. Forget this, and you are He. Make a little difference there, but that difference counts so much. The world has come up along with the mind and everything which is not necessary.

Everyone knows I am naked under my clothes. Everybody. Taking off the clothes is not needed. Everyone understands, "I am naked under my clothes." Understand it is not true, be naked in that way. Will you become naked when the Reality is there? Where does it go? It cannot be experienced by anybody. When you say that you have understood the Reality, you have not gone to that place or seen that place. When the ego comes how can you know Him? The ego is the only hindrance.

The sun was there but the clouds came. You couldn't see the sun. The clouds have not erased the sun. The ego has not erased the Reality. The Reality is everybody and everybody is He. So I always say, "You are He, why do you worry?" But you don't want to be He, what to do? You like the pineapple, but you don't eat the pineapple. What is the meaning of it? You like it but you can't eat it. Why? You become a pineapple.

Questioner: Why are we doing so much in this world?

Maharaj: Because Knowledge always wants more and more, but Knowledge is not true. When one dies, what remains? When you take the birth again, where has that Knowledge gone? It goes away in a fraction of a second. When you sleep you forget the whole world, body, and mind. But even one thought won't allow you to sleep. Thought is the mind's work. So, forgetting yourself is the best. Forget that ego. Unless the ego goes off, you can't know Him.

Krishna told Arjuna after he won the battle that although he won the battle, he can't sit on the throne until he kills his son. Who will kill his son to sit on the throne? The son means ego and then you can sit on the throne. Forget that ego. Kill that ego and you are He. Krishna was not a foolish person. Arjuna's son was born from himself, but still he has to kill him. Understanding should come. The son has come from him. By Knowledge the ego has come. Kill that ego and you are The Master of Illusion." Be "The Master of Illusion." But you always accumulate what is not.

Questioner: On one side, the Self is called the unknown knower. On the other side, it is said to be self-revealing. It reveals the Self all the time. But you say you can know it.

Maharaj: What is your name? (Tobin) Any need to say that again and again? "I am Tobin, I am Tobin." Any need? No need.

Questioner: But isn't that just a reference to the empirical self, the personality?

Maharaj: Her name is Brigit. Any need to say it over and over, again? Once you know, why to say again and again? People would consider her to be a mad woman. Your Self is nameless. There is no name for you. You have no qualities. And if you know something, how can you know Him? There is only one way. Forget this (Illusion), and you know Him. No words for it. Forget the Illusion and He is there.

You remember Illusion, always. After knowing if you say, "I know, I know," it means you don't know Him. He cannot be known by anybody. But still He is so open to everybody. Follow me?

Questioner: Yes, but it sounds like an empty abstraction.

Maharaj: When you know yourself, what is there to say again and again?

Questioner: Maya is an instrument of the Self. Thoughts are part of Maya. So I prove my existence on the basis of Maya and not of my true Self.

Maharaj: Reality is always open. Unless you know the Illusion, you cannot know Him. What is Illusion? It is what is not true, it is "Maya." It is not. When you say it is not and don't take it true, your Self is so open. Who says it is not true? That is your Self.

Questioner: Do you know yourself by deduction, or is the Self, self-revealing? What you said before feels like you deduce that you are He. I wouldn't call it self-revealing if it shows itself on the basis of deduction, or logic.

Maharaj: Forget this, and you are He. Short and sweet. This is Illusion, it is not true. You know that which is not. That which is not, what do you have to know? Nothing to know. What is nothing, what to know? You know what is nothing. No question of deduction comes. He is so open there.

If you see the picture, the picture is true. If you see the screen, then the picture is not true. There is the difference. No question of deduction comes. That which is not, is always not. You take it true, and I make it not. It is not like that. He is so open, no need to say. That which is not what to deduct and what not to deduct, tell me? Nobody is here from Kashmir, so we say nobody is here from there. All others are here, so we can say that. It just means that they have not come.

Same way here also, you say true when it is not true, so we have to teach you it is not true. And when you understand it is not true, how much do you need to deduct. If you deduct twenty minus Zero, what remains? Twenty remains only, but the twenty never existed. Deduction is only required when you say it is true, then you have to deduct it. When you say Illusion is true then you have to deduct Illusion. And that deduction means Zero. Deduction means that you take it true. Do you give value to that, or not? If you deduct B from A and the value of A is ten and the value of B is seven, you are left with 3, but still it is nothing.

When you give value to something you have to deduct but when you don't, what to deduct? So if you don't give any value to A or B? So what is not, no deduction comes. That is the main point: He is always there and everywhere He is. He is here also, but you don't know Him. So Saint Ramdas said, "What has never happened, why do you ask for that?" Understand deduction. It is Zero and you are He, or not? When you say it is true you are lost.

He asked if you can become a pineapple. How he did he get that in his mind, I don't know? How can you be a pineapple? If you eat fish, do you become a fish? What you eat you cannot be.

Questioner: The common man takes this as true. It is only when you investigate what is real that you see that what appears has no substance.

Maharaj: So you can understand or not? You may be a man of action, I agree, but still you can understand it is not true. Can that understanding come to you or not? Do all actions, but say that I have not done anything. Otherwise a realized person could not stay in the world. He should die. If he dies who will tell you? What to do? Questions always arise. I know it is nothing and I enjoy nothing, a realized person can say that.

You all cry. You all cry in the Illusion. The realized person laughs at Illusion. That which is not, why to worry about it? If you say it is true, deduction comes. You are always He. Don't give value to A and B. then deduction doesn't come. You are ever open, understand this way. The common man can understand also.

Questioner: When you find out that nothing has value, is it by negating? But negating is also a process.

Maharaj: Yes, say it is nothing, negation. But when it is nothing what sort of process is there? If this person is mad, forget him. You know he is mad, so do you forget him or not? In the same way, when it is not true, forget it. You want to find out something. What is it? How can you find out what is not? You make Zero larger and larger. It only makes Ignorance. Knowledge wants to expand but it comes from Zero. Knowledge cannot expand when you say it is not true. That ego wants to know, crush down that ego.

Kill the watchman, the ego, and then can you go inside or not? How much time does it take? You should kill the watchman. Then you can get the master of the house, or kill the master. The ego is the only factor that doesn't allow you to know the Reality. So, what you have learned up to now, leave it. You are not a man or a woman, you are nothing. All are equal, all are One. What remains to be found out now? If everything is gold, what is bad and what is good? If understanding comes, the ego goes off and you are open.

There is no screen between you and Reality. If there were a screen there, I would have to open it. So, no screen. When the clouds are there you can't see the sun. Remove the clouds by understanding. When the clouds are there, let the rain pour out, then you can see the sun. In the same way, let go of everything you have accumulated. Say that nothing is true. You don't exist but you have to go up to Knowledge. Then let everything pour down, including yourself, and you are He. It is an open fact. If you know yourself, then nothing to know. Nothing remains to understand or know. Leave the picture, and is the screen there or not?

When you go to the cinema, after three hours, what does the screen say? Go! But does the screen remain or not? The picture goes off. The picture has no value. You have paid so many rupees for a seat. That is the value of the picture and then you have to go home, you can't sit there. But the value is still not true, because they ask you to go away and you don't take anything from there. The screen shows everything and that which you have seen goes, but still the screen says, "I am still here." You can only deduct from the Illusion. Nothing can be added or subtracted from the Reality. Understanding should come, that is the main point.

Questioner: I know that choice doesn't exist, that it is an Illusion. But sometimes I don't know what to do and I am like in a jail. I don't know what to choose and what not to choose.

Maharaj: You take it true so you have to choose. When you say it is not true, what to choose? Nothing to choose. Everything is nothing, or Zero, what to choose, tell me?

Questioner: I know this but I do not have the strength of mind.

Maharaj: Your mind doesn't accept so you are a slave of the mind. One has to become free, but you run after that when you know it is not true. Suppose you are in a dream, a good or bad one, and after awakening you remember it again and again. What is the use of it? Nothing. You see all these things but finally where do they go? When you sleep what remains, tell me? The mind always runs after that, but it is a dream. The mind always wants to know something, but when you awake you say the dream is not true. In the same way, when awakening comes here, everything is not true. That is the base! Unless the base is there, you will be affected by anybody. Anything can attract you. Even poison attracts someone who wants to leave this world. You don't want to live so even poison can attract someone who wants to be out of this worst Illusion. When you want to destroy the body, do you take it true or not?

No need to take poison. Be brave and accept that is not true. You have to stay in the Illusion but understand nothing is there. That you should feel. When you feel that nothing remains, there is no need to take anything, but you are attracted by the poison, the worldly things. You are attracted by many, many things in the world. What won't attract you, you cannot say. Ask your mind what you don't want!

If you ask your mind what you don't want, it will say, "I want everything." Can you get everything? Impossible, no? Everything is not true, it is Zero, and when you accumulate Zero, what will be your position? Lots of Zeros. But when you understand, Reality shines. Forget that Zero and Reality shines always. It is so open, why to worry? You worry because you don't understand the Reality, or what is the positive. The mind should be positive and that which is not, is not positive, it is Illusion. You're interested in what is not, and that is the liking of the mind.

Forget the mind and you become He, a Saint. How much time does it take to have a degree of a Saint? This is very difficult for an ordinary person. You can say it is not true, but it is difficult to put into practice. The one who says, "I don't care for anything," then he can put it into practice, otherwise not. Understanding should come, nothing else. If understanding comes, then nothing remains. When you say it is Zero, what remains? It is not, no?

Suppose that you say that anything you like is beautiful. Can you eat that? I ask you? It is very beautiful. You cannot eat what is beautiful. By mind you say it is beautiful. If you eat that will you become full? Understanding should come, that is the main point. Understand it is not true. You take it true and then you talk. Say by mind it is not true. When you say it is true you are in it, and when you say it is not true, you are out of it. To enter this room, you have to cross the doorway, and then you are in. Then you become a trespasser. I can say you are a trespasser, but if you put one leg outside, then I have no right to tell you that. I cannot say you are a trespasser.

With Ignorance you say it is true, and with Knowledge you say it is not true. That ends the matter. Unless you understand that, how can you put an end to it? Suppose there is a bottle of poison, who will taste it? If you do, it will mean your death. So who will taste it? Nobody will taste it because you know it's poison. In the same way, know that it is not true. You keep money in your pocket, many different notes, 100 rupees, 500 rupees. It is just paper and they never say that I am a note. Will they say?

Nothing says I am beautiful but you say beautiful, what to do? Nothing is beautiful and nothing is bad. What you say is bad is also not true. Bad is beautiful and what you say is beautiful is bad. The mind likes it, no? The mind likes it but it is not true. What the mind doesn't like is bad. Put your mind in the right position. If you put your mind in that position, you are always He. Nothing to worry about.

* * * * * * * * * *

February 15, 2000

Questioner: Is it necessary to fulfill very deep desires to get rid of them?

Maharaj: If you feel that it is not true then one will not have any desires. Desires do not remain. If the poison bottle is there you don't touch it, no? In the same way, you have the habit since birth to have desires. You have to forget the desires in the beginning because you take them true. If you feel it is not true then?

In darkness you see a string as a serpent. You fear it, and when the light is on, then you see the string is not a serpent. Therefore, if you are awakened by the mind, you will feel for yourself "Why should the desire come?" In the beginning, one has to put an end to the desires, then you can say afterwards that desires are there. Let them be there but you don't take them true. Instead, you take your desires as true, but they are not.

When nothing is there, will any desire come? Does anybody desire to eat the shit in the toilet? No, because it is a bad thing you think. You throw off the shit from your body. You never desire that, but if a pig is there, he likes to eat the shit, because the pig has no brains. You have the brains. One should understand that nothing is true. Suppose you dash your head on a stone, it is sure to break. In the same way, desires are there and one should break them by understanding, and then forget the desires.

What is there in desires? It's your thought only. You have no desires but the dream comes. If you like the dream and somebody awakens you, you think, "It's a nice dream," but still you can't get that dream again. It's not possible. When a man is dead what remains for him? Can he see the whole world? It's not possible. He forgets everything. Daily you are dying but you don't know it because you wake up again. When death comes, you forget everything, and it is the same when you sleep, you forget everything, your body, your house, your mind. Everything goes when you sleep.

So forget that way. You have to practice that in the beginning. If you want to understand the Reality, these bodily deep desires you must forget them. So it is told in our language, "Saam, Daam Dand & Bhed."

<u>Saam</u> means "the simple way"; the humble way

<u>Daam</u> means "by force"; put some force over it.

<u>Dand</u> means "punishment" or (penalty) Say to your mind, "Don't think of it!" But still you think of it, so you have to punish the mind and then you have to say that you are wretched.

<u>Bhed</u> means "difference" or discrimination. You don't know what the Reality is. You don't want to know the Reality. That means that if you do accounting and

you have made some error, you have to pay something to the government if you have made a mistake on your taxes. It means if you don't know the difference between what is and what is not, then you have to pay the consequences.

So, in these four ways you can stop your mind. You lull your mind, what to do? Lull means pamper the mind, as you lull the child to sleep. Don't lull your mind. You have to forget and when you are strong enough, attack it. It's okay to do your duty, no harm.

In the beginning you have to give punishment to the mind. If you don't give the punishment to the young boy he will do it again. You have to say to him, "Don't do it." You have to say to him that he is better than that, than his behavior. The mind has to be punished. Desires are there due to the habit of many lives and many years. These desires come again and again in the mind.

The realized person can crush the mind. The realized person can say, "I don't want what you want." He has that much power! If the boy goes to the poison bottle, you check him or not? The boy does not know, and he does not like to be told no, so he goes again and again. Try to know your thoughts and what your desires are. Once you understand, the question of desires does not arise then. Bodily desires are there but one has to forget them.

What do you get when you desire? You get nothing, you lose yourself but still you are happy with that. Everybody loses, what is the use of it? Try to preserve your Power, and that Power can bring you to the Reality. Unless you understand the Reality it's of no use. In the beginning you have to do something. Punishment has to be given to your mind, "Don't do it," you must say. Punish your desires. Try to forget, why not! If you want to forget you can forget, but you don't want to forget because you think that you are the body and the mind. All these things should be eliminated from the mind. The mind should be averted. Nothing is true!

When you travel on the train and look out the window, you see many scenes. You have to leave the scenes behind or not? Many scenes are seen there, good or bad, whatever it may be. You have to end your journey. In the same way, leave your thoughts. Once you leave your thoughts, then do you get happiness or not? When you sleep, do you get happiness or not? You spend the night dancing and drinking and then get tired of it, but after you sleep, are you not fresh the next day? You go to the Reality then, but you don't know it. The remedy is to go to the Reality and then you are satisfied or fresh. Freshness comes from where? You go to Zero when you sleep but still that freshness comes. How do you become fresh in the morning? You have forgotten everything including yourself. Try to understand. Unless you understand, or try to understand, thoughts are going to come again and again, they have got that habit.

So, desires should be thrown off in the beginning. These are all bodily affairs. After understanding you feel everything is okay, but you understand that nothing is true. After understanding, you don't care for anything but first you have to forget the desires. Desire is for what? For what is not true. Is anybody satisfied? After one desire is satisfied, another desire comes. If one day you take a good lunch, the next day your body asks for it again. The mind wants it because what you have taken the day before goes off. It doesn't remain. One has to control the mind. Have you got the control over the car or not? When you are driving the car, you know when to stop. You put your foot on the brake and it stops, otherwise an accident may happen. Life is an accident, take it for granted. Don't do anything rashly. The mind is very rash. Accidents can happen, especially if the road is not good, so you have to go slowly. Everybody wants everything to be fast, as fast as possible. Everyone wants the birth as fast as possible, but one has to wait. Try to understand the Reality.

Reality has nothing to do with all this nonsense because all this is Zero. If the body dies, let it die. You want to preserve the body and enjoy it. It's impossible! If you go to the doctor for respiratory problems and he says not to eat this and that, and if you decide not to follow his advice and eat ice cream, you can die of pneumonia. Desires are always there. You have to keep them in check. If you want the Reality, then understand the Reality. Forget this Zero. It starts from Zero and ends in Zero.

When the body dies, where does it go? It becomes the smallest particle and goes away. We Indians cremate, and you people put the bodies in boxes and think that Christ will come for you, but he hasn't come in the last 2000 years. All these dead bodies have gone to ashes, they have become dust. All these are wrong beliefs that come from your mind, because you don't know the inner meaning of what is written in the Bible. Awaken yourself, you are the Christ. You give the light to Christ, otherwise he cannot be seen. So you are the father of Christ, or not!

One should understand that death is the penalty for all human beings. The sage goes beyond death, so no death for him. If the body dies, he doesn't care. Why should you worry for this body, so many bodies are yours or not? Say, "I enjoy in everybody." Why should this body enjoy for personal pleasure? It is ego. So you want to preserve the body, which is not, and which can be rotten any time. If you keep fruits for a long time they will rot. Don't keep the perishable. Say that the body is a useless thing. Unless you get the understanding that everything is useless, you can't be a king. If you play with the marbles how can you be the king? If you want to become the king, then forget the marbles.

In the same way, forget the deep desires. They have been there for many years, I agree. Have you got satisfaction? The serpent enjoys for one and a half hours. How much time can you enjoy, tell me? Four, five, six minutes at the most. How much do elephants eat? 1 mond per day. (One mond means twenty-eight pounds or fourteen kilograms.) Can you eat that much? You want to eat but you cannot digest. So, when old age comes, people want to eat more, but they cannot digest.

Old age is second childhood. The child also does not know, and when he eats too much he gets stomach pain. In the same way, old age is also second childhood. You can't walk, you can't go up fast when climbing steps. The body deteriorates. So, why to lull this body? This is a dead body at the moment. The connection is there, so it speaks. So, you run after that which is not true and doesn't last.

The deer runs after the mirage of water. If you say, "Don't run, there is no water," he will say, "You are a foolish person, I see water." He sees water, and he runs, but he does not get the water. In the same way, people don't get satisfaction. Are you satisfied at anytime with anything? In the paper it was written that some English woman spent thousands of dollars on her wedding dress. Is she satisfied? If someone has a better dress, she will not be happy. The mind always wants something more and better.

Try to understand your mind. If you understand your mind it takes you to the Reality and then you are satisfied. One who is realized says, "I don't want anything," but still people give, what to do? Can't help it. If you beg you can't get. One who does not beg he gets so much. The world is like that. So one should not run after many, many things. Try to understand, then do your deep desires go off or not?

When you understand that all this is nothing, then renouncing comes in the mind. Desires don't remain there, and finally you understand what to renounce when everything is nothing. When you know that everything is Zero you become the Master of the universe, why not! Try and understand your mind. The mind is the greatest factor and also the most mischievous. When the mind says, "I don't want anything," you become its Master and then deep desires don't remain. Forget everything because it is not. You take it true like the deer the deer that runs after water (in the mirage) and then you feel that you have been unlucky.

In the same way, you don't know what is happiness or satisfaction. When you sleep, is happiness there or not! You are in Zero and you forget everything. If you don't get sleep for three days you have to go to the doctor for insomnia. Sleeping becomes a disease if you don't get it. Try to forget yourself. You don't exist! And when you don't exist what remains for you? One who is dead, what remains for him? He may have many dollars but can he send a check to anyone? Impossible! As long as the connection is there, it's okay, but then the ego comes. "I've done this, I've done that." But the human body has a limited time span so you must understand the Reality as soon as possible.

Why do you worry for these deep desires? When you worry they remain forever. Suppose someone takes poison and dies. He has committed suicide because he has so many debts or what-not. So he has to do it all over again in next birth. What is the use of dying that way. Don't die, have the courage to oppose all of the things in the world. Be brave enough to accept whatever happens, and stand like a rock. Whatever happens let it happen, the rock doesn't mind. Understanding brings everything, and the Master gives that understanding. No need to give understanding either. Your Self is He, but you have forgotten yourself, the Reality.

You give yourself names and say, "I am Mr. So-and-so," or "I am Miss So-and-so." The names have no value at all. When one dies, what is written? "Mr. So-and-so died," and that ends the matter. The name goes and the shape of the body goes. You never die! So why should one worry about death? Death is to the body. Okay?

Try to understand your mind. So, deep desires should be averted. They come as long as the body is there, they are sure to come. Oppose them! Mosquitoes come, so you have to put something on to stop them. In the same way, desires are all mosquitoes. Try to avert all deep desires. If you get understanding, then you get real happiness. The world is not true, so have the wish for Reality, and that Reality is not wrong. Have the wish for Reality and become wishless. Say that all of this is not true. When you say that you can leave the world in a fraction of a second. You have that much power, but you are so much engrossed in this tiny world. And this tiny world doesn't remain when this body dies, so why do you worry for this body?

The deer runs all round for Kasturi, (A deer that has this musk in his navel and it runs around wondering from where this smell has come), but it does not know that Kasturi is hidden in his naval. Go to that point, that navel, and you can enjoy. In the same way, the Power is with you, you are the Reality, and that Reality is in you. Try to understand that Reality and be out of all this nonsense which is nothing. It is just temporary pleasure, so try to forget all these useless thoughts. Any other questions?

Questioner: If I want to be free now and that is not experienced by me, does that mean that I really don't want to be free and that my desire to be free is not strong enough?

Maharaj: It means that your desires are running over you just like a moving car when you stand in its way. They are your desires and they are so strong that you forget yourself. If you are there, then the desires are there, otherwise from where can the desires come? When you take the birth, then the desires come. If you don't take the birth, then? When you say that you are birthless and deathless what desires remain for you? But, if you keep the desires in your mind, then the car overruns you and you die, what to do?

Questioner: If I cannot reach the Reality is it because my desire for Reality is not strong enough?

Maharaj: Yes! You take this as true again, what to do? All the desires, or thoughts, you take as true. Why can you not get it? You are He, so if you can't get yourself, whose fault? You don't know yourself. You are running after these small, small things. A child runs after marbles to play. He is not interested in making money at that time, only later on does he want something else. He grows up, and you can do the same. You can grow and grow, why not! You are He, so forget your desires.

How long are your desires going to stay? Desires come and go. You want to eat but can you eat for the whole day? Impossible! Understanding should come but you don't want to understand. Why? Due to the desires in your mind, the mind stops you. Solve the mind. My Master, what did he do? He said, "I don't care if I die. I will achieve my goal!" He achieved his goal and at the same time he got a strong case of diabetes, and no medicine was available at the time. He didn't care what happened. At the age of 48 he left his body.

He gave the understanding and threw off the body. When you want to achieve something you have to be very hard. You have to do your duty so strongly. Due to your desires you cannot overcome your thoughts and you forget yourself. You are the Reality at the moment, I tell you. Everyone is the Reality. People don't know, so the Saints have to say it again and again. "Be the Reality. Be the Reality. Understand you are the Reality." But you say "No, I want to be a small creature," and then nobody can help you. Desires, thoughts, mind, all come over you, and you are suppressed by those desires due to the body. The body is the greatest factor. It brings all desires, all thoughts. No body, no-mind. If you forget the mind, what remains? Try to forget your mind. Thoughts are sure to come. Forget the thoughts. Say that "I don't want you." You have the habit to entertain your mind. The mind is a beggar, and begging is a poverty.

In 1928 there was this blind boy and he was begging always on the same corner. When he died they found one lakh of rupees but he was still begging up to the last moment. He could not enjoy and the government took the money. When the habit becomes your master you can't do anything. You cannot overcome those habits.

If you say, "I am the body," how can you be the Reality? Forget the body, and say, "I don't care for this body. I want to accept the Reality." Why not! You are He at the moment, that is the main point. When understanding comes everything goes to Zero. There is no America, no India, no France, everything is just earth, nothing else. In Sedona, Arizona we went to the Grand Canyon one day. It is a valley. (Maharaj points out of his window which is on the 3rd floor.) This is also a valley. If you stand at the window this is also a valley! Understanding should come, then all of this goes to Zero. Nothing is true, how much time does it take?

A big cyclone comes from space and makes havoc, and then it goes back to space. Zero has so much Power, and it shows everything. You don't want to be Zero, you want to be rich. Money has no value, the Reality is rich. Reality is ever there, just like a screen. Pictures come and go and the screen doesn't care. Everything happens on the screen but the screen remains as white as anything. The screen doesn't take the touch, but you have the habit to touch. You touch the world and confusion comes. Adam told Eve not to touch, but she did, and you all have the habit to touch, what to do? You, yourself are Adam and Eve. You want to see, you want to know the flavor of the poison, so you die. The world is a poison so if you touch it, you have to die, that is the result. In the same way, you want what is not, so how can you get happiness from that? Everything starts from Zero and ends in Zero. Zero is space, and when you understand that this is nothing but space, then you are beyond it. When understanding comes then nothing is good and nothing is bad. Make the world a Zero by understanding. Any other questions?

Questioner: What do you mean when you say that you have the choice to open the door?

Maharaj: Open the door! If you don't open the door, how can you go and stay in the house? Nobody knocks on the door. Someone in Germany said, "I saw the door, but I didn't knock!" Whose fault if you don't knock? If you knock on the door someone must answer, no? Your Self is He, then you become the owner of the house, but you don't want to knock because you think "I will lose everything." But Reality is there, and when you are inside, then there is nothing left to find out. If you don't knock how can Paul (a disciple), come out?

If I want to meet Paul I have to knock. There is nothing to see also. Knocking on the door means that you understand that everything is Zero. Say everything is Zero, and then you are there. When you say that nothing is true you are always He. When everything goes, do you remain or not? When the guests go, you remain. All have gone but all are myself.

Try to understand. Nobody goes anywhere and nobody comes from anywhere. Have that much courage to accept that you are He, but you don't want to be He because you fear everything will go off. "What will people say?" (Maharaj looks at his Master's picture.) My Master takes you to that place where understanding doesn't remain and where Knowledge and Ignorance don't remain. Let everything be there, no need to change anything, but say it is not true. Forget the sense of the world, which is nonsense, then you get the real sense, and Reality opens up for you.

* * * * * * * * * *

June 4, 2000

Questioner: I have the feeling there is no progress and the ego is an Illusion, that it doesn't exist. And with faith in the Master concepts vanish. So how does

Maharaj who is just like us, in the body and has perception of the world, how does he see the world?

Maharaj: He says that the world is Zero, that it doesn't exist. It is just like a dream. You see the dream, nothing exists there. You say upon awakening that yourself was just a dream. An ignorant person always sees the world as true. The realized person says the world is not true. That is the difference. It is just like darkness and light. When light comes, darkness goes off, and when darkness is there, you cannot see the light. In the same way, one should understand that what you see is your mind. That is your ego. When you take it as true, you see everything as true. One who understands that it is not true, or Zero doesn't worry for anything. That is the difference. It depends on the person now.

There is a woman. Someone says she is my wife, someone says she is my sister, and someone else says she is my mother. She is one only, so it depends on your thoughts, your mind. So, in each one's mind, she is quite different but she is still one only. Try to understand your mind. So, the question was "How does the realized person see the world?" He doesn't see the world, what to do? So, in darkness you see something, but when the light comes there was nothing there. Darkness means what? That there was nothing there, but still you felt it. It is due to the mind. It depends on the person now, nothing else.

If you are realized you will say it is nothing. If he is not realized he will say you are a foolish person. "We see everything, we do everything and still you say there is nothing." An ignorant person will not agree with you. It is quite the contrary to the way they think. It is just like a coin. If you stay on one side you see the heads and if you are on the other side, the opposite one, you say it is tails. There the coin exists, here nothing exists but still you say it is something.

A realized person gets hungry just like everyone else, but he says the body gets hungry not myself. Good and bad thoughts come to the mind and not to me. You take of the touch of it and you say, "Oh, bad thoughts have come and now I must go and pray to God and ask him for forgiveness."

So, Friday is confession day. You do everything and then confess to the priest. He says, "Go, don't do it next time." But still you are doing the same thing, what to do? What right does he have to say you are free? Because he knows that you have not done anything. Only the mind and body have done it, but nothing has happened. You take it true by body and mind, but it is not true.

In a dream you may see a bad or good picture, but does it remain? When you awaken it automatically goes off. You see the whole picture on the screen and when the picture is over, where is the picture? Is it there on the screen? Here Knowledge is the screen, and Knowledge sees everything. But a realized person is beyond Knowledge. He says that Knowledge is not true. So, when you see a dream, and as soon as you awake, you say that it was a dream and not true. Same way here also, when you are awakened by the Master you say that nothing is true, so why to worry. You won't worry for anything. The Master doesn't see, or worry, or feel that anything has been done. That is his understanding.

Suppose he kills somebody, the worst of the worst actions. He knows that he must be put to the gallows. And when he is being put on the gallows they ask for his last wish. Do you know what he will say? "Put me on the gallows as fast as possible." And other ignorant people will say, "I've got this wish, and that wish, and that wish." He doesn't worry for what has happened. He says, "I wanted to kill him, so I killed him." Everything is ended. So, action at the moment becomes no action. You feel in the mind that I have done good or bad. And that is called in our mythology "Karma." Karma means action. When an action is completed in the mind that is called "Akarma." And when you keep thinking in the mind about good and bad actions, that is called "Vikarma." Vikarma means what you feel that you have done something, but one should understand that "I have not done anything."

These are beliefs, nothing else. In India there is a belief that if you commit suicide then you will have seven births and seven more suicides. Who will count? Why do they say that? Why to worry, what is there! Why to fear the world? So the idea is that you should not commit suicide, but nobody is going to count. How can you remember your last birth, and that I committed suicide? Do you remember? Death puts an end to everything. Death means that you forget everything, Knowledge and ignorance, and ego. All go off.

Suppose you are a king and you die, nothing remains. Nothing. You go to Zero. When you leave this body, you think that I must have another body, so you take another birth. That is called reincarnation. So one must take the birth, I tell you. Suppose you leave your house and move to another house. You love that old house so much and you say to the old house, "Sorry I am leaving you." The house doesn't mind whether you leave or stay, it doesn't mind. The house doesn't mind, but you feel according to your mind, "It is my house. This was my father's house and I have lived here 50 years," but the house doesn't feel anything. Does the house feel anything?

So, that was the question. The Master doesn't do anything. You feel something, but he doesn't feel that I have done anything. So, he is out of the action. The mind discriminates good and bad things. Bad and good both are wrong because you don't do anything. The picture shows that the screen is singing, but when the picture is over the screen doesn't sing, because it throws off everything at the moment. In the same way, when one understands it is not true, he throws away everything. What is there! What is going to remain there now? That which is nothing, is always nothing.

You yourself create the bondage, nothing else. Bondage and liberation are your feelings and you think that the Master can liberate you, but the Master says that you are never in bondage, and "Who am I to liberate you!" He gives you the understanding that you are never in bondage, but you feel that you are, what to do?

A good example is how to catch a parrot. You make a triangle with string and a small hollow pipe and put it on a tree. As soon as the parrot sits on it his head falls toward the ground and he feels he will fall, so he holds tight onto the pipe upside down. He forgets the fact that he has wings. So, the parrot catcher comes in the morning, picks up the triangle and puts the parrot in the cage. You also do the same thing due to ignorance. When the parrot is in the cage he feels some support now, but then he wants to fly away from there. He tries and tries but cannot find a way.

You have taken the birth and that is the bondage. You have taken it yourself by Ignorance, and you go round and round trying to find a way out, nothing else. In a cage what happens? He goes this side, he goes that side. So find out the way to go out. The world is a maze nothing else. Once you enter you can't go out. Don't enter into Ignorance that is the best way. Forget everything. Due to Ignorance you say that everything is true. Say that nothing is true and that is the real mantra given by the Master. You feel you are in bondage, and the Master does what? He gives the mantra that means you are not in bondage. That is the mantra.

When you go to school you put your name on the record sheet. You are bound to go then. You have to go. Same way here also, you go to the Master and ask how to live in this world. It is really a mystery. "How am I in this world?" Now you say that you have taken the birth and that is a mystery. So, the world itself is a mystery and you cannot go out of it. Once you enter it, it is just like a maze, and when you find the door it is not the right door and you can't get out of it. So the Master, or guide, he gives understanding and that is called the mantra. Enter by this way and go by this way.

Mantra means nothing. Master gives the understanding. Come through this door and go out of it. For the ignorant person it is a maze he cannot come out of. Unless you come out you cannot be happy. You are just like a parrot in a cage. The parrot tries to find out by his beak, he pokes here and there. By beak he wants to know where to go. He cannot. You also do the same thing. You have no beak, but still you want to know "How can I go? How can I realize? How can I go to God? I am in bondage," and you go here and there with your beak. Beak means thought.

So try to understand, nothing else. The Master says that you have done nothing. "No, I have done," you say. That is your ego. In your sleep you kill somebody, and when you awaken do you still say that I have killed? "No, how can I kill, I have no revolver!" Awakening is the only thing, so the Master awakens you. He awakens you by saying that you are not this. You are not the body, not the mind, you are something other than that. Why do you worry for what the body and mind have done?

The world is always the same. It is just like a scale. If you feel that you have done something, you have to pay for it. You put the corn on one side, and you put a weight on the other, otherwise you can't say the price. It's the same way here also. You feel that I have done something, and the Master says that you have not done anything. You have not taken the birth also, why should you worry? You feel, you experience, "I am So-and-so, and I have so much trouble." But you have not taken birth. The body has taken the birth. Be out of the body. Understand this way and you are out of the danger of the enemy.

The Master gives the caution sign. It is just like a sign you see for electric wires. If you touch it you will die. The Master gives the caution, "Don't touch." You take the touch, and you are in so much trouble. You take the touch of the body and you say, "I'm this." That is the touch. Many bodies have come and gone for you. Why you should worry for this body?

An actor works in pictures and asks for a different part. He wants to be a Saint, and wants to know how to play that part. He wants to know, so he becomes a saintly person there. He is not saintly, no doubt. He takes the part of the Saint, and he tells people not to do this and that. Play your part, nothing else. As you have taken a part, you do everything according to your part. Just understand that it is a part. You take the body and say, "I'm this" and that is the greatest Ignorance.

Forget the body. So many bodies have come and gone on you. You take the touch of the body and say "I am the body." You take bondage on yourself when you say, "I'm the body." You are not the body, you are the Power in the body, and always free. Try to understand the realized persons, what they say. They say that they have not done anything in their life.

Suppose someone kills someone in the picture, who will be sentenced to death? Tell me? Which person? You see everything, but still, who will be sentenced? Nobody is there, it is just a picture after all. It's the same way here, if something is wrong, the body gets affected, you don't get affected. You take yourself as a body and you are bound by that. Then you feel you are lost now.

He is not going to kill anybody. The Master knows myself is everywhere so whom to kill? Somebody says how can you say this? Many, many questions come in the mind. Can he kill, why not! He has the right to kill anybody. He may not kill, that is okay. The Master kills you. Your ego is taken out by him. You are not the body, he makes you understand. That is killing or not, tell me. He kills everybody, but still he is not a killer, because he doesn't kill anybody. What is wrong has been taken out, nothing else. The doctor operates on you, a nice cut here. Is he called a killer? No! You do it willingly. "Make me all well" you say.

So, he sees the world as nothing. You, an ignorant person see the world as something true. This is a vast difference. He does everything as you do, but he understands that everything is Zero, and you don't understand that. You take it true and feel bound, but you have not done anything. In a dream, what have you done? When you awake do you say "I've done something"? You have done nothing. When you are asleep your eyes are closed 99.9% of the time, but you see the whole dream. By which eyes did you see it? Tell me? Sometimes you can have a dream where your dead father or grandfather comes in the dream and he wants some fish or mutton. Where to put the fish or mutton, tell me? There is no entity at all. If there is an address there in the dream, where can you send it?

So everything is nothing, everything is Zero, when you understand. Then you are out of what? No doubts remain in the mind. You become doubtless. An ignorant person doubts everybody. If you meet someone on a plane or train and he sits with you, do you doubt or not if this person will do anything like take my money, or "God knows what he is going to do." Doubt always remains.

It's the same way here also, if you say that it is true, doubts always remain in the mind. Is it true or not? Doubts always remain in the mind because the world is incomplete. It is never complete. Illusion is never complete. Reality is always complete. So, you become complete yourself and you never feel anything. He understands that everything is myself. He may be a mad chap, no? Still he says that all is myself.

So, understand and be out of the clutches of Ignorance. Ignorance goes off and you are always in Reality. So, doing and not doing doesn't arise for him. In a dream if you drink four bottles of whiskey and you wake up, is there any kick there? So, an ignorant person thinks of good and bad and reaps the fruit. You feel the fruit is there, but it is not. Nothing is there because it is not true. Try to understand the realized person and then you can be out of it, otherwise not. Okay?

Questioner: We are one, I am Reality and you are Reality. So everything is One. Still our minds are different. So how to reduce that gap between our minds?

Maharaj: Forget your mind and accept my mind. You have done many, many wrong things due to Ignorance. What I say is my mind, so accept it and we will be the same. You want to keep yourself intact, and then you want something else. How can it be? If your house is full of everything and you want to keep everything, how can it go away? Empty your mind and take what I have got in my mind. Take it, why not? My mind is full, but nothing is there. It is full with everything, but nothing is there. Can you accept that? He says "I am not the body." Accept it! Why not! You are He. Everybody is He, why not accept it! A drunkard is drunk and you are not drunk. How can it be equal? He has got some kick in his mind. The kick of ignorance is there in your mind. Throw off the kick of ignorance and you are myself, why not? No difference.

You feel yourself to be a woman, and I say that you are not a woman. Can you accept that? No man, no woman, nothing. These are all bodily affairs. You have become a woman and you never leave that. That is ego. Finish it off. Say, "I am not a woman, I am He!" That is your greatest obstacle, what to do? You don't allow what the Master says to come in. Accept you are not a woman then you are He. How much time does it take, tell me!

From birth your mind has been filled with this nonsense. You work with Knowledge and a man also works with the Knowledge. Both have Knowledge in common. Try to understand, nothing else. You are a woman, it's okay. Bodily you are a woman, but you are not a woman. That Power that is in you is not a woman. The Power is there and you can use that Power anyway you like. That depends upon you now and it depends upon your thoughts.

So everybody is one, and mind is also one. Difference comes when you take the touch of something. The mind works with the Power and Knowledge. Understand the Knowledge and the mind goes off. It doesn't remain. You have taken the body of a woman but you are not a woman. The Power is the same in everybody and everyone has the same Power. Understand that way. Then the phrase, "Frailty thy name is woman," won't come to you. So I always say and it is my quotation: "Who works with the mind is man, who woos that man is a woman."

In foreign countries all people like to put on the dress of a man (pants). Nobody says anything. It is very difficult in foreign countries to find out if it is a man or a woman. In India it is very easy. A woman puts on a dress. Okay? So forget yourself and say that "I am the Power." Have that understanding. And if you are not the Power, tell me, as I am responsible.

Questioner: A poet described the experience of Reality this way. It is like to have the head in the stars, the cosmos, and the heart open to the invisible world. Is that a good way to describe it?

Maharaj: The poet said that your heart is open. If you feel like that do it, experience it. How can it be true? Here your death is required. Die yourself. Erase yourself. Ego is for the anatomy. So they say in the military: "Not to question why, not to make a reply, do your duty and die." Same way here. The Master doesn't make you die, but he says to die yourself. If you are not there, how can the poet understand that Reality? Is it possible? Head in the stars, heart open, these are all thoughts.

Suppose you are sleeping on a terrace and you see the cosmos there, is your heart open? You see and say many things like this, but it is not the Reality. Reality is quite different. It is like you. Reality is like you. Agree? Don't say that I am the body. If you say it's the body, it's not like that. It's like you. You are the Reality. So, what to open and what not to open? Poets can only write. They don't know what they say because they are only poets. The experience is quite different.

In Indian mythology so many things have been written and so many examples have been given, but people cannot understand the inner meaning of these things. Arjuna eloped with the sister of Krishna. He brought her to his mother and he bowed down to her. So, the mother said to him that he was to share whatever he brought with his five brothers. What is the meaning in it? Can you say? The mother knew she was coming, but what is the inner meaning of what she said? There were five brothers and one woman. How can they share? Can she be cut in five pieces? How can you understand the meaning?

All the five elements are in everybody. The Knowledge is there. No Knowledge, then this cannot work. Otherwise how can you share? It's impossible. Everybody has got five elements in his body. They are working with what that Power. The mother wanted to say that, but people don't understand the inner meaning of it. Otherwise she is a prostitute or not! If you understand the inner meaning, you can bow down to what has been written, otherwise you will think this is just a story.

The poet has written all these things, that was the question? The cosmos is in you. The cosmos is nothing but a state and the state is in you. But you are stateless, you are thoughtless. What you see and perceive is a state. Understand that way then the cosmos opens, otherwise how can it open? How can the heart open? Understand in mind that everything is in me. Knowledge brings everything, understanding brings everything. Understand the Master, and understand the right way, then everything is okay. Okay?

Questioner: Tukaram said to always be in the company of a Saint. What does he mean?

Maharaj: If the Saints are there, they give the right understanding. Why are Saints required? To give the correct understanding. What is the world, who are you? The Saints are capable to say what you are and what you are not. All the ignorant persons, your father and mother, and everybody say that you are the body. He says that you are not the body. So, that kick of Ignorance is there, so you cannot understand what Reality is. So, the Saints give the understanding of Reality.

Saints make a proclamation (Maharaj quotes from the morning arati): "I beg from you, grant me that I should not forget you. I shall never forget you. I sing about you with this loving song." He makes a proclamation that he asks God, "If you want to put me in the body I am willing to go, again and again. But my conditions are that I should not forget you. All the people who are in my vicinity, I shall tell them to sing about you and your greatness. I don't want liberation, I don't want money and I don't want prosperity. I don't want anything from you. Give me someone who can guide me correctly."

In foreign countries it very difficult to know where you are going. In India it is very easy, you just ask somebody if this road is correct. You don't ask. If you ask it is very easy to get the place. Saints are the real pointers. They show you, "Go this way." Try to understand. "I don't want money, liberation, nor prosperity." What is liberation? It is just your thought. Then you can say that you can put me in birth, I don't care. But my conditions are this. They don't mislead you, they take you to the right point, nothing else. He should be a real Saint otherwise it is all nonsense. Some Saints say to do this or that, but without doing anything you are He. Don't do anything and you are He. So, I want the Saints with me to take me to the right place.

Hammer one thing and make two pieces. You should know how to hammer. What is right, and what is not right? That you should find out, and that is hammering. So, the Saints are of that type, they hammer and make two pieces. "This is not true, this is true, go!" So, Saints are required. Anything else? So foreign people take out the map to know where we are, but the Saints are more than a map. Sometimes you want to go here, but sometimes you forget where east is, or where west is. Why are Saints required? Because they give you the right understanding. Maps can be wrong too. Saints make you understand the Reality and who are you.

Questioner: Why does the wife say to do this and that, and that this is wrong, and the husband feels the same way?

Maharaj: Because minds differ. A woman's mind and a man's mind both differ always, what to do? The minds are always different. Mind means thought only. "What you have done is wrong, and what I have done is right." That is the meaning in it, and you always blame each other. Wives and husbands always blame each other. Why? They want to make some priority in their mind. He wants to show that "I am something" and she also wants to show that "I am something," nothing else.

It is human nature to blame others and not take any blame on yourself. So she says to her husband that he is doing wrong things, and he says to her that she is doing wrong things. Who is right? According to your mind you see, according to her mind she sees. Who can find out? It is very difficult to find out. Say that both minds are one and both are correct. Go, don't worry about it.

Always the wrong things come to the mind. Nobody is right, all are in Ignorance. The minds differ always, but the Power is the same. Electricity is not right or wrong. The two wires are one cord, and they make the machine work. Electricity doesn't know, but the Power is the same. So what I do is correct, and what others do is wrong, that is ego. Forget the ego, say whatever they do is okay. So don't blame each other if you want to live in harmony with each other. I have no wife and no child. It is human nature to blame each other. The mind is not one. The mind differs always, so it is called mind. Try to understand your body first and then you can know other bodies. Due to ego you say that "I am this, the body" and that "I'm correct," but only shit comes out from this body. So you are the manufacturer of shit, nothing else. You say, My name is this, I am the manager of this shit mill." These are all bodily affairs, it has nothing to do with what is true. It is all nonsense. So we meet tomorrow.

* * * * * * * * * *

July 26, 2000

Questioner: Maharaj,. when you leave your body, how do we go beyond that gap? It is so nice to be here with you and to see you everyday. We learn so much by the way you live your life and learn so much by the way you scold us and teach us casually. I feel there will be such a gap when the Master leaves the body. There must be a gap.

Maharaj: No gap!

Questioner: An adjustment?

Maharaj: No gap. Your body makes the gap.

Questioner: Yes, I know it does but I can't help it at the moment.

Maharaj: When you understand yourself, that you're not the body, how can the Master be a body? He is not! Understand this way. Why do you feel like that? It is due to some ignorance in the mind. You still take the body as yourself. When you say, "I don't exist," it means, "I don't exist!" That includes the body. This is said for everybody, I just don't tell you.

Some spices are there and then chutney is made and you say it is spicy. In the same way, understand "My body is spicy, and these spices give me trouble," but don't throw off the body, no need. You can love your body but still say that "I am not this!"

One man's wife died and he had a two year old son. Somebody told him to get married again but he said, "Oh, I don't want to get married because if some woman comes she won't care for my son the way his real mother did." But one woman agreed to be his wife and she said, "I'll do everything for him, more than his mother." And she was doing just that, but her inner-most thought was: "It is not my child."

So, that subtlest point remains and that subtlest point should be taken out. The woman was correct. She was doing everything very nicely, but in her mind what was there? That subtlest point, and that is ego. That subtlest point you have to break down, and that can only be done by yourself. No one else knows your ego. How can they? And when that subtle ego goes you don't remain. What is there? Where is my existence? Only He is there and by thinking again and again and practicing, the world becomes clearer. When you don't exist nothing remains. Nothing!

If an ant follows a bee and it has full faith, then one day it will surely fly. But if its understanding is that, "I can't fly," then that understanding has to be changed. Try to understand the Master. Accept his understanding. Forget yourself and that is the right way.

The Master doesn't want anything. Whether he is in the body or not, the Master doesn't feel anything. He gives the understanding and the disciple takes that up only. The bees take the pollen from the flowers and make honey out of it. Others may just take the honey, enjoy the honey and say, "Very nice, very nice." But the one who takes the essence, who wants the Reality will do so even at the cost of his life! So one has to kill oneself, the ego, and once that conviction "I don't exist" is there, then Illusion never comes back to you. How can it come back to you? Only if there is some mistake in the mind. The Master can rectify that mistake. He has his ways.

The body doesn't exist, agree! But He exists in everybody and everywhere, and except Him there is nothing. Then you have a clear cut understanding. What the Master says is correct and with his understanding you can do it. The Reality is always there. It doesn't go anywhere. It is yourself but you don't know that, and that is the difficulty.

So, who to appreciate that Reality, tell me? So you can appreciate the Master only as long as his body is there, okay. He has given the understanding, and when his body goes away, the Master remains with you in your heart by understanding. And that understanding makes so much love out of it.

There is a fountain and some stones come into it. Take out those stones, stones are ego. At the cost of yourself, you have to achieve what your Self is, and that is the real appreciation of the Master. Anyone can do it! Don't worry, just say "I don't exist," no need to tell others, keep it inside. One can live vacant inside. Even if people say you are a very great person say, "Okay, okay! Enough!" But no need to say anything.

If you do it in this way, you are He. How much time it takes? You are He. You are He forever. Nothing to do then, and that is the real appreciation of the Master. The Master does everything but doesn't take the touch. "I don't do anything, I don't exist," that is his understanding. Do everything for Him, or the Master, or anything, but say that "I don't exist," otherwise the "I" can come at anytime. The "I" is so cunning, the ego is very cunning. By understanding you can kill it. That is the main point.

* * * * * * * * * *

The End of Volume II of Illusion vs. Reality